KING OF THE OUTBACK

BILL KING

This book contains names and images of people of Aboriginal descent who are deceased.

First published in 2011

Copyright © Bill King 2011

All rights reserved. No part of this book may be reproduced or transmitted in any form or by any means, electronic or mechanical, including photocopying, recording or by any information storage and retrieval system, without prior permission in writing from the publisher. The Australian *Copyright Act 1968* (the Act) allows a maximum of one chapter or 10 per cent of this book, whichever is the greater, to be photocopied by any educational institution for its educational purposes provided that the educational institution (or body that administers it) has given a remuneration notice to Copyright Agency Limited (CAL) under the Act.

Allen & Unwin
Sydney, Melbourne, Auckland, London

83 Alexander Street
Crows Nest NSW 2065
Australia
Phone: (61 2) 8425 0100
Fax: (61 2) 9906 2218
Email: info@allenandunwin.com
Web: www.allenandunwin.com

Cataloguing-in-Publication details are available
from the National Library of Australia
www.trove.nla.gov.au

ISBN 978 1 74237 695 0

Maps by Ian Faulkner
Index by Sue Jarvis
Set in 12/15 pt Bembo by Bookhouse, Sydney
Printed and bound in Australia by Griffin Press

10 9 8 7 6 5 4 3 2 1

The paper in this book is FSC certified. FSC promotes environmentally responsible, socially beneficial and economically viable management of the world's forests.

To our beloved son Russell who, at the tender age of 22, with maturity far beyond his years, became a Bill King's Northern Safaris Tour Leader, pioneering Australia's virgin outback and taking people where nobody had taken them before.

*Now you are on the road again.
The endless highway in the sky,
and even though you're not with us now,
'Boss' will never die.*

CONTENTS

Foreword   vii

CHAPTER 1	Becoming a real life bussie	1
CHAPTER 2	In search of Burke and Wills	11
CHAPTER 3	The colonel, three ladies and me	29
CHAPTER 4	Opals and oddballs	41
CHAPTER 5	In search of Captain Charles Sturt	47
CHAPTER 6	Holiday in Copley and cattle kings	59
CHAPTER 7	Hippie headaches—The age of Aquarius	70
CHAPTER 8	The old days of outback hospitality	81
CHAPTER 9	The painting schools	99
CHAPTER 10	And the rains came	107
CHAPTER 11	Hips, ticks and unions	116
CHAPTER 12	Spreading our wings	126
CHAPTER 13	America—Here we come	141
CHAPTER 14	About 'Burke's bones'	148
CHAPTER 15	From Lasseter's Cave to the northern frontier	156
CHAPTER 16	It's hard to get good help	168
CHAPTER 17	All about business, beds and barramundi	177
CHAPTER 18	Hitting the big time	187

CHAPTER 19	Into survival mode	193
CHAPTER 20	The German expedition	201
CHAPTER 21	In search of Skylab and people gone missing	209
CHAPTER 22	The end of an era	221
CHAPTER 23	An audience with the Grim Reaper	229
CHAPTER 24	The global market—On our terms	239
CHAPTER 25	We build the 'mogs'	249
CHAPTER 26	Changing times	255
CHAPTER 27	New direction	266
CHAPTER 28	Kimberley cruising	273
CHAPTER 29	Gone west	280
CHAPTER 30	In search of my family	291

Postscript	297
Further reading	300
Acronyms	301
Index	302

List of Maps

21-day Burke and Wills Safari route	13
12-day Sturt Safari route	50
12-day West of Alice Safari route	131
16-day Gunbarrel Safari route	132
23-day Leichhardt Safari route	134
In Search of Harold Bell Lasseter	158
30-day Northern Frontier Safari route	161

FOREWORD

AFTER MY WIFE AND kids convinced me that I should write my memoirs, I began to seriously think about how to do the same. I cannot spell, I have no academic track record and I have certainly never passed an English exam, so it took me years to get this document started. The hardest part was deciding where and how to begin my life story.

I had several of them actually—lives, that is. I got swept out to sea when I was a young bloke and without the help of a lifeguard I would have been a goner. I had a coronary thrombosis in Berlin when I was 51 years of age and I would have been a goner then, too, but swift intervention by the medical profession got me going again. I had a pulmonary embolism in Los Angeles in 1993 and thought, 'This is it,' but had another escape. Then, in 2000, I had another brush with the Grim Reaper—a heart attack that needed a triple bypass. Apart from a second heart failure in 2007 that necessitated the installation of a pacemaker, I feel pretty good.

Oddly, it was only when I began to put all the stuff that I had in my head down on paper that I realised I had actually lived many lives, and while they did not necessarily coincide with the health problems I encountered along the way, they may have had some bearing on decisions I made from time to time. Anyway, a lot of people over the years have said I have been blessed by good luck. But there is no rule that says all luck has to be bad luck.

I asked advice from many people on how to write a book—my niece Susan King and her partner, Helen Razer, who are both journalists, my editor, Cathy Alexander, publishing agent, John Ross, and publisher, Stuart Neal—and in the main the message was write it all down and sort it out later.

Essentially this is a story about Bill King's Northern Safaris, an idea that had its beginnings in the 1960s when I began taking people to the outback. Not easy in those days either, with two-wheel-drive vehicles along dirt tracks. 'Ayers Rock or bust' was the adage, and sometimes we got there and sometimes we didn't. It is also a story about Australian tourism and its evolution from a cottage industry that after World War II grew into Australia's largest employer of human resources.

The stories contained in this yarn were accumulated over time and many of them concern the young men and women we employed. Bill King's Northern Safaris also gave me the opportunity to work with my kids in later years: Russell as a full-time tour leader, Martin as a backup tour leader, Melissa in reservations, and Bradley worked in our maintenance depot in Alice Springs. Furthermore, I must note my appreciation for the dedication and pride all of our people displayed when going about our business. I always said that it was not our intention to be the biggest in the industry, but let it be known that we would move Ayers Rock (as it was called then) to ensure that we were the best.

We believed that, we really did. We were the elite, and while our competitors handed out community singing leaflets to entertain their passengers, we were distributing literature for our travellers to absorb. Each itinerary had recommended reading in the documentation and it was also available on the vehicle. There were guides to Australian birds, wildflowers and trees. We also carried books on the explorers in whose footsteps we were travelling and on the Aboriginal mythology that was significant to our regions.

FOREWORD

Our crews had studied the literature and absorbed the contents. Imparting that knowledge became their life. Their work was not just a job; they were selling 'creative leisure'. It was an educational experience, having a holiday and learning a little at the same time. I went to an industry symposium a few years back and heard a guest speaker talking about eco tourism, a couple of buzz words that appeared from nobody seems to know where, and he said it was a movement that started in the late 80s. Now if he was talking about biodegradable dunny paper, solar energy and the like in accommodation houses, he was probably right. But if he was talking about travel with an emphasis on Australia's unique natural environment, he was 30 years too late.

We had white (plastic) tablecloths to cover the folding tables, too. We served table wine with the evening meal: it may have been 'Chateau Cardboard', but nevertheless it gave a touch of sophistication. We had fresh food storage for five days and a company cookbook with recipes that were workable in a primitive environment.

So here we go. As this book is a historical narration I believe it is imperative to tell the story as it was, so the name Ayers Rock has been used where historically accurate; the change in name throughout the book reflects its transition over time. I also have changed a few names and places to protect the guilty, so only they will reflect on their misdemeanours. I may have got the odd date wrong here and there, but it is how I recall it all happening. For those who take the trouble to turn a page, I hope you enjoy the ride.

Bill King
October 2011

CHAPTER 1

BECOMING A REAL LIFE BUSSIE

MY BEING INVOLVED IN an enterprise that was so far out of the ordinary has prompted many people to ask, 'How did you ever get into such a business?'

Well, I grew up at a time when families ate their meals sitting at a kitchen table; my father carved the roast, told the little people at the table to mind their manners, and talked about the old days. He told us stories about our family pioneering the North West Cape of Western Australia, about my grandfather prospecting the Bangemall and Coolgardie goldfields, and my great-grandfather, Juan Bancells, a Spanish immigrant who became a brumby trapper and horse breaker, shipping remounts to the British army in India. I was always an avid listener, enthralled by his many stories of the outback, and thought, 'One day I'm going to go there.' And I did.

My father, Billy, as he was known, was a great raconteur who harboured a passion for everything Western Australian and forever talked about our family's involvement in the founding of the Swan River Colony. After leaving school in Perth he took his first job as a jackaroo on the family property, Exmouth Gulf Station. Later he became manager of Yardie Creek Station on the Indian Ocean side of the Gulf and later again licensee of the Bangemall Inn.

My grandfather, Joe King, was a true pioneer and jack of all trades: carpenter, fencer, shearer, miner, bore sinker, soldier, windmill builder and publisher of the *Miners Right* newspaper in Kalgoorlie in 1897. But most of all he was a prospector and sold his strikes to miners with the capital to develop a project, or collected a government reward and moved on.

In 1899 he began fossicking in some old workings in Greenbushes, south of Perth, where he successfully set up a tin-mining enterprise. He did well with the tin mine and sold the lease in 1908 to enter into a partnership with his half brother, William, taking up the lease on 200 000 acres of virgin country on the North West Cape of Western Australia to establish Exmouth Gulf Station.

Then in 1925 Joe got a grass seed in his sock; growing wool and meat had never been his go. Gold was bringing a good price and he'd heard of some good strikes in the Gascoyne, an area he had worked 30 years earlier. Joe went back to the Bangemall goldfields and began mining the Eldorado. Unlike its namesake—a fictitious lost city of gold in the jungle of South America—Joe's mine was a treasure trove waiting to happen and in 1928 he 'struck it rich'.

The Bangemall Inn was up for sale, so Joe bought it with a view to running his enterprises as a family affair. That was how my newly wedded parents came to be living and working in the Bangemall goldfields, one of Australia's more remote settlements.

By mid-1929 the inevitable had occurred and my mother was pregnant with yours truly. At five months she said she'd had enough and made the decision to return to Melbourne to have her baby. There was no way she was going to have a January child in that environment, especially when daytime temperatures in the 40s were normal and a 50 now and again was not uncommon, and there were no medical services on the goldfields. I wouldn't have enjoyed it much either, I should imagine. She left Bangemall in September 1929 and, even though the goldfields were thriving, my father left in December to join her in Melbourne for my birth. So here I am, conceived in Bangemall, born in Melbourne and raised on my father's stories of the outback.

Now you could legitimately wonder, 'Where the devil is Bangemall?'

Well, it's not on maps these days. It's now called Cobra Station and it's a bugger of a place to get to, more than 400 kilometres inland from Carnarvon.

I'll never forget going from Meekatharra to get to Bangemall and then across to Carnarvon, over 800 kilometres on the roughest track I have ever driven on. There had been rain about and the potholes and tyre marks had dried out and set like concrete. What's more, the track hadn't seen a grader since cocky was an egg and the corrugations were dreadful. We called it the track that never ends. That was in 1999. Goodness knows what it was like in the 1920s.

•

In Melbourne my folks rented a house in Grange Road, Ormond, and my old man got a job driving a truck for Strang Brothers in Richmond. In later life he always said that he never had any fear of being sacked, or, for that matter, anyone ever coveting his job, which was carting hides from the abattoirs in Newmarket to a tannery in Richmond. The hides were dripping in blood and fat and stank to high heaven, and had to be loaded and unloaded by hand. His one regret was being shunned by fellow human beings when he travelled home from work on the train each day. But my father got his own back on hot days. Driving through the city on the way to Richmond his truck would be pursued by hordes of drooling blowies and smell so bad that people would put handkerchiefs over their noses when he stopped at intersections. He drove the truck for the first few years of the Great Depression and during this time he developed a burning ambition to drive a bus, the only means of motor transport he had ever seen where the load took itself on and off the vehicle.

There was a bus that ran past our door in Ormond. Continually pestering the owner of the bus service for a job eventually paid off and my father became a bus driver, piloting a Reo Speed Wagon along the length of Grange Road. That was about the time I began to have memories: my old man parking the bus out the front in his meal break and me climbing in to sit on his knee and hold the steering wheel and play with switches, and later sitting in the corner next to him on his Gladstone bag for a ride to the terminus and back. It seemed I was destined to be a bus driver.

It came to pass that a bloke named Wally Laidlaw and my father started talking about forming a partnership and in 1938 they took up the licences of the Coburg Heidelberg Omnibus Company, with four Federal buses and a garage and workshop in Bell Street, Preston. My parents rented a house on the corner of Banksia and Cape streets in Heidelberg. Soon after that, the bus company obtained a school contract driving kids from the Heidelberg area to Ivanhoe Grammar School, so my parents decided to send me there and my father could take me to and from school.

Changing schools is never easy, but Ivanhoe was different. The headmaster was the Reverend Sydney Buckley, 'Cobber' to the boys, and he knew everybody by name from the first time he met you. He really was a lovely man. Only today I opened my mail and there was an invitation to the annual lunch reunion of 'Buckley's Boys', and I left school 65 years ago.

•

My first job was at S.R. Evans Motorcycles in Elizabeth Street, Melbourne, in 1947. I had been fascinated by the two-wheelers ever since my father bought the bus company in Preston. Tom and Stanley Woods, the two mechanics who maintained the buses, both had Rudge Ulster bikes that they raced regularly on the dirt track.

My first bike was an ex-military model Royal Enfield 350 side valve. The former army dispatch rider's machine was poor in power, used a lot of oil and handled very badly—in fact some experienced riders said it was bloody dangerous—but it was all I could get for 40 pounds, a year's savings. I soon succumbed to temptation and upgraded to a really flash road bike, a 1937 Levis 500 D Special. It had a 21-inch speedster wheel and alloy cycle guard on the front, an 18-inch 'fatty' on the rear, and heaps of chrome—a real head turner.

I left S.R. Evans in 1948 and started working for my old man at the bus depot in Bell Street, Preston. The four-vehicle business he bought in 1938 had expanded fourfold. I began in the workshop as a motor mechanic, working with people from all over the world: Greeks, Italians, Calabrians, Sicilians, Yugoslavs, Maltese, Dutch, British, Germans, and Joe the Latvian. I really enjoyed getting to know those blokes. Conversations in the lunch room would be about faraway places with customs or foods that were so different to Australia's. Most of the blokes had been displaced in the Second World War, so there was never a shortage of stories, some amusing, some horrifying.

•

Leisure time in those days revolved around motorbikes and I bought a 1938 249cc Empire Star BSA (Birmingham Small Arms Company), and with some help from the Woods brothers stripped and prepared it for scramble racing, an event similar to today's motocross, only undertaken around bush tracks.

When there were no races on I just took off for a ride with a few mates to wherever. Favourite destinations were the Great Ocean Road, Phillip Island, or the Black Spur in the Great Dividing Range. It was exhilarating stuff.

Wednesday and Saturday nights became very special. Billy Glennon promoted the dance at the Heidelberg Town Hall, and I wouldn't miss it for quids, always hopeful that I would meet a girl. There was a particular girl who was always noticeable because she was a good looker, could dance well and wore really smart clothes. One night the barn dance, one of those where you change partners throughout the dance, finished with me opposite this girl and we introduced ourselves. Valerie West, her name was. We had a bit of a chat and when I asked her for the next foxtrot, which happened to be the last dance for the night, she said yes. Then, when I asked if I could give her a lift home on the bike, she also agreed, but said that I would have to drop her off down the block from where she lived as her father forbade her to ride on a motorbike.

Johnny Grayden, a local bloke with a real groovy band, had a gig at the Preston Town Hall on a Wednesday night, so I asked Valerie if she wanted to go. She said yes, but again I would have to pick her up down the block. On the night, I got toffed up in my best gear, looking sharp, but the Levis wouldn't go. I messed about with it for a while, but there was no way I could get a kick out of it. No option—I grabbed a torch and some insulation tape and affixed it to the forks of the BSA racing bike as a headlamp and rode off to pick up my date.

It was a freezing night and as conversation was not possible I remember thinking to myself as we were riding across Bell Street, *No wonder I can't get a girlfriend*. Even a good bike was second-class transport on a date; a BSA racing machine was ridiculous.

Then, as we pulled up at the traffic lights at Plenty Road, a police car slid up alongside us. Valerie immediately burst into tears, pleading with the cops not to tell her father she was on a motorbike. They weren't paying her the slightest bit of attention, but were taking a real interest in my bike, which was unregistered, had no tail light, no proper headlight and an open megaphone exhaust system.

I was fortunate that our bus depot was only 600 metres down the road. We pushed the bike there and left it, walking the remainder of the journey to the town hall. We left the gig early to catch the bus home, Valerie got off at the Military Hospital to walk back to her house and I continued to Heidelberg station. And that was how the romance started.

I bought my first car soon after that for 60 pounds, a 1928 Singer Porlock Sports. It was a boat-tail two-seater with 27-inch wire wheels and a timber-framed fabric-covered body, built like the early aeroplanes. It was a bit sick when I bought it but looked really smart when the renovation was completed. I didn't have the Singer for long, though, because a bloke came up to me in the street when I was parking it one day and offered me 125 pounds for it. 'It's yours,' I said, as I snatched the money out of his hand, and so began a long history of buying cars to renovate.

I continued to see Valerie and we got engaged when she was seventeen and I was twenty. Was that not what life was all about? Get a girlfriend, get engaged, get married, build a house and have kids. That was how it was supposed to happen in the 1940s, and that is exactly what did happen.

Soon after this we saw a land auction advertised at Macleod and went with my father to have a look. It was the last block of about ten for sale and the auctioneer was struggling to get it to 190 quid. 'Buy it,' said my old man. We ended up buying the block for 196 pounds and were lucky to get it for that, because it left me with only 4 pounds in the bank.

It was a 50 by 150 foot house lot with electricity but no water, no gas, no sewerage, no stormwater drains, no phone, no road, just two wheel tracks leading to four survey pegs in a paddock. That was what you got in outer Melbourne in 1950.

Val and I got married on 5 February 1952 at St James Church of England in Ivanhoe. It was 105 degrees Fahrenheit (about 40 degrees Celsius) by 11 a.m.—a God-awful day with a howling north wind. Fortunately a weak cool change did arrive just before the ceremony, which made it bearable for people in suits, collars, ties and all the paraphernalia.

The bride was late and that got me stressed. My best man, Alan Cromb, said, 'Don't worry, they're supposed to be late,' but that didn't help. Val eventually arrived with her three bridesmaids, looking gorgeous in the long white wedding dress she had made for herself, even though her features were concealed behind a veil—the custom at the time.

We had a reception at the Preston Town Hall, with Johnny Grayden and his band playing, then went to the Prince of Wales Hotel in Fitzroy Street, St Kilda. It was a swanky address in those days, but the trams nearly drove us to distraction. We were unaccustomed to city noises. We took off the following morning to drive to Surfers Paradise for our honeymoon. It was no Gold Coast back then, just Cavill's Surfers Paradise Hotel and a few beach shacks owned by Brisbanites.

Val and I lived in Macleod for six years, had two boys, Russell and Martin, and developed a great relationship with our neighbours. We all built our own homes and had kids at about the same time. We played cards or square-danced on Saturday nights. The cricket test in England was eagerly awaited and listened to on the BBC until the early hours, and the Aussie tradition of getting together with an armful of beer and a plate of sandwiches was the routine.

It was around then that I got serious about renovating cars and bought another Singer sports, a 1938 model, to be followed by a 39 model, before an Austin 8, an Austin A40 and then I got into big horsepower when somebody told me about this 1939 Ford V8 Mercury sedan on a farm out at Rockbank. The 39 Mercury was a really smart car and I went to look at it with great expectations, but arrived at this run down property to find the car in a hay barn covered in chook shit from the hens that had been laying their eggs in it, and rat shit from the rodents who were after the eggs. What a mess! 'Belonged to me old man,' the bloke said. 'He carked it a couple o' years back and I ain't got no money to fix it, mate.' As if it would cost money to wind up the windows.

Anyway, I bought it, renovated it, kept it for a couple of years then replaced it with a 1948 Mercury and later a 1950 Custom, followed by a 1955 Ford Sunliner. I grew to love Ford V8s and still do. I now have a Mach 1 Mustang as my boy's toy.

•

My father and Wally Laidlaw decided to dissolve their partnership and sell the Coburg Heidelberg Omnibus Company in 1960. Wally wanted to retire and the old man wished to stay in business, so they sold the main part of the operation, the Bell Street route, and my father retained the licences for extensions in Glenroy that had yet to be fully developed. I was not privy to my father's financial status, but I assume that when he cleaned off all of his debts and purchased the licences and buses, there was bugger all left.

We certainly did not start off in Glenroy in a big way. We rented an old barn on a rural property in Westbreen as a depot. It had three tin sides and a tin roof, and was big enough to fit two buses to work on, but it had a dirt floor that could flood in winter and choke you to death with dust on a windy day in summer. The mud and dust problem was not just confined to our depot either. Half the roads we ran our services along were little more than dirt tracks. Ted Wimble, another driver, and I built a 12 by 12 foot lock-up building alongside the shed that served as an office and store. The dunny was out in the back paddock and serviced by the 'night soil' man.

My job? I was a bus driver, motor mechanic, body repairer, coachbuilder, panel beater, spray painter, and doer of anything else that needed to be done.

We had four 20-year-old Federals and two ten-year-old Bedford buses to call a fleet: four pieces of shit and a couple of fair vehicles. The Federals were built by coachbuilders Cheetham and Borthwick in Carlton, with lightweight sheet-steel panels screwed to a timber frame on an extended American Federal truck chassis. Much of the timber frame had rotted or come adrift in the joints after two decades and the bodies flexed all over the place as they went down the road. It was only the sheet-metal skins that held them together. The front mudguards flapped about as we drove them through the potholes—we called them 'friendly fenders' because they waved at the passersby.

It fell to Ted Wimble and me to solve the problem. We bought a bench saw, found a source in Coburg for good quality kiln-dried hardwood, and—as a pair of bus drivers—set out to build a bus. We stripped all the panels off the first Federal and gave the framework a kick, and it fell off the chassis—it was that bad. But we were not to be deterred. We rebuilt the four buses in eighteen months, as well as driving our regular shifts in the morning and afternoon.

Later we bought an industrial site in Walter Street, Glenroy, and constructed a purpose-built maintenance facility and office. By then my brothers Ron and Alan had joined the company and the old man gave the three of us a share in the business. Ron looked after the office, Alan the maintenance and I looked after the charter operations, which included rostering the drivers and allocating the vehicles for the following day's work, and I also drove one of the buses.

I was a real live bus driver. I left home at 5 a.m., started work at 6 a.m., and finished at about 6 p.m. They were long hours but it was just how life was. But every day was exactly the same, every day was an ordinary day, I felt ordinary. I was getting bored, there was no time for renovating cars. I needed a project, and that's what I got—though it wasn't one on wheels.

After five years in Macleod the time came for us to move on. Val and I had two kids and another on the way, so our two-bedroom house had become crowded. We eventually found our ideal block of land, a 4-acre lot on Main Road, just near the Lower Eltham park. We designed our new home as a replica of the Bangemall Inn, of which I had a photo, where my parents lived after they married in 1928 and where I was conceived. And we decided to build it ourselves as owner-builders.

The house was to be a rectangle with a hip roof, belled out over a verandah all around, and constructed of all natural and recycled materials where possible. So after the site was excavated and we had the clay on hand, we got hold of a couple of mudbrick boxes, one for Val and one for me, and on weekends we became mudbrick makers.

During the week I had a lot of waiting time with drop-offs and pick-ups all over Melbourne, so with a copy of the page advertising demolitions and building materials in Saturday's *Age* newspaper, I was able to haunt sites all over the city. I spent more than twelve months gathering stuff, much of it from the demolition of Presbyterian Ladies College in East Melbourne and the grandstand at the Melbourne Showgrounds, and I also haunted Whelan the Wrecker's yard.

It was a very eventful time, and a lot of hard work, but eventually our home was built, and we lived there happily for over ten years. Today the property is known as La Fontana Ristorante.

CHAPTER 2

IN SEARCH OF BURKE AND WILLS

I WAS AT THE depot one day doing what I always did, writing out running sheets, rostering drivers, allocating vehicles for the following day's work, when a bloke walked into the office and said, 'You got a job for me?' Now that question really took me by surprise. John Knox was a one-vehicle operator trading as Starliner. His main source of income was an overnight trip to Thredbo on Fridays, carting fresh produce for the ski lodges and weekend skiers to the snowfields. He had a good business going in winter, but seasonality had him struggling to maintain a viable operation.

John had actually walked in the door at the right moment with a proposal that was right for the time. Our midweek charter business was a real growth area. We had bought two new Leyland VK 43 chassis and Alan Denning, an up-and-coming Brisbane coachbuilder, fitted custom bodies to them. Alan then designed and built his own monocoach, the prototype of the Denning coach that in later years would set the standard for extended touring in this country.

John's proposal was that we would start selling charters to groups, social clubs, schools and whomever else on ski weekends and begin operating tours to Ayers Rock during school holidays. It was a plan that would virtually ensure a 7-day operational schedule for the vehicles throughout the year. This, of course, was new to us. We had never gone out and sold travel; we just satisfied the needs of those who walked in the door.

It was when I began to take tours to Ayers Rock that the seeds my old man had planted in my mind began to germinate. I was fascinated by the land itself: what lived in it, what grew in it, who discovered it, and the people who had pioneered this very different country called the outback. I had been camping with the old man many times when I was a little tacker, exploring the back country of New South Wales and Queensland, but this was different.

Talking about these things with folk on our Ayers Rock tours convinced me that there were a lot of people out there who shared similar interests to mine. Not content to just look at the country, they wanted to 'feel' it, to 'live with the earth', to be 'touched by it', to go where no tourist had ever been before, leaving nothing but footprints and taking nothing but photographs, before moving on to the next adventure and the next destination.

There were no 'off the beaten track' operators in the eastern states at that time. There were a couple of blokes in Adelaide, but they concentrated on the Flinders Ranges and Cooper Creek zones. So I began putting itineraries together on paper, following the journeys of Robert O'Hara Burke and William John Wills, Charles Sturt, Ernest Giles and others, also looking at four-wheel-drive equipment in order to embark on this pioneering venture taking people to the Red Centre, Arnhem Land, the Kimberley and along Cooper Creek.

I spoke with family members about the project. They saw merit in it, and so we settled on a Series 2 Land Rover safari wagon, carrying four passengers and a driver. I felt I was achieving something. There was, however, still much work to be done: survey expeditions to assemble workable itineries, and sales aids like brochures and display material to introduce the mysteries of Australia's inland to the city dweller.

It was 1968 when our first survey mission got underway, with just four of us making up the 'team'. John Knox and I would be lead

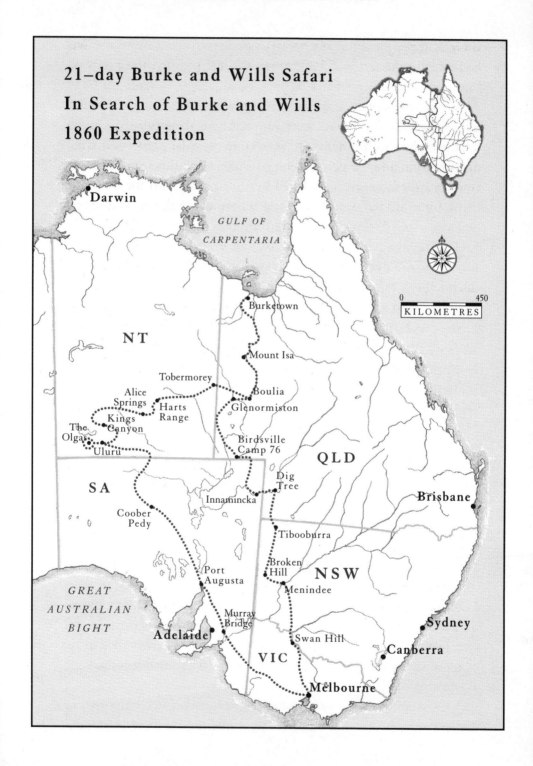

drivers in this venture. Graham Rose, a mate of mine, was camp cook; he would also learn the ropes as a future backup driver. 'Rosey' had spent many years working in shearing sheds in southern New South Wales. Rennie Ellis, an aspiring young photojournalist who had just arrived back from overseas, was to make a twenty-minute 16-millimetre movie. It was to be simply titled 'Outback Australia' and we planned to screen it at social clubs, educational institutions, travel agents seminars and the like.

We couldn't believe our luck when we found Rennie, his price was so much cheaper than anyone else's. Rennie told us he had worked on movie sets overseas and had already made one documentary, but all that turned out to be bullshit. He had never had anything to do with moving pictures other than sit in a cinema. But that was our Rennie, a great bloke who could talk himself in and out of anywhere. We became firm friends and I was to work on several projects with him over the years. I got him to help me write the introduction to our first brochure because he understood my message. He had never been in the bush before, but he had felt it:

> It's true that for most Australians, indeed the majority of people throughout the world, life is becoming a continuity of pressures and frustrations. Relaxed and mentally refreshing holidays are becoming increasingly necessary for the urban dweller, yet he or she is finding the holiday resorts a repetition of the environment they are trying to escape—the crowds, congestion, pollution.
>
> This is why so many people are turning and returning to a holiday with Bill King's Northern Safaris. In Australia we still have room to move. We still have frontiers where man is not just a cipher in a system.
>
> We at Northern Safaris have the knowhow and experience to open up the remote areas of our country and share the outback experience with you.
>
> Living close to the earth, following bush tracks and century-old camel-train paths, absorbing nature's gifts and the peace of the

bush, and swapping yarns around the evening campfire create a new quality of life that is only revealed to those who travel beyond the fringe.

That message about life and leisure was written 40 years ago. Nothing much has changed, has it?

•

Our main itinerary was to be the Burke and Wills expedition. We were to follow as closely as possible the explorers' route, starting at the bluestone cairn in Royal Park in Melbourne from where the expedition departed on 19 August 1860, to the Gulf of Carpentaria, then return via Ayers Rock.

The departure of the Burke and Wills expedition was one of the biggest events Melbourne town had ever witnessed and was hours late leaving because it was so cumbersome. It took them seventeen days to get to Swan Hill and another month to get to Menindee, where they set up a major depot. Burke took a room at Maidens Hotel while the base camp was being set up. The pub was still in the hands of the Maiden family when we went through Menindee in 1968. They had kept Burke's room intact: the iron bed, cedar wardrobe and chest of drawers, wash basin and water pitcher were all there. But you won't believe it—the Maidens sold the hotel some years later and the new owner knocked out the wall adjoining Burke's bedroom, tossed out the furniture and extended the bar to install a pool table. It makes you wonder about some people, doesn't it?

We were then to drive to Broken Hill en route to Mootwingee to familiarise ourselves with what the 'Silver City' had to offer the visitor. Broken Hill was to be the hub of our operation, where people coming from Adelaide on Greyhound buses and Sydney on the Indian Pacific train would join the tour. So it was an important part of the itinerary.

It still is a fascinating place and, apart from the legacy of art left by Pro Hart and the Brushmen of the Bush, Broken Hill is historically significant for many reasons. It was where the boundary rider Charles Rasp first discovered silver in 1883, and that led to the establishment of Broken Hill Pty Ltd.

It was where war was declared on Australia for the first time, by two immigrant hawkers from Afghanistan and Pakistan on New Year's Day 1915, in retribution for Australia going to war with Turkey. They opened fire on a group of Broken Hill picnickers en route to Silverton on the Silverton tramway. Six people were shot dead in the attack before the culprits were killed in a shootout with police. There was a sizable Muslim population in Broken Hill at that time, a legacy of the camel trains that were the only reliable form of transport in the early days. In 1891 they built their own mosque, utilising the popular construction material of the time—galvanised iron. It is now a heritage-listed building.

The settlement of nearby Silverton is unique. Regarded today as a ghost town, it is inhabited by about 50 people living in renovated ruins who are in the main associated with the tourist trade. Silverton is now known for its film sets—*Mad Max, The Adventures of Priscilla Queen of the Desert, Razorback,* and 30 or so other Australian movies and TV programs have utilised the pub and surrounding desert country in their productions.

The Silverton pub is an institution, the epitome of an outback watering hole. I was there one day and a horse that was wandering around the street stuck her head through the door and peered in. When her eyes became accustomed to the gloom she stepped in and breasted the bar. She was not a small horse either, and had to stoop to get in. Misty was a regular and came in every afternoon for a couple of pots of draught that the publican poured into a bowl on the bar for her. 'Whose horse is it?' I asked as Misty quietly lapped up her beer.

'Dunno, mate. She just wandered into town one day and has been here ever since,' said a bloke.

When the horse had finished she began staring at the publican, licking her chops and looking for another one. 'That's it, mate, no more. Bugger off,' said the publican. With that the horse turned around and headed out the door, but as her back end passed through the doorway she lifted her tail in a most unladylike fashion and let out a resounding fart. I assumed it was to voice displeasure at being refused another drink.

Misty has gone now, off to that big pasture in the sky, and whether there is a friendly pub up there for her to enjoy a couple, who knows—but she is close to her beloved watering hole in Silverton, interred in the beer garden with appropriate recognition of her contribution to the local culture.

We followed the expedition's route, which took us to Mootwingee, where the New South Wales Parks and Wildlife Service in the early 1960s had constructed quite a remarkable visitors centre, with excellent displays and a theatre that showed a film depicting the life of the desert people. It was appropriate because the Aboriginal artwork in that region was unique.

Now I have always subscribed to the theory that the quality of Aboriginal art is governed by the availability of food; the less time needed to hunt up a feed, the more time available to pursue the arts. In Arnhem Land and the Kimberley, where there are superb examples of paintings, or the islands north of Darwin, where Tiwi people carve elaborate Pukamani poles, tucker is easier to come by. Desert art is much simpler; in particular the desert people of Central Australia told their stories with stone arrangements, intricate patterns of rocks laid out on the sand, using the only material that was abundant. I only ever saw one, a real one that is.

We had stopped for lunch on the Mereenie Track next to a small watercourse. A fire had recently passed by and the ground was bare. I went for a stroll along the watercourse, looking at stones on the ground, and I noted they were in a line and of similar size. Then I saw another line, stones of a different size, then lots of lines. We were also beneath an escarpment, so I scampered up to the top and there it was, probably 20 metres across, a very elaborate pattern of pathways, like a maze, leading inwards to a pattern of circles (the sign depicting water).

On one of the pathways you could see a serpent; on another a goanna, the rock depicting the head narrowing a bit, then fat rocks depicting the belly, with smaller ones making its skinny tail. The dozen or so people on that trip were really privileged. I later asked some rangers if they knew about it: they didn't, and didn't seem to care much. I never told anybody else and after the first bit of rain it disappeared under the herbage again. But in all likelihood it is still there, although the sighting was 40 years ago.

As we know, many artists of Central Australia continue to produce 'sand painting' on canvas, using dots and lines to represent stones, sticks and tracks. It was an art form introduced in the 70s by creative people to bring to the world their interpretation of the primitive desert art pursued by their ancestors. Now, elaborate works on canvas by famous artists like the late Clifford Possum, Emily Kngwarreye, Gloria Petyarre and Minnie Pwerle are worth thousands of dollars and are hung in many state and national public buildings as well as private galleries.

While there are examples of rock art found in many places in Australia, it is in the harsh environment of western New South Wales where the most spectacular rock 'peckings' are found. Rock peckings or etchings were created with the use of stone implements—rocks with varying degrees of hardness to use as hammers and chisels. Flakes of quartz, for example, were widely used by the desert people of New South Wales as chisels, spear points and the like. I make the point that the rock 'peckings' at Mootwingee are so elaborate they must come from a much more lush period in that part of Australia. Life-size emus and wallabies painstakingly etched into huge slabs of rock suggest a plentiful food source.

The rock art at the top of the Bynguano Range overlooking the surrounding plain is also a classic. A giant serpent surrounded by the hands of the tribe etched in ochre, it is among the best and certainly the largest example that I have seen.

Early pioneers used the place, too. They could fence off the gullies in the ranges to hold stock, and in one of the gullies near an old campsite there is a bit of authentic graffiti, including the signature of Ernest Giles. Those old blokes never ceased to amaze me. Giles worked on stations in New South Wales in the 1860s before heading off to South Australia to do the same thing. In 1873 he manned an expedition to Central Australia to explore the country west of the telegraph line. He took another expedition in 1875 and again in 1876, and on two occasions rode across the Gibson Desert to the West Australian coast and back. He covered more country on horseback during those years than most of the four-wheel-drive enthusiasts of today do in their lifetime.

•

We discovered all sorts of interesting things on that survey trip. There was an old bullock trail that went from Broken Hill to the White Cliffs opal fields. If you looked hard you could still find signs, like the occasional oxen shoe, rock work bolstering the tracks on the hillsides, and marked trees. John Gerritsen, the ranger at Mootwingee, had told us about this waterhole to look for. It was a huge outcrop of rock and in the top was a deep fissure that was never known to be dry. In the old days they once found the bodies of two people who had died of thirst lying on the shady side of it. Poor buggers—they were only a few metres from life.

We stayed by the waterhole that night, and I got the biggest fright of all my born days. Can you imagine the sound of a steel trestle table with pots, pans, tin plates, cutlery and food supplies on top being rattled about in the middle of the night? I poked my head out of the tent I was sharing with Graham Rose and there was this great wild boar up on his hind legs, trying to steal our grub. Then he bowled the whole lot over on top of his sow, which let out an ungodly scream and backpedalled straight into our little two-man tent in which there were now three of us. The dopey pig couldn't find her way out. We all ended up tangled in the tent and rolling around on the ground. Rosey and I yelled out for help, which sent the sow into a frenzy and the boar into a nasty mood, charging the other blokes when they stuck their heads out of their tents. Thank God the sow's razor-sharp trotters tore the tent to shreds and they both raced off.

It was possible in those days to traverse New South Wales from south to north across stations and disused mining tracks to Milparinka and Tibooburra in the Corner Country. Milparinka was in a time warp, a remnant of the Golden Era in the latter part of the nineteenth century. Deserted historic buildings were still conspicuous in the 'town' that included the perfectly preserved stone courthouse and gaol and the ruin of the Commercial Bank and the bakehouse. The only inhabited building was the Albert Hotel. Built in 1885 at the height of the rush, it was the home of the Garland family, Alan, Jenny, and their two kids. It was an outback pub (and a petrol pump) where a cold beer had a flavour all of its own. The Albert is the last of four licences in Milparinka. It's hard to imagine that the region was once home to more than a thousand miners.

•

In later years we began to operate painting schools. I would select a destination that offered impressive subjects and landscapes and retain a known artist to accompany the tour as a tutor. We would provide all the equipment and knowhow; the participants only had to bring themselves, some gear and their paint case and easel. I advertised on Saturdays in the arts section of the Melbourne *Age*. And I will say to you without fear of contradiction that there was nobody in Melbourne's art world in the early 1970s who did not know about Bill King's painting schools and the unique destinations we chose. It was such a different concept of travel and we received a huge amount of free publicity and editorial space. At first they were all bush camps, and we had people on board who would never think of going on a camping holiday, yet it became fashionable to travel with us.

The tutor would do a demonstration each morning and then the students would go off and do their own thing, with the tutor checking in on them occasionally during the afternoon. Each evening prior to dinner and with the broaching of the 'Chateau Cardboard' they would bring their work out for discussion and critique. Some of the work was truly bad, but they didn't care. They were away in the peace of the bush pursuing their hobby in a manner that had never been available to them before.

We ran our first painting trip to Milparinka and took Alan Martin as tutor. He was a well-known Eltham artist from the Max Meldrum School who lived not far from where I did. I had met Alan years before and was well aware that he loved the bush as he regularly went off on painting trips on his own. He was a bloody good teacher, too, the perfect bloke to kick this thing off. Alan was a short fellow, very short, and had a mop of jet black hair and a bushy black beard above which a white nose protruded and two dark eyes peered: he answered to 'The Black Stump'.

I should say that the main participants in our painting schools were little old ladies, with a few younger ones and fewer blokes. On that first trip, we set up pretty good amenities. Our camp was only about 100 metres down the track from the Albert Hotel and we had done a deal with the Garlands to use their showers and toilets.

I always tried to serve good meals in the bush, meals that would surprise people and that first night was barbecued lamb. We had picked up the meat from a station owner I knew on the way through. He had cut it into chops ready for a barbecue. It was beautiful meat, too, raised on salt bush and desert herbage, a very different flavour from the grass-fed meat we get in the far south. It smelled magnificent on the barbecue and I reckoned I had cooked it to perfection, just pink.

We had a crew of three on the job: Rosey, Riley Stevens, a young Eltham girl I was training as cook's help, and myself. When it came time to serve up dinner, Rosey put the meat on a tray while

I dished up the veggies. 'Bring over the chops,' I said, and behind me I heard Riley mutter, 'Oh fuck.'

'No, she hasn't,' went through my mind, but she had. I turned around to find Riley had dropped the chops on the floor of the cooking tent and most of them were scattered in the sand. The three of us tried to wash the things in a bucket of water, but all we did was ensure the ones that weren't covered in sand didn't miss out. We cranked up the barbie to heat them up again and by this time the campers were so hungry I thought they might start eating each other.

It was the worst meal that we had ever served—lamb à la grit is no bloody good, it's a wonder it didn't take the enamel off their teeth. Embarrassing moments, tell me about 'em.

Unlike our dinner on that first painting school, the bush telegraph was working very well—well enough to get out to Theldarpa Station where they were shearing. The station was about 80 k's away, not far after a day in the shed, so it wasn't long before they lobbed up at the Albert in clouds of dust. We were still tidying up camp after dinner when the painters took off to absorb the local culture and, I must say, for city folk it was an educational experience.

By the time the crew and I got over to the pub, the local lads were in full flight. 'Toby the Camel' was drinking his warm Melbourne Bitter out of 26-ounce bottles because it made him drunk quicker. Hookey, the shed boss, was telling a couple of blokes in no uncertain terms that they couldn't shear one another's boof heads and if they didn't 'speed it up a bit' they could fuck off out of the shed. Alan Garland, the publican, was yelling at the mob to tone it down. Toby the Camel had latched on to one of our ladies and she was obviously enjoying the attention, even though Toby was no study in oils, with his two front teeth missing. (I was to notice over the years that some people do behave differently when on holiday.)

I soon got sick of the noise and was still grumpy about the meal being stuffed up so I headed off to bed. Hookey was hanging over the front verandah of the pub throwing up. 'Bit crook, Hookey?' I said.

'Nope, just don't want it,' he replied, heading back to the bar to top up again.

In the morning the lady sharing the tent with the woman Toby the Camel was eyeing off in the pub told me, 'Jill didn't come back last night.'

'Really,' I said, not wishing to get involved and not knowing if she was telling me out of envy or indignation.

•

The next stop on our survey was Tibooburra, just up the road. It is another old gold town and home to Barney and Jos Davies. Barney had worked on cattle stations all his life and 'retired' to town to take up the lease on the Family Hotel, famous for the murals by Sir Russell Drysdale, with his 'Drinkers at the Bar' sketched on the wall, and later for Clifton Pugh and Sydney artist Frank Hodgkinson's work. There was also a Fred Williams on the bar wall. The art was worth far more than the pub.

Clif's mural was huge and covered one whole wall in the main bar. 'The Bacchus' was a sort of self-portrait of Clif, with devil's horns on his head, sitting on a stool enjoying a drink. He was naked with his legs apart and his willy in full view and his 'orchestra stalls' hanging well below that, and he had several semi-naked female figures draped all over him. That was the original version, but the local cop freaked out and called it pornographic, instructing Barney and Jos to cover it up. They stuck a tea towel over the offending parts until Clif's next visit. He then painted a vine leaf over them and later, when the cop retired, Clif replaced the family jewels.

On our survey and film-making expedition we were also keeping our ears open for stories about Ludwig Leichhardt—wishful thinking, I know, but if you don't talk to people about these things something might slip by. I used to get around to raising the subject of early explorers with everybody along the track.

Leichhardt had left Brisbane in April 1848 with four white companions and two Aboriginal trackers to travel to the Swan

River Colony in Western Australia, and they were never heard of again. Four years before, he had successfully manned an expedition from Brisbane and reached Port Essington, on Australia's northern coastline, so it seems logical to me that Leichhardt would use a route he was familiar with on the first part of his 1848 journey. He would then break into new country south of where Tobermory Station is situated today, on the Queensland–Northern Territory border, and that was where we were.

After we had visited the historic Burke and Wills sites along Cooper Creek and Camp 76 on the Diamantina River near Birdsville, we veered off along station tracks skirting the fringe of the Simpson Desert. We were heading out through Cravens Peak to Glenormiston Station when we came across a stockmen's camp.

There were three Indigenous stockmen with a big string of horses and a fair mob of cattle settled in by a waterhole. They were working deep into the Simpson Desert, rounding up scrub cattle for Glenormiston. They had shot a steer and invited us to stay for a feed. Why wouldn't we? They had meat and we had beer. They'd been out in the bush for ages, so even a warm stubbie was seen as nectar from the Dreamtime.

That night around the campfire we had a really interesting conversation. The stockmen were locals, born in that country, and the two older blokes had heard about Ludwig Leichhardt. Stories had been handed down to them from their ancestors about white men and horses coming through their country.

Then the conversation got even more interesting. It appears that many years before, the same two blokes were rounding up scrub cattle deep in the desert and stumbled across the remains of a campsite gone terribly wrong. Under the lee of a huge dune they found skeletal remains, saddlery and gear. The leather was so old it was brittle. There were also iron stirrups, buckles and other relics.

Excited by their find, they poked a stick into the top of the dune as a marker, took a rough bearing of where they were and got on with earning a living, vowing to return and investigate further.

They informed the powers that be about the discovery, but it was many months before a group from Brisbane arrived to research the site. However, they couldn't find the dune marker again—which is understandable in thousands of square kilometres of desert country where every sand dune looks the same—so it is a mystery that in all likelihood will never be solved.

•

Burke and Wills of course never actually made the waters of the Gulf of Carpentaria. They reached impassable mosquito-infested mangroves and headed back to enact the tragedy at Cooper Creek. We continued north through Cloncurry to Burketown on our journey, then turned south and travelled back through Camooweal and Urandangi.

Urandangi is another of those strange locations with no reason to be where it is. It's a pub and a petrol pump located 1600 kilometres northwest of Brisbane, with a population of about 50 people who are probably there because they have nowhere else to go. It was established in the 1880s and went past its use-by date when the cattle drives ceased coming down the Georgina stock route to the rail head in Dajarra. Road trains with the capability of picking up and delivering stock at the station gate put the rail service and the drovers out of business.

We were after a feed of meat as well as fuel and beer, and when the publican told us they'd killed a steer a couple of days before, I bought a big lump of hindquarter. We had no refrigeration, but fresh meat in a sugar bag on the roof rack with a bit of air getting to it will last three days or so. We already had some spuds, onions and a small pumpkin so Rosey announced that roast beef and veggies were to be the fare for the night, and he got his cooking fire going in the hole he had dug.

We settled in for a few tinnies, waiting for the coals to slow-roast our dinner in the camp oven. It's not a process that can be hurried so a lot of tinnies had passed by and a lot of lies had been shared before Rosey said, 'Grub's up!' We all agreed the meal was absolutely delicious and Rosey's 'special sauce' was really something.

'Bloody beautiful. Compliments to the chef. It's an appropriate night to open our Macquarie port,' I said, rummaging in the back of the truck for a bottle I had secured in a safe place for a special occasion, and there it was—empty.

'Which one of you buggers has been drinking the port?' I asked. Silence. I couldn't believe it. There were only three of them and they were all shaking their heads. 'Okay, where did it go then?' Rosey was looking at the ground sheepishly and shuffling his boot about in the dirt.

'You bastard!' I said to him. 'You drank it!'

'No, I didn't,' he said. 'I cooked the beef in it. You said it was for a special occasion, and this meal was special.'

Spare me.

We turned west down a couple of wheel tracks heading into the Northern Territory near Tobermory Station. Our plan was to reach Harts Range, about 350 kilometres along the track, then go south over the mountains, using old mining tracks into Alice Springs via Arltunga. We were well on our way, heading around this dune, and were dumbfounded to find that sitting on a claypan on the other side was an old flat-sided Land Rover utility, and there sitting in a deck chair was this bloke surrounded by 'stuff', more than you could ever imagine, coming out of the ute.

He was dressed in a blue boiler suit and a blue beret like the RAAF ground crews had in the Second World War. He had a big black beard and there was a pipe sticking out of it. 'G'day,' he said as we pulled up. 'Alby Shultz,' he introduced himself.

'You in trouble?' I asked.

'Nah, I was. I blew a top radiator hose and didn't have a spare, so I shot a kangaroo and skinned his tail to make a sleeve to patch it up.'

He's kidding, I thought, but the bonnet of his vehicle was up, so I walked over for a look and sure enough there was this furry radiator hose bound with insulation tape. Bloody hell!

'Now I don't have enough water to fill him up,' Alby said. 'Gotta keep a bit to drink.'

We topped up the radiator and he tried to start the Landy, but the battery was too low so we jump-started it. I checked out the radiator hose and it had billowed out a bit, but there was no leak. 'Genius,' I said to myself.

'Wouldn't have any spare meat, would you?' he asked. 'I've eaten all me roo.'

'Aw, yeah,' said Rosey, and pulled the bag off the roof rack to cut him off a lump.

'Wow, that's a good piece of meat,' said Alby, when Rosey handed him the lump. 'I'll just chuck it in the fridge.'

Among the huge pile of stuff that surrounded Alby was a small household refrigerator, of all things. There was no generator to power it and I was wondering if he'd invented some other power source when he said, 'Been below zero at night here, so I leave the fridge door open at night and shut him in the day—works fine.'

But this wasn't the end of the Alby Shultz story. We move on about twenty years and Melbourne *Sun* journalist Keith Dunstan and cartoonist Jeff Hook went off to the United States to ride bikes all over the place and send stories back to the newspaper. I was reading *The Sun* one morning and as I turned a page I was confronted with a sketch of this bloke in a boiler suit and beret with a big whisker and a pipe sticking out of it. 'Bloody Alby Shultz,' I said to myself, and it was. Dunstan and Hook had come across him in the Mojave Desert or some such obscure place. He was an international character, our Alby.

•

We returned from the outback armed with the information we needed to operate an educational expedition following in the tracks of Burke and Wills. We had enough 16-millimetre film in the can to produce a feature twenty-minute doco and stills for a high-quality brochure. We were ready. So we ran our first advertisement in

Walkabout, a prestigious Australian magazine at that time, and it worked—we received nearly three hundred reply coupons.

Then one day the old man arrived at the depot and said we needed to talk about the direction the company was taking. 'Okay,' I said, wondering what might be different to the status quo. So I sat down with my brother Ron and he proceeded to tell me that we were going to cease the public touring and concentrate on the charter and route services.

'There's no future in public touring,' he said.

I couldn't believe what I was hearing. We had established the foundation for this new business and Ron was telling me there was no future in the tourist industry. I was in shock, really; the dream of establishing Northern Safaris, our concept of creative leisure, was no more. There had been no warning—it was just out of the blue. The significance of what had been said began to sink in. I was back to being a bus driver, back where I started. Not that I believe there is anything wrong with being a bus driver, but I didn't see that as my career path.

It came to me all of a sudden; there was no planned decision. I just thought, *That's bullshit*, as I walked out the door and in through the next to speak to my father. I started with: 'Ron believes there's no future in the travel industry. He believes the business is best suited to charter and route operations. I believe there is a future in public tours so I wish to sell my share of the business and I'll purchase the Denning, the Land Rover and the sales aids we have produced.' And that was it. All those proceedings took about an hour—an hour that changed my life for all time.

So, I have related the first 39 years of my life and cannot even fill 39 pages, a very ordinary life indeed; it was to me, anyway. But it wasn't without some trepidation that I considered the future: 'Now, you're on your own, sonny boy, with a wife and family to feed, no business, no income and the biggest project of your life.'

CHAPTER 3

THE COLONEL, THREE LADIES AND ME

I CANNOT REMEMBER WHAT I said to Val when I arrived home that evening. I could not even comprehend what I had done myself; it was like the beginning of a second life, and nothing would ever be the same again.

In reality we had not bought a business—we had no customers. We had bought a bus, a Land Rover and (hopefully) more than a good idea at the time. While we had a brochure featuring four-wheel-drive tours, there was nothing for the Denning. We needed a coach tour brochure in the marketplace really fast and we needed that part of the business working to carry the off-road stuff until we became established.

That was also the day that Val discovered she was going back to work. We began advertising in the dailies, so there were brochure requests to be fulfilled, reservations and documentation to be managed and travel agents to be serviced. Later on it became her responsibility to ensure tours were appropriately provisioned and crews briefed on passenger requirements prior to departure.

Fortunately we had a couple of enquiries from an advertisement in *Walkabout*, and my first tour was the 21-day Burke and Wills expedition, setting out from Royal Park in Melbourne, where the original explorers departed in August 1860. I had four passengers to collect that day, all single bookings, one man and three women. I was bloody nervous, I can tell you. I had been carting people all over the place for years, but this was different. Much as I said to myself it was all the same, it wasn't.

I didn't really know what I was doing. I had been driving large groups, including school kids, for some years, and that felt sort of impersonal. They were the punters (the trade expression for passengers) and you were the crew and it was mostly to the same destination—Alice Springs and Ayers Rock. This was another story and very personal. I would be living closer to these people than I would with my own family, 24 hours a day for the next 21 days, and the trick would be to make them think I knew what I was doing.

Our pick-up point was outside the Princes Bridge railway station where Federation Square is today. The passengers were all lined up when I arrived in Flinders Street. 'Colonel Mac Dawson, US army, retired,' was how the man introduced himself. 'Ex-military,' I thought, 'that's good, he's been on a bivouac or two—he'll be handy around the camp.' As it turned out, he wasn't. The colonel had grown up in Texas, gone to military academy then went straight into a military advisory group attached to the White House. He remained there for the whole of his career, served under a succession of presidents and never left Washington, D.C. His main reason for participating in our expedition was to accumulate a photographic record of significant sites to accompany the lecture he was to deliver to his historical society back home.

The three females on tour were all in their 30s. Alison was a physiotherapist, Helen a secretary and Jill a nurse. They seemed well travelled, I thought, and that turned out to be true.

The colonel was sitting in the front seat with the three ladies in the back. In the rearview mirror I could see their eyes swivelling backwards and forwards, checking one another out, and then looking at the colonel and me. I had sunglasses on, so they couldn't see me checking them out. When one glances into the rearview mirror on a coach, all you see is a sea of faces. When I looked back in the Land Rover I saw a physiotherapist, a secretary and a nurse. I was on my own very steep learning curve.

We were headed for a bush camp somewhere between Balranald and Mungo, the archaeological site in southwestern New South Wales. The day passed uneventfully until we pulled up at this lovely claypan, clean as a whistle, no bindi-eyes and no water about to bring the mozzies. As I began unloading the gear, the colonel came up and said, 'Excuse me. Where's the bathroom?'

I thought he was kidding and poured him a mug of water from the jerry can, of which I had two. 'There you go, Colonel. You can clean your teeth in it, bathe in it, drink it, or if you're really clever, all three.' I immediately understood from the look on his face that he was very serious and took him through the 'shovel dunny' procedures.

Those unaccustomed to the ways of the bush always seemed to share the same difficulties as little kids, getting the hang of dropping the aforesaid problem on the proper spot from such an unfamiliar posture. Improvisation is also required. Is it too hard to dig a hole? I'd be surprised if there were no stones about, and a small monument to one's thoughtfulness is most appropriate. These were suggestions I included in my education process and most people got the message.

The problem with the colonel was that he had been on safaris in Africa, where there are facilities set up along the way and half a dozen bearers to look after the customer's every need. He assumed it would be the same in Australia, and I learned another lesson: provide more information to overseas visitors and eliminate the assumptions. The girls, though, were fine. They knew all about bush-style camping.

There was a phenomenon that occurred that evening which I had never seen before, and have never seen again. The sun had just set on the horizon and we were sitting around the campfire having a drink while the grub was cooking, when this strange noise gradually welled up. Coming from the west, it grew louder and louder. 'It's a bloody train,' somebody said.

Suddenly, this huge black cloud came straight towards us at an ever-increasing speed. Illuminated in the evening glow, it changed shape constantly as it rose up above the mulga. It was a massive flock of budgies; the sky was black with them, thousands of beautiful little birds. The roar from their flapping wings was almost deafening as they flew overhead and settled at a waterhole about 500 metres from where we were camped. If I had known the waterhole was there I wouldn't have stopped for fear of the mozzies, but how lucky we were that we did.

There had been a long period of drought during the 1960s, and waterholes were scarce. I can only assume that the birds spread out all over the countryside during the day to feed on the plains then teamed up as they flew towards their waterhole to camp for the night. I have only seen big flocks of cockatoos and parrots on two other occasions, once at a water tank near Frewena on the Barkly Highway and once at a water tank on the Nullarbor, but nothing like the size of this mob. My passengers were impressed.

•

The following day we were off to Lake Mungo and the Walls of China, where for thousands of years nature has been eroding the landscape into weird and quite spectacular formations. This is a really interesting area. Erosion is still exposing the bones of prehistoric animals, birds and humans, calcified plant life, ancient stone tools, and remnants of cooking fires that went back thousands of years.

Mungo is a treasure trove for archaeologists. In the year of our visit Professor Jim Bowler and a party from the Australian National University in Canberra unearthed the remains of a young female whom they named Mungo Woman, and carbon dating showed that she lived on earth some 30 000 years ago.

Then five years later, not 500 metres from the original find, they came across the remains of Mungo Man, a discovery that has stimulated debate between archaeologists ever since. Mungo Man was estimated to have lived more than 60 000 years ago and was ritually buried with his hands covering his family jewels, no doubt to protect them on whatever journey his relatives thought he would take. Not only that, the skeleton is of a fine structure, not unlike modern-day humans, and far different from any other prehistoric human skeletons discovered in Australia.

Even more intriguing was that after a study of his DNA, scientists arrived at the conclusion that his cells bore no resemblance whatsoever to other ancient skeletons, either Aboriginal or European. That conundrum is still to this day being debated by academics, because it seriously weakens the 'out of Africa' theory of evolution. If Mungo Man left Africa in the last 200 000 years, his DNA should be similiar to everybody else's, but it is not.

From Mungo we travelled across to Menindee to visit Burke's room, then still original, at Maidens Hotel. About a kilometre from town is Dost Mahomet's grave. He was one of two Afghan cameleers—the other being Esan Khan—who were brought to Australia by George Landells. Landells was a horse trader who sold his remounts in India and so was in an ideal situation to import camels and cameleers specifically for the Burke and Wills expedition.

Dost Mahomet was a young man of only 23, and he and Esan Kahn—both devout Muslims—had great difficulty with food, insisting on eating meat killed in the traditional halal method. Dost was one of three men left with William Brahe on Cooper Creek to await the return of Burke and Wills from their expedition to the north. Brahe was one of Burke's trusted lieutenants, a German immigrant who had arrived in Australia some eight years prior and was recruited for his experience with horses and cattle. After Brahe made the decision to abandon the Cooper Creek camp and return to Menindee, Dost was attacked by a camel that shattered his right arm, leaving him handicapped for life. He never left Menindee. When the expedition packed up to return to Melbourne he obtained employment with Ah Chung, a baker who had set up a business in the settlement. Dost died in 1880 and locals have preserved his grave and its headstone, which is an important relic from our past.

Another important link to the past is the old Kinchega Station. Its historic woolshed built from red gum and blackbutt is the centrepiece of the nearby Kinchega National Park. More than 6 million sheep were shorn in this shed, which in its day stood 26 blade shearers.

Today it is a hop, skip and jump from the New South Wales border to Cooper Creek. Not then; it took us nearly two days to get to the Dig Tree, the old coolibah carved with directions to locate the provisions buried nearby. Arriving at that spot is always a tremendously moving experience for me. After standing before Sir John Longstaff's painting in the National Gallery of Victoria, I always have this feeling that I was sort of there. The painting, commissioned in 1907, is indelibly etched in my mind and depicts the absolute despair of the explorers after their arrival back at the depot on Cooper Creek on the evening of Sunday 21 April 1861. It is huge (286 by 433 centimetres) and shows Burke standing with slumped shoulders, gazing into nowhere, Wills collapsed against the Dig Tree in bare feet looking at the ground, and John King, lying prostrate, a picture of hopelessness that could not be more real. The poignant message is depicted, carved into the trunk of the coolibah tree that today is a national icon:

DIG
3 FT. N.W.
APR. 21 1861

Animal dung and footprints that they saw were evidence of the fact that Brahe and the support group had only recently left the site. It was in fact that same morning. Brahe had waited months for their return and, believing that Burke and Wills and their party were never coming back, missed the rendezvous by only nine hours.

Burke wrote in his diary:

> Our disappointment at finding the depot deserted may easily be imagined: returning in an exhausted state after four months of

the severest travelling and privation with our legs so paralyzed so that each found it a trying task to walk just a few yards.

Poor buggers.

Burke, Wills and King made up their packs with 30 pounds of supplies left by Brahe in each for the thrust through Sturt's Stony Desert to Mount Hopeless, but the waterless terrain was unrelenting in its hostility, and they made only about 40 miles. Too weak to continue, they returned to the Cooper where they wandered aimlessly for months until 1 July 1861, when Burke died. He passed away on the north side of the Cooper, east of where Innamincka is situated today, and later the site was marked with an ornate cast-iron grave surround. Wills died just days later, a few miles west of the Cooper crossing, though whether he died on the north or south side remains in doubt.

I had Brigadier Lawrence FitzGerald travel with me on one occasion. He was chief of the military mapping mob during the Second World War and author of the book *Lebanon to Labuan*, a story of mapping done by the Australian Survey Corps from 1939 to 1945. Laurie was also a student of Burke and Wills history, and had devoured every piece of available material on the subject. He firmly believed that Wills died on the same side of the Cooper as Burke, although the marker indicating the site was on the opposite side. So, who knows?

King stayed with the Yuntruwanta people, who cared for him until he was found. He contributed to the food supply by shooting birds. He was rescued on 15 September 1861 by a Mr Welch, a surveyor with Alfred Howitt's expedition, who had been sent forth by the powers that be to find out what actually happened to Burke and Wills. Welch's horse had bolted for whatever reason, running through a group of Aboriginal tribesmen who were camped on the Cooper, and when they scattered out of the way there was this solitary figure, looking more like a scarecrow than a human being. John King was taken back to Melbourne, but did not enjoy good health and was only 34 years old when he passed away.

That was still not the end of it—there was to be a very public atonement, and Howitt was dispatched back to Cooper Creek to gather up what remains the dingoes had left of Burke and Wills and bring them back to Melbourne for a proper burial. There were quite a lot of missing body parts by the time Howitt arrived back at the Cooper, but he dutifully loaded what was left onto a camel and set off to Melbourne via Adelaide. He certainly covered some country, did Mr Howitt. And what of the bones? That's a story I will write about later.

•

We were camped on the Cooper, the colonel, the three ladies and me. It was the first water we had seen for three days, so you can imagine what we looked like. Although the Land Rover was a sturdy little vehicle, it was probably the most uncomfortable machine ever devised for the carriage of man. The seats were hard, there was little leg room, engine heat transferred directly into the cab, there was no adequate dust sealing or air-conditioning, and the weather was hot. We were perspiring freely and travelling through clouds of swirling red dust. We had hair and faces streaked with red dirt and sweat.

I delivered the instructions: ladies upstream and gentlemen downstream. It was bath time. The news was well received. With a scrub up and change of clothes we all came up looking pretty good, I thought. The girls, in fact, had put on the lippy and all the stuff that goes with it and looked very smart indeed. The colonel had silver hair and a droopy moustache, so with a shave and a trim, his western-style shirt and broad-brimmed hat, he looked the epitome of the southern gentleman. I had changed into a fresh uniform, which was khaki shorts and shirt with epaulettes and shoulder patches with a soaring eagle, surrounded by the words BILL KING'S NORTHERN SAFARIS on each arm. It was a functional and stylish uniform, or people kept telling me it was.

We were sitting around the campfire after dinner, enjoying our Chateau Cardboard. The colonel was only a one-glass drinker but the girls had developed quite a thirst. All of a sudden there was an unholy noise coming from a flotilla of pelicans that had moved on when they saw us set up camp. I'd heard it before so I knew what it was all about. It was the noisy habits of pelicans when they mate. I was doing my best to pretend it wasn't happening while wondering how, if asked, I would explain it to my polite guests, when, right on cue, one of the girls said, 'Good God. What was that?'

'Pelicans copulating,' I replied as matter-of-factly as possible.

There was silence for a minute, then she looked at the Colonel, then at me, then at the other girls and said, 'Half their bloody luck,' at which time they all fell about shrieking with laughter. They were very funny ladies, particularly after the broaching of the Chateau Cardboard.

After the first day I had begun rotating the front seat every half day, which became the custom for these tours. It's the best seat in the house, so to speak, so everybody got a go, and it also allowed me to get to know people and their special interests, if any. If a person was into rocks, for example, I could put some emphasis on that subject—not that my knowledge of geology was that great, but I knew where there were unique features, like the remains of petrified forests near the Cooper, Coober Pedy and not far off the Oodnadatta Track, or marine fossils in the north of South Australia. The big plus for me, of course, was that many of our passengers were authorities on a particular subject. I was being educated on every expedition that I drove.

I learned more than I already knew about Burke and Wills from Brigadier FitzGerald, and in later years I was to find another devotee of the Burke and Wills story. Manning Clarke was an academic, one of Australia's most eminent historians, and a lecturer at the Australian National University in Canberra. He was also the recipient of the Companion of the Order of Australia, our highest award, in 1975, and was Australian of the Year in 1980.

I met the Clarkes during one of our 'Summer in the Mountains' programs. We were parked on the peak of Mount Kosciusko, as you could in those days with a four-wheel drive, and he came up to us and introduced himself as Manning Clarke and his wife, Dymphna. She was also an academic, a linguist lecturing in German at the university. They were on a walking holiday and had climbed from Thredbo village to the summit of Kosciusko on that day. They were very active mature-age people.

While my group went off looking at wildflowers, the Clarkes quizzed me on our tours. I told them about our philosophy of creative leisure; have a holiday and learn a little at the same time, living with the earth and getting the feel of the country. I also told them that we created itineraries around the journeys of the great overland explorers, Giles, Sturt, Burke and Wills. Professor Clarke said he was writing the fourth volume of his *History of Australia* at that time and it had always been his ambition to travel in the wake of Burke and Wills and experience the country where the tragedy happened in 1861.

I received correspondence from the Clarkes and they travelled with us later that year. In 1978 the professor published his fourth volume—*A History of Australia: The Earth Abideth Forever—1851–1888*. In the preface he writes: 'I would like to thank Bill King Safaris for helping me realize the ambition of a lifetime, to travel over the Burke and Wills country and camp on Coopers Creek.'

It took me no time to realise that my education was just beginning—after 39 years of ordinariness—and now with the birth of Bill King's Northern Safaris I was being exposed to all sorts of people with diverse backgrounds, interests, cultures and creeds. I did confess in the beginning of this story that I was never born to be an academic, but through the people I met I did become a jack-of-all-trades but master of none. Apart from historians, cartographers, photographers, writers and astronomers, there were geologists, herpetologists, ornithologists, anthropologists, botanists and probably a lot I have forgotten.

After travelling through the Queensland outback and the Northern Territory to Alice Springs I took the colonel and three ladies to Ayers Rock and Kings Canyon.

A mandatory stop on that route was Pete Severin's Curtin Springs Station. In the early days there was only a dirt track, just two wheel marks in some places, from Alice to the Rock, wending its way through huge patches of red bulldust, churning over sand dunes through washaways among huge stands of desert oaks. Pete's place was a welcome respite and a convenient camp if you were not going to make the Rock that day.

Central Australia in the 60s was nothing like it is today. It had endured drought for fifteen years, and Ashley Severin, Pete's son, was fourteen years old before he saw proper rain. The spinifex had died years before and just blown away, the desert oaks had dropped half their needles, it was the dead centre, and the Severins battled to survive.

Curtin Springs covered well over 5000 square kilometres. 'You would call it a ranch,' I told the colonel.

'Ranch, you say?' said the colonel, turning to Pete. 'Raising what?'

'Cattle,' said Pete.

'God, man. What do they eat?' asked the colonel, looking at the parched bare landscape.

'Rocks, mate. Only the soft ones, though. The hard ones break their teeth.'

The colonel did have a sense of humour: we just had to educate him on the Australian version.

Pete Severin is still a funny bugger. Val and I caught up with him again at the opening of Longitude 131, the luxurious retreat at Uluru, in 2002. As three 'living legends', Pete, Ian Conway from Kings Creek Station and I were invited as guests of honour. Pete's dry sense of humour had not diminished and he told the assembled guests a story from the days when he took over the lease of Curtin Springs in the 1950s.

There was little water on the property and for it to become viable there was a desperate need for the precious liquid. A million acres is only as good as the number of bores you can spread over the place. Pete was advised to contact some government department or other for primary producers assistance with funds on a reduced interest rate and some other department that would organise geologists and the necessary drilling team to set up bores. *This is brilliant*, thought Pete, until he discovered these blokes went through money faster than the water they couldn't find. They were collecting and studying scientific data and putting down test holes here and there, but still no water.

One day Pete heard a vehicle heading for the station homestead at great speed. It tore into the yard in a cloud of dust and out leapt the head honcho on the drilling rig. 'We've found it! We've found it—the best one yet. It's a bloody beauty!' Pete was over the moon and jumped in the truck with the bloke to take a look.

Bloody hell! Where's he going? Pete thought after they'd been tearing through the scrub a while. But finally they scrambled over this huge dune, and there it was, right in the middle of a claypan, water flowing all over the place.

'How's that?' said the head honcho smugly.

'No bloody good,' said Pete. 'You're five miles inside my neighbour's property.'

So much for government assistance. Pete sacked the lot of them and with what money he had left bought a drilling rig and some gear at a clearance sale. So, all set up with the proper gear he set out with his own plan to discover water on Curtin Springs Station. The geologists were always saying there were 'signs' here and 'signs' there and sometimes they got a show and sometimes they didn't. Well, Pete thought, 'Bugger that.' I'll drill in the spots on the property where I would really, really like to have water.' So, regardless of the 'signs' the geologists had marked on the property Pete went to work. And guess what? The results were exactly the same; sometimes he found it and sometimes he didn't.

CHAPTER 4

OPALS AND ODDBALLS

WE LEFT AYERS ROCK on our journey south and headed for Coober Pedy, our last port of call before returning to Melbourne. Our formula was working well—taking in the tourist attractions and then adding a little more off the beaten track.

Australia is the world's largest producer of precious opal and responsible for 95 per cent of the world's production, and Coober Pedy and Lightning Ridge make a significant contribution to this statistic. I had met a bloke in Coober Pedy on a previous trip who worked for the mines department. He told me to give him a call when I came through with a small group and he would take us out to a working site, something that couldn't happen with tourist buses. True to his word he took us to a site where they were working an open-cut system with heavy equipment. Did I say heavy? They were using a Komatsu super dozer, the biggest machine I had ever seen, and the driver was a gem in his own right, scraping the floor of that mine with the finest cut, just a couple of millimetres, using a massive blade. They were 'on' opal.

Tourism-wise, most of the coach companies would stop at Faye Nayler's Opal Cave. She and her partner, Sue, were not only pioneers in the town of Coober Pedy, they were pioneers in the fledgling tourist trade. The Opal Cave, I believed, was the best attraction in town. On that first tour we were privileged to share tea and scones in the double-decker bus that Faye and Sue called home.

•

The opal fields were discovered in 1915, when a bloke named Jim Hutchinson and his fourteen-year-old son, Willie, were camped in the area prospecting for gold. Young Willie went off looking for water and came across this pretty stuff lying on the surface. The first claim was made on 1 February in that year. It became known as the Stuart Range Opal Field, after John McDouall Stuart, the first white man to pass through that area many years before. The Indigenous people from the Mutuntjarra called the place *Kupi Piti*, which translates to 'white man in a hole'. The field became known colloquially as Coober Pedy, taking on the name officially in 1920.

Coober Pedy drifted along until 1946, when an Aboriginal woman named Tottie Bryant made a spectacular find at a field called the 8-Mile. This stimulated a new rush that continued through to the 1950s, swelling the population with the arrival of immigrants from all over the world—from Europe, North America, South America, and even, as Faye Nayler told me, an Eskimo.

Coober Pedy was certainly a mixed bag in those days. On driving into the place you would read signs like MOONLIGHTERS SHOT ON SIGHT. Moonlighters meant the thieves that raided mines at night if there was any whisper of a miner being 'on colour'. There was no police station either, as it was yet to be established; the nearest was in Kingoonya, 270 kilometres to the south. There was the tale of the two Yugoslavs who were found in the bottom of a mineshaft with a soccer ball. The silly buggers went out to play football in the moonlight: that was their version of the story, anyway.

One of the many characters was Crocodile Harry. He had spent years as a croc shooter in the Gulf Country until it was banned, then headed off to Adelaide but only got as far as Coober Pedy. The next pub was in Kingoonya and that was too far, so he stayed.

I first saw Harry on a visit to the settlement in about 1968, and he was hard to miss. He was as thin as a yard of pump water with grey hair and a long flowing grey beard and he just loved a drink. He was at the bar with a clear space around him, hanging onto the edge with his rocking shoes on. Harry was getting a bit stroppy and bad words were flowing freely so Giovanni, the publican, said, 'No more, Harry. Time to call it a night.'

'Just one for the frog 'n' toad, Giovanni,' slurred Harry.

'Nope,' said Giovanni, and turned away to serve a customer.

With that Harry wrapped his arms around the till on the bar, picked it up and, staggering along at an angle of nearly 45 degrees, made for the door. He was pulled up short by some people coming in and the next thing he was teetering backwards across the floor with his arms still wrapped around the till. By now Giovanni had spotted him, jumped the bar and made a grab, but only succeeded in hooking his arm through Harry's, sending him into a wobbly pirouette. As Harry was spinning around he raised the till above his head then dashed it on the floor. The drawer flew out, scattering notes along the way, before hitting a table leg and sending coins all over the place.

There were 50 or so people in the pub and you could have heard a pin drop. Harry stood there with a malevolent glare on his face. Giovanni gaped at his till on the floor before turning on Harry and shouting, 'Out, out, you bastard. You're banned for life. Get out!' Harry saw the look on Giovanni's face and knew he was an outcast from his favourite watering hole. 'I said life, but you're banned for life and ten years after that, Harry, you bastard!' Giovanni added as he bent down to pick up his money. He really was pissed off.

A couple of months after that I was back in Coober Pedy and there was Harry, as large as life, standing at the same spot at the bar, rocking shoes on, a clear space around him and bad words were flowing freely again. I said to the bloke standing next to me who was obviously a local, 'The last time I was here Harry buggered the till and Giovanni banned him for life.'

'I remember that,' the bloke said. 'It was only a week before he got back in the door because Giovanni got frightened he would leave town. Harry made a lot of money on the crocs and there's no way Giovanni was going to let him take it with him.'

•

We had a couple of experiences in Coober Pedy over the years with passengers 'gone missing'. On the first occasion we were camped at the Opal Cave, and as usual the punters were warned that it was unsafe to walk anywhere but on a road, as the area was pockmarked with disused mines and airshafts.

Just as the camp had come to life in the morning, a group of agitated passengers said that two of them had not come home last night. They were last seen walking home from the pub, hand in hand, then veering off and walking up through the mullock heaps behind the Opal Cave. Well, it didn't take much imagination to understand what had happened. It took Faye Nayler an hour or so to organise a search party of town folk. The search party wasted no time either, and scoured that hill for hours—nothing. By evening everybody was really worried. There was a distinct possibility that it might be days before they were found. Then one of the searchers was walking home and, by pure chance, heard a weak cry for help. The searcher followed the voice to an abandoned mineshaft that had been driven into the side of the hill and there were the two missing people lying exhausted at the entrance.

The story was this young couple had fallen several metres down an air vent and landed, he first and she on top of him, on the floor of the mine. They were so lucky to even be alive, although she had a badly broken pelvis and he had injured his back. When dawn came the glow of light from above revealed a shaft leading away from where they had landed. So he began pulling himself along on his belly, dragging her behind him. For hour after hour he dragged her along that shaft in total darkness. Fortunately he was a very fit young man; otherwise the outcome might have been very different. Naturally the incident became the talk of the town, and the conjecture began as to whether he would be remembered for his bravery or his stupidity.

On another occasion my friend Howard phoned to see if I had a seat available on a sixteen-day tour to the Red Centre which was departing the following morning, and it so happened that I did. Howard's wife, who was French, had a niece visiting, a 21-year-old university student from Paris, and thought it would be good if she could have a look at the real Australia. 'That's nice,' I said. 'No problem.'

Eight o'clock the next morning I was at the departure point in Flinders Street, checking passengers off the list and loading luggage, when I got a tap on the shoulder. It was Howard, and he introduced me to Cathy. 'She speaks very little English, Bill, so keep an eye on her for me, will you?' Keep an eye on her? It was hard to keep your eyes off her—she was a stunner.

As it turned out I didn't need to babysit Cathy because she teamed up with a couple of Australian girls of similar age. I just mentioned a few things to her over the journey and she just said, 'Oui, Beellee,' or 'Non, Beellee'.

When we arrived in Coober Pedy a bunch of punters said they were going to walk up to the town to see what there was to see and maybe visit the clubs or the pub. 'Just be careful of blokes trying to sell you opals at bargain prices—they buy cheap doublets and triplets at the souvenir shops and sell them at outrageous prices in the clubs, and be wary of any "miners" inviting you back to see their mine. There are some real scoundrels in this town.' After listening to my lecture and taking no notice whatsoever, off they went.

The next morning, we had a big day ahead so I was up early, packing away gear, when Cathy's two Aussie girlfriends came up and just stood in front of me. 'What's wrong?' I could see they were worried.

'Cathy didn't come home last night.'

'WHAT!' I could feel myself going pale. My head was in a whirl. Where do I start? What am I going to say to Howard? 'Where did you last see her?' I asked, as I began securing stuff and slamming locker doors to crank up the coach and go looking for her.

'At the Greek Club.'

If I was concerned when they first told me Cathy was missing, I was now bloody horrified. I alerted Faye Nayler to my dilemma before heading off to the Greek Club to see if there was anybody about. But I hadn't gone 500 metres when I saw Cathy walking, no, swaggering, down the hill, hands in the hip pockets of her jeans, nose stuck up in the air, boobs thrust out.

I felt a flush of anger, compensating for the anxiety attack she gave me, I suppose. I opened the door of the coach and she hopped up onto the step and just stood there with this determined look on her face, her eyes flashing, just daring me to say something. I didn't. Then she pulled her hand out of her pocket to reveal a handful of the most exquisite opal you could ever imagine.

I looked up from the opal and she said, 'What is more, Beellee, 'ee was beeutifulle.'

Another lesson: always mind your own business, my mother used to say. And mums know best.

•

Thankfully there were no such problems on my tour with the colonel and three ladies. They seemed to appreciate the personal attention which can only happen in a small group and the varied and unique itinerary.

As well as the well-known and less frequented opal sites, we also visited the Breakaways, an area that typifies the region's stunning desert scenery, and walked where a petrified forest of fallen logs and stumps had been exposed by weather and time.

We left Coober Pedy and headed off on the last phase of my first Burke and Wills expedition. We had all become quite chummy by then and I did reflect in later years that I was lucky to pick up such easygoing folk on my inaugural tour in the Land Rover.

CHAPTER 5

IN SEARCH OF CAPTAIN CHARLES STURT

OUR FIRST YEAR IN business was a financial disaster. We carried 30 passengers and lost $9000, which took a huge lump out of our savings and the balance of funds I was to receive from my share of the family business. We had one year left to get it right.

I had all sorts of people giving me all sorts of advice on all sorts of issues: developing a business plan, formulating a budget, creating a marketing strategy, costing an advertising schedule. I knew I had to get my head around all that stuff, but first I had to get the product right and get more wheels.

I believed we were on the right track because the people we were attracting were the ones we had set out to appeal to, but obviously we needed more of them. Agency intelligence told us that one tour of 21 days duration was too long. We needed two-week and one-week arrangements as well. I also needed more seats on the four-wheel-drive tours, another vehicle, and more flexibility so we could have two tours operating at the same time, or alternatively two vehicles in convoy. I had four months to get all that together and launch us into the 1970s—with no money coming in and plenty going out.

One big plus was our property in Eltham. It had an area where I could park any number of vehicles, the huge barn which sufficed as a store for gear, tents and the like, as well as a workshop. We also used our dining room as an office, so we had no rent or associated bills.

I bought an ex–postmaster general Land Rover 4-cylinder van and an ex–Australian Army C1300 International ambulance at a government disposal auction and set about converting them to passenger-carrying vehicles. I had gone to the auction to buy one vehicle but the International was so cheap I bought that, too. A Land Rover is a bit like a Meccano set. You can buy all the bits and pieces and they either bolted or riveted into place, so I bought a near-side rear door, frame and guard panel, and a Holden bench seat at a wrecker's for the rear compartment, and created a four-passenger-plus-driver vehicle. The International was a backup vehicle and only needed seating. I split and hinged the front bench seat so that it folded forwards to give access to the rear, and put in a secondhand pair of coach seats behind the driver, another pair behind that and a Holden rear seat across the back. That gave us eight passengers plus a driver. Finished and sign-written, they were lovely acquisitions.

Next I had to rectify the Land Rover 6-cylinder motor; that had given me a lot of heartache because it didn't like the heat and had burnt engine valves twice. But a bloke in Geelong had designed an adapter plate to fit a Holden engine to a Land Rover, so I fitted a brand new one. The 'Red Holden' motor, as it was known, was the sturdy, reliable, and all but indestructible engine that General Motors Holden used for 17 years. It was the solution to my problem. I then set about reseating it, moving the rear bench seat to the back compartment and replacing it with a pair of Mini Minor bucket seats, which gave access to the rear between them, and lo and behold we had a six-seater plus driver vehicle, with a trailer attached for gear.

Passenger comfort? There wasn't any, but it was never an issue. People didn't care in those days. We were venturing further and further off the beaten track, where no tourist had ever been before.

While the reorganising of equipment was going on I was also getting my head around itineraries, brochures and how to market our tours. Rosey took out the next tour, another 21-day Burke and Wills, while I set off on a survey mission to follow Captain Charles Sturt's 1844 expedition to find the 'great inland sea'. My objective was to research some shorter itineraries. I had advertised the 'survey expedition' in the Melbourne *Sun* and was pleasantly surprised when I picked up four starters to accompany me. The practice of advertising random survey expeditions became quite successful in later years.

•

Sturt's third expedition—eighteen years before Burke and Wills—intrigued me, and I was keen to seek out historic sites. His party left Adelaide on 10 August 1844, and in the next eighteen months suffered unbelievable hardship and privation brought about by searing heat, lack of water and poor diet. There were seventeen people in the expedition, including John McDouall Stuart, the first white man to cross Australia from south to north and return, and John Eyre, the first to conquer the Nullarbor Plain. Sturt obviously had an eye for good men.

It was, however, a large and cumbersome expedition comprising five bullock drays (four teams of eight and one of six) and two horsedrawn carts (one of three horses, the other of two). There were also six spare horses and 200 sheep. Did I say cumbersome? Oh, and they had a boat on top of a wagon to sail on the great inland sea.

The expedition followed the Murray River upstream to the Darling junction. It was summer by then and bloody hot. At the junction Sturt turned north and this took them through harsh waterless country, more or less following the route when driving from Mildura to Broken Hill and Tibooburra today. It was now midsummer and they were fortunate indeed to find a watercourse that Sturt named Evelyn Creek, then even more fortunate to find a deep waterhole, which he named Depot Glen. There they were,

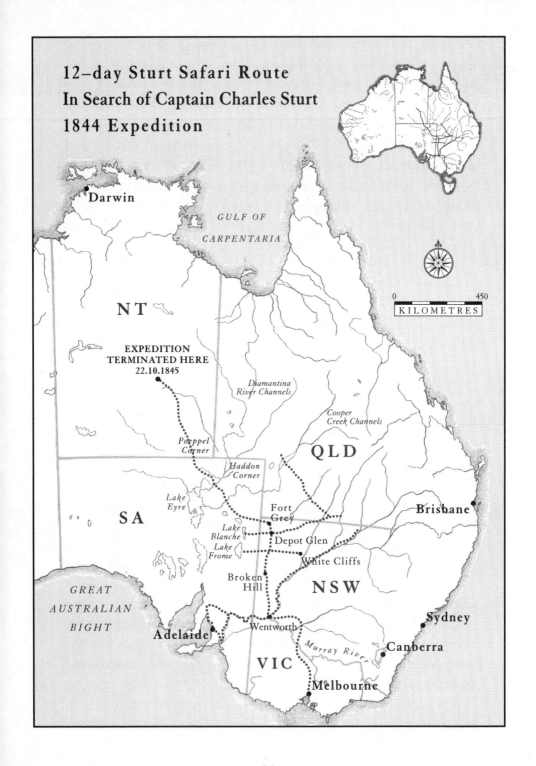

stuck for more than six months in temperatures well in excess of 37 degrees Celsius, unable to move forward or back until rains came.

Sturt wrote in his journal of the men's hair and fingernails falling out. He had to log his journal at night because the ink dried on the pen before he could get it to paper during the day.

Sturt named the highest point in the region Mount Poole, after his first assistant, Mr James Poole, and had his men, who were bored nearly to death and becoming restless, carry rocks to the top and build a cairn, just to keep them occupied. One of Sturt's crew, a bloke named Daniel Brock, who kept a diary, confirms the order:

> 15th March. Although poor Mr. Poole is very ill, he plans work for us—Today we have commenced to build a pyramid on a hill distanced about 4 miles to the north east from our camp. It is to be of stone, twelve feet high and ten feet around the base. Our boots suffer fearfully through the stones, which are as so many knives.
>
> 16th March. Busy rearing the stonework of the pyramid. 11–1/2 ozs of bread per day gives us but little strength to lift stones in their place of 4 and 5 cwt. This has to be done.

On the Sturt survey we set up our camp at Depot Glen to get the feel for the place and the following morning set off to climb Mount Poole. I couldn't believe how big the cairn was. It's bloody huge. At the top of the cairn I saw a piece of weathered timber, hardly noticeable between a couple of rocks. Clearing a few aside, I could see adze marks, then more weathered timber. What we had discovered was Sturt's original survey marker with the N, S, E, W letters carved into the adzed timber pointers that fitted through a mortice on the top of the post. We were pretty excited about our find so we assembled the directional markers and installed them in their proper place. That, however, proved to be a bad idea because the next time I visited the markers were gone. Spare us from the work of thieves and vandals.

Mr James Poole's health continued to deteriorate. When he died they interred him beneath a large beefwood tree near Evelyn

Creek and Sturt marked the tree 'J.P. 1845'. I was there nearly 40 years ago and the beefwood was looking very tired indeed. Maybe now it's dead, too.

Shortly after Poole's death the long-awaited rains arrived and Sturt pushed the expedition forwards to the next big waterhole, where he set up another depot, naming it Fort Grey. The lake was bone dry when we were there, but the remains of the old Fort Grey homestead were in excellent condition. Also built with what was to hand, the construction was rude timber, with adobe brick made from mud on site and a thatched kangaroo-grass roof. It was a charming relic that was unfortunately inundated by exceptional floods in the early 70s. Today there is not a single remnant to be found at Fort Grey other than a tree marked by Sturt to indicate the depot's position.

•

There is all manner of interesting stuff in the Corner Country, the area around Cameron Corner, the border junction of Queensland, South Australia and New South Wales. On another journey, Rennie Ellis was with me again. He was collecting shots for a new business venture he had underway. Scoopix was to be a photo library available to anyone who needed shots of a particular subject, and Rennie was keen to have a big section of photos of outback Australia. Also with us was Wesley Stacey, a photographer friend of Rennie's from New South Wales, who was collecting photos of Australian woolsheds for a book he was publishing.

There were three woolsheds in particular that I had told Wes about and he was keen to add them to his collection. The first one was at the old homestead at Lake Mungo, formerly Gol Gol Station, which was beautifully crafted by Chinese workers in the 1860s out of native pine, held together with handmade wooden pegs. The second was the historic shed at Kinchega Station near Menindee that stood 26 blade shearers in its heyday. The third was located at Waka Station at Cameron Corner, and few people knew about this one.

The old Waka woolshed is a classic. Built over a rudimentary timber frame, it was made entirely out of thatched kangaroo grass and would look more at home in Europe than in the Australian outback. Wes was enraptured. It was his pièce de résistance. He was a real oddball, was our Wes. When he saw something that excited him he'd run over to have a look, run here and look, run there and look, check his light meter and look, squat and look, lie down and look, run inside and look, then just stand with hands on hips and look and look. Truly, the ritual could take half an hour before he would set up his camera and start shooting. Rennie was much more casual; he just strolled about, taking shots.

The three-state border was the extent of that journey. Today there is a roadhouse with all mod cons; in the 60s there was nothing but the corner survey marker. It was surveyed by and named after John Cameron, who spent two years marking the border between New South Wales and Queensland. Cameron Corner was of great interest to Wesley also. He had a burning desire to stand on the demarcation marker on the Corner and pee in three states with one swivel of his hips. Strange ambitions some blokes have.

•

The plan for our Sturt survey expedition was to head across to the Strzelecki Track through the Cobbler Desert. The homestead of Bollards Lagoon Station is just a few kilometres from the border, but when we went past it was deserted. It was still furnished and livable, but the doors and windows were open, the place was full of sand and there was no stock. Somebody must have just walked away.

From there it was only 80 kilometres or so west to the Strzelecki Track. We followed the only track leading in that direction, but this stopped at a broken-down bore a couple of kilometres from the homestead.

So there was no alternative—we'd have to go cross-country over those monstrous dunes if we wanted to make the Strzelecki. It was really soft sand and one dune ran straight into another. Our progress was painfully slow and by nightfall we'd only made it halfway.

The following morning we topped this enormous dune and miles off to the right we saw what I thought must have been a huge windmill. Without changing pace, because the Landy would have bogged in sand, I turned towards the thing and we could see it was a giant drilling rig.

Then it happened—the top of the dune gave way and we slid over the edge. The Land Rover was leaning over at a 45-degree angle, sliding sideways at ever-increasing speed towards the bottom, about 30 metres away. We hit the claypan with a tremendous thump and the vehicle teetered on two wheels for ages, trying to make up its mind whether to fall over or land upright. There is no rule that says all luck has to be bad luck—we fell upright.

We then tried to navigate our way along the claypans to reach the rig, but there was nothing to take a bearing from. So we picked a big dune and ground our way to the top. With great relief we could see the rig was now only a few miles away and we could get there along the top of the dunes.

The oil rig workers had seen us coming from the south, and, boy, were they surprised. 'Where the bloody hell did you come from?' said a bloke who introduced himself as the site manager. 'Been drilling around here for six months and you're the first people we've seen.' He apologised that they couldn't offer us a beer—one of the blokes had flown down to get some from Lyndhurst but wouldn't be back until about four. 'You're welcome to stay the night, though,' the manager said. 'We've got mobs of tucker.'

'Thanks all the same, but we're behind time,' I said.

'Well, have some lunch. I'm about to blow the whistle.'

Even though these blokes lived an extremely isolated existence, they had basic comforts and a Cessna 206 'workhorse' to ferry people and supplies in and out. There were ten of them plus the pilot accommodated in Atco blocks of single air-conditioned rooms, with a shower and toilet on the end. There was a mess hut, a 'rec' room with a pool table and an office—a good set-up way out in the desert.

We gratefully accepted the lunch invite and the camp cook served up corned beef, salad, fresh bread, cake and tea. I should add here that I like my bread, and the tucker I really missed in the bush was proper fresh bread. All you could get was white sliced stuff frozen after it left the oven, frozen (sort of) in transit and then frozen again at its destination until ready to eat. They're just like slices of cardboard by the time they hit the table.

Over lunch the manager explained that they had towed the rig in from the Strzelecki Track with a bulldozer six months prior, so there was a flattened path heading west. 'Just drive straight down the airstrip and keep on the dozer track and you'll hit the Strzelecki,' he said. He also invited us to drop in again. You just never knew what you would come across in those days, and that was not the end of the fellows from the drilling rig either—more about them later.

The route we took after reaching the Strzelecki Track went northwest, through where the Moomba gas field is today. After crossing Cooper Creek, which Sturt named, we headed north across the desert and believe me it was tough country—sand and gibbers as far as you could see in any direction, with not one blade of grass or clump of herbage.

This was where I saw my first western taipan. The snake is found in the Cooper Creek region and its venom is the most toxic known. This one was nearly 2 metres in length and as thick as my arm. With a dark head, yellowy-orange neck and light-brown flecked body, he was a monster. He was heading towards Cooper Creek, probably for a feed of fresh water rats. I stopped on the track across his path and he just kept coming straight towards us.

I was looking at him with my head out the window and—bang—he just reared up and struck the door of the Land Rover. He was so angry he had another go. I was safe and transfixed as I watched him vent his hatred on my wagon. He had a really ugly knotted scar behind the head where something or somebody had given him a dreadful wound, maybe a dingo, or perhaps he had been in contact with humans. We took off and left him to his own business while we got on with ours.

We got as far north as Kings Lookout, a giant dune where one can view the seemingly endless desert moonscape, and from there we struggled out to Coongie Lake. The track was so slow, but it was worth it when we got there. There was more bird life than I had ever seen in one place. Sturt went on into the Simpson Desert and reached a point on 8 September 1845, just north of where Birdsville is today, where he called it quits. He made a little excursion east along Cooper Creek on the return journey, but he was spent and returned to Adelaide a sick and bitterly disappointed man. He never found the inland sea. We called it quits also, and headed back down the Strzelecki Track and through the Flinders Ranges to home, with enough research accomplished to launch our twelve-day Sturt expedition.

•

Charles Sturt was travelling in the wake of Major Thomas Mitchell, surveyor-general of New South Wales who, incidentally, was quite jealous of Sturt's success as an explorer, particularly his success in following the Murrumbidgee River down to the Murray in 1829. Mitchell had on three occasions, in 1831, 1835 and 1836, followed waterways south of Bathurst towards the Murray, but for whatever reason was from time to time in conflict with the Indigenous people.

Sturt was well aware of this, and as he was travelling north through the same country he took two 'native' trackers, as Sturt referred to Mr Nitebook and Mr Tuando. Their job was to assure the natives they encountered that they meant no harm. The two trackers did their job well. As Daniel Brock wrote in his diary: 'The natives we encountered seemed to be breathing peace and kind feeling.'

Daniel Brock was an educated man with a young family who only took the job with Sturt because he was hard up for cash. He was also a devout Methodist, a misfit among the bullockies and stockmen who accompanied the expedition. His intolerance of the men's crude and blasphemous language left him with few people to communicate with, and on reading his diary it's clear that Sturt was not one of them. At the same time Brock was a very impressionable fellow, with a good command of English. His sympathy for the natives was very different from the language of the journals kept by some early explorers: Thomas Mitchell, in contrast, referred to them as 'fire-eaters' and 'daring and bloodthirsty'. Mitchell, however, was accused of mistreating them and had every reason to be vigilant.

On 16 October 1844 Sturt's party came across an Indigenous tribe who were preparing to make an attack on them, and it was only the intervention of Mr Nitebook that saved them from an unwanted disaster. It was a tribe that had been badly wronged by Mitchell's party.

In his diary Brock wrote:

> I will relate the circumstances. As was customary Mitchell had camped two or three miles from the river. One of the men on coming to the river for water had an interview with a female native and promised her a kettle if she would satisfy his lust. A day or two later the wretch again came to the river and the poor creature, which had an infant on her back, came for her kettle, having with her 2 or 3 others. It appears he first knocked her down, and she, as soon as she could, ran for the river, but as she was jumping in the brute fired, and instead of jumping in she fell back on the bank a corpse. The white fellow came up to her and finished his butchery by taking the child by the heels and dashing its brains out on a gum tree. And then observing the natives crouching behind a tree on the other side of the river he fired a volley at them.
>
> To conclude the scene—one of those behind the tree was a young lad—he is now a tall fine young man named Topar—he has shewn us the grave, the tree where the child perished, the tree behind which he crouched, in which were the marks of three balls.

The Daniel Brock diary was released in the book called *To the Desert with Sturt* but wasn't published until 1975. It was in the possession of the Royal Geographical Society in Adelaide for goodness knows how many years and was only discovered on an anniversary of Sturt's death. Brock's account agreed factually with Sturt's journals, only there is one great difference—it was written with emotion.

CHAPTER 6

HOLIDAY IN COPLEY AND CATTLE KINGS

As I mentioned earlier, that wasn't the last of the blokes from the Cobbler Desert drilling rig. Leap forwards a couple of years. We had four vehicles away at that time: the Land Rover 6, the Land Rover 4 and the International were all heading for the Cooper on Burke and Wills and Sturt expeditions, and I was taking a tour to Alice and the Rock in the Denning.

We had departed from Melbourne on Boxing Day and were on our fourth day out. That morning we had left Wilpena Pound to take a route through Blinman and the northern Flinders Ranges to Copley, then up the Oodnadatta Track to camp in the bush somewhere.

There were 34 punters and three crew on board: yours truly, our cook Riley Stevens, and Ray Moore who was co-driver and rouseabout. Ray was known as 'Rag-mop', or 'Rags' for short, because of his unruly blond hair that always looked like a birch broom in a fit. It was Ray's first trip. I had knocked about with him in my late teens when I lived in Eaglemont, and had seen little of him in later years until he came to me about a job. He had been driving heavy vehicles but had fallen on hard times due to an alcohol problem, and was ready to make a fresh start.

We were going to Copley via Balcanoona and it was the first time I had taken that route. On other trips I took either Brachina or Parachilna Gorge. The track was full of steep dips and pinches through the creek crossings. *Easy does it*, I thought. I knew I would have to be very careful not to over-rev or my GM V653 two-stroke diesel power plant wouldn't like it.

It was late morning when we arrived. Copley at that time, I might add, was a pub run by a very elderly lady whose name escapes me and her bachelor son, and next to the pub was a post office and store run by a bloke and his wife—and that was it. We stopped for refreshments and I was sitting in the driver's seat with the engine running as the folk were filing back. When Riley returned she said, 'Hey, Bill, there's oil dripping out under the engine.'

Oh no, don't tell me. What had I done? Over-revved it and pulled the top off a piston? I hoped not. I went around to the back and slid underneath, and there it was, compression and oil coming out of the breather tube. We were going nowhere. We were parked right outside the front door of the pub and that was where we would stay until we fixed it.

'What's the problem, Bill?'

'Can you fix it? Do we have to get another bus?'

'What are you going to do, Bill?'

'I'm going to have a beer and a think,' I said, so I bought a stubbie off the old dear at the pub and sat on the verandah to drink it.

'Are we going to stay here?'

'How long will it take to fix it?'

'Have you worked out what to do, Bill?'

The questions never stopped.

'Leave him alone, he's thinking,' said a protective one.

Now when one has a breakdown in the sticks with a load of passengers on board, one needs to create a sequence of events to resolve the problem in the most efficient manner, and one cannot ever have a preconceived plan because one never knows what the problem will be.

So I had learned back in history that the best thing to do was to sit down with a stubbie and consider the priorities and the options. I never used to drink on the job, at least not until after the daily chores were done, but when I was in deep trouble I found it helped. I had my stubbie, maybe two, and put the plan into action. The priority was to get the punters out of my thinning hair.

Option one: put a camp up near the pub so they are close to all amenities. It's all easy. Unload the stuff and they can carry it out the back and away they go. But, if any yahoos got around the pub it could be a nightmare. We had about twenty women in our group, some of them American school teachers who were imported by the government of the time to overcome a teacher shortage in Victoria. Imagine the yahoos getting wind of that. They'd be like crows around a road kill.

Option two: a bush camp at the river crossing about 5 kilometres down the road; good shade, plenty of firewood and no yahoos, but I needed to borrow the old Austin tray truck from the bloke in the store to get the people and the gear down there. The old jigger had high cyclone gates on the back and sides for carrying a couple of steers and that was good, we could get a load on it. The bloke in the store said no worries, so option two was underway.

I called Detroit (the agents in Adelaide), explained the problem, and got them to have a technician and parts ready to head our way when we found out what was needed.

Young Riley was in charge out at the camp; she recruited a couple of volunteers to help get grub ready while Ray and I set about stripping the motor. The truck owner said he would take a run down to the camp after dinner to see if anybody wanted to come back to the pub for a while. About half of them took up his offer.

We had the engine stripped that night to discover that my intuition was correct, and the following morning the Detroit engineer was on his way with the required parts while we looked forward to a boring day—it would be well after dark by the time he got to Copley. Luckily the old dear at the pub told our mob she had organised a dance that night and all were welcome. They had a piano in the lounge and her son could play, so a great night was planned for all.

Well, the bush telegraph was on fire in Copley—by about six o'clock the bar was busy and, you wouldn't believe it, there were some blokes off that drilling rig who I had run into out in the Cobbler Desert. They weren't working the same site any more, but were still in the region and had come from miles away when they heard about all the 'sheilas' in the broken-down bus. The bloke from the store ferried my punters to the pub on the back of his truck and by eight o'clock the place was full with locals from far and wide, 'in' for the big event. The engineer had arrived and told me to get lost as he knew what he was doing, but I left Rags with him to fetch and carry so he didn't get tired.

The publican's son could really play the piano, and could sing, too, although he did go downhill a bit as the amber liquid he insisted was essential to keep his vocal cords lubricated started to have some effect. He grew tired and put on a record so he could have a rest, although the first thing he did was make a bee-line for one of the girls to ask her for a dance. By this time not only had his voice gone downhill, he had got his Cooper's Bitter Ale legs on, and the girl did a good job steering him around the floor. Then he got the gropes, so she gave him the flick.

He fronted up to another girl who must have given him the rules, because I saw him nodding away as he dragged her onto the dance floor, but the dopey bugger couldn't help himself; he was at it again, hands everywhere. The old dear was onto him in a flash—she grabbed the beer-sodden towel off the top of the bar and began flogging him with it in the middle of the floor and yelling at him to get back to the piano.

The blokes from the drilling rig were choirboys in comparison, and managed to keep their hands off the women. It was good to catch up with them again.

By early afternoon the next day we were fixed up, packed up and on our way up the Oodnadatta Track. And do you know what? If you asked anybody who was on that tour what the highlight was, they would tell you it was their holiday in Copley.

•

All that country around the bottom of the Oodnadatta and Strzelecki tracks is full of history, but the story that intrigues me is the one about Harry Redford, the man who first traversed the Strzelecki Track. This story is an Australian classic, yet not well known.

Harry was born near Sydney in 1842 and was thought to be the son of convict Thomas Redford, who was shipped to the colony in 1826. Harry went bush at an early age and took up droving; he became an excellent bushman and worked all over western New South Wales and Queensland. It was while he was working near Windorah that he became aware of the giant cattle run at Bowen Downs, near where the settlement of Muttaburra is today. The property of nearly 2 million acres was said at that time to be running some 70 000 head of cattle.

Harry reckoned if a station had that many cattle, maybe they wouldn't miss a few. So off he went to check out the lie of the land and found a secure watered valley on the Thomson River system. Harry's plan was to duff a small herd and take them off to market, but he was confronted with two problems. The first was he needed some help; the second was that many of the cattle were branded with markings that would be recognised in New South Wales and Queensland.

Not to be deterred, Harry recruited four blokes to assist with the project and systematically began stealing stock and storing them in his watered valley. When he had precisely 1000 head he said to his men, 'That's enough.' To solve the problem of the brands, Harry told the men they would need to drive the stock to Adelaide, where the marks were unknown, and he would become Mr Henry Collins, a grazier from Queensland. It was more than 2000 kilometres through uncharted country. 'No bloody way,' two of them said. But the other two agreed.

So began Harry's epic journey, with two helpers and 1000 head of cattle split into two groups to keep the dust down. They followed the Thomson channels to the Barcoo channels, and then the northern side of Cooper Creek to a point near where Burke and Wills had set up their base camp at the Dig Tree to make a crossing. He headed south down an Aboriginal trading route that had intermittent water soaks, and that's how he opened up the Strzelecki Track.

By the time they arrived at the northern reaches of the Flinders Ranges they were desperate for supplies. Then out of the blue they came across a property called Hill Hill Station near the waterhole at Artrocoona. It was the first sign of civilisation they had seen since their journey began. Harry had a prize white bull in the mob, a very well-bred animal imported from England, with distinctive markings. He hadn't really wanted it from the beginning and tried to get rid of it, but it fell in love with some of his cows. In hindsight he should have shot it, but Harry must have thought it was too valuable. So he traded the white bull and two other branded steers for supplies at Hill Hill.

The drove continued down the Strzelecki Track until they came to Blanchwater Station on the George Creek, just south of Lake Blanche. Suddenly it was payday. The manager at Blanchwater was a bloke named Mules and he offered Harry 5000 pounds for the 1000 animals, using a promissory note from the Bank of Adelaide, redeemable in six months. Harry was delighted to get rid of the cattle before they got to the saleyards, and he and his men continued down to Adelaide to have a nice time and wait for their money.

One can only wonder at Harry's skill as a bushman; to set off with 1000 head of cattle on a journey through the unknown for 2000 kilometres and arrive at the other end still with 1000 head was some feat. But all was not going to plan.

The manager at Bowen Downs Station had eventually missed the white bull and suspected that other cattle had been duffed. When word came to him of tracks left by a big mob of cattle moving south down the Thomson River system, he and two other employees set off in pursuit. They got to Hill Hill Station and there was the white bull in pride of place in the yard and the new owner showing them a bill of sale confirming what they already suspected. By the time they arrived at Blanchwater Station the disaster was complete. Most of the cattle had been sent to the Adelaide market and sold, and there was no sign of Harry and his mates. However, there was enough evidence available to have warrants issued for their arrest.

The warrant was issued in Queensland in January 1872 and when Harry eventually turned up in Blackall the cops nabbed him. Now the one mystery in this story is what happened to the 5000 pounds. Harry made no admission that he received it, in fact he made no admissions at all, so the only people who know if Harry got the money or was dudded by Mr Mules are the two of them, and if Harry was ripped off there was nothing he could do about it anyway.

Despite the overwhelming evidence against him, including the white bull, which was shipped from Hill Hill in South Australia back to Roma in Queensland for the trial, Harry Redford was found not guilty. There was uproar in the court, uproar in the town of Roma, and uproar in Queensland.

Harry's amazing feat in opening up the cattle markets of Adelaide to the beef growers of Queensland with his pioneering of the Cooper Basin and the Strzelecki Track is now in the annals of Australian folklore. The people of the outback were fascinated by his bushcraft and daring and made him a hero. To this day horsemen pay tribute to his legacy with the annual cattle drive along the 200-kilometre Redford Trail, a renowned event in the Australian outback.

Another of the greatest cattle drives in Australian history actually involves one of the owners of Bowen Downs Station at the time Harry knocked off the cattle. Nat Buchanan was an Irishman, born in Dublin in 1826, and was famed for taking 20 000 head of cattle from southern Queensland through unknown country to Katherine in the Northern Territory and opening up the Barkly Tableland. This Northern Territory pioneer was also known for many other feats of endurance, droving big mobs of cattle from the Northern Territory to the Kimberley and further south to the Murchison River.

Yet another remarkable story is that of the Duracks. Patrick Durack and his family were subsistence tenant farmers in Ireland who came to this country with little but hope, and through hard work and foresight founded a dynasty of pioneers who built a cattle empire across half of known Australia. The Duracks originally arrived in New South Wales then made their way south to the Victorian goldfields. Patrick had a couple of good strikes and in 1868 went bush and built Thylungra Station on Kyabra Creek, a tributary of the Cooper near Quilpie, which was no mean feat at that time. In 1883 Patrick set off with 7500 head of breeding stock and 200 horses on an epic journey to reach the Ord River in the Kimberley. It was the longest cattle drive in Australia's history, covering 4800 kilometres and taking two years and four months to complete. Patrick's granddaughter Mary wrote the book, *Kings in Grass Castles*, and on the first page is a stand-alone quote attributed to Patrick in 1878:

> 'Cattle Kings' ye call us, then we are Kings in grass
> Castles that may be blown away upon a puff of wind . . .

Never a truer word was spoken.

While we're on the subject of cattle it would be remiss of me not to write a little about Sidney Kidman—'The Cattle King', as the author Ion Idriess called him. Kidman was born to a farming family in South Australia in 1857 and ran away at thirteen years of age with 5 shillings in his pocket and a one-eyed horse he had purchased with his savings. He began working as a drover, then as a stockman and rouseabout in saleyards and on stations. He was fascinated by the stories of the overlanders, squatters, adventurers and early explorers like Sturt, Burke and Wills, and Stuart.

A hard worker, Kidman, still at a young age, became a trader, buying and selling stock, equipment and anything he felt he could sell at a profit. His grand ambition was to become a squatter and that opportunity arose during the economic downturn in the latter part of the nineteenth century. Unfazed by the drought and weak economy he bought a cattle station, then another, and another, at bargain prices to fulfill his vision. He bought wisely and saw his land holdings as a 'chain' through the Channel Country, linked together along the Darling, Cooper Creek, the Diamantina, the Georgina and their tributaries. This gave him the ability to move his stock more easily to good feed in times of drought and to markets where cattle were bringing the best prices. Even though he was said to have lost more than 70 000 head of cattle in the big drought of the late 1890s, he still survived and prospered.

Sidney Kidman controlled an empire that reached from Cape York to Adelaide, with more than 100 stations, taking up well over 250 000 square kilometres of land and stocked with cattle that numbered in the hundreds of thousands. It was said that he could move them from the Gulf of Carpentaria to the Adelaide markets without crossing another person's property. He was by far the biggest landholder Australia has ever seen.

•

Having added the Sturt expedition to our program, I needed to get my head around brochures, distribution and how to market our two distinctly different products: four-wheel-drive expeditions and coach tours. While they targeted two different price brackets and markets, our concept of 'creative leisure' was a common denominator and this had to be clear in our printed material. We presented a unique product. We had introduced recommended reading with each itinerary for people to familiarise themselves with the region through which they were going to travel, and I had a library of reference books (among those listed in Further reading) in the vehicles.

We had steel-legged trestle tables we made to fit each vehicle that folded to almost nothing, and white heavy plastic tablecloths and custom-made boxes for storage of such items as the Chateau

Cardboard. We reckoned tablecloths and wine with the evening meal to be a sophisticated touch, plus you could check every brochure on the travel agents' shelves and the nearest place you could get a glass of wine on safari was in Africa.

I used to take pride in the food that we served along the track and we wanted to be better than the others. The coach tour operators in the main used canned and freeze-dried stuff, but our objective was to feed our folk fresh meat all the way. I had discovered some ex–US army 'food boxes' in an Aussie disposals store. They were ingeniously designed, well-insulated aluminium boxes about the size of a small suitcase, with three 6-litre sealed containers in each. Designed for use in the Vietnam War, their purpose was to deliver hot and hygienically prepared food to troops in the front line from kitchens well to the rear. I figured that if they could hold hot food they could also hold cold food. So I bought a commercial freezer, we packed meat in order of use, separated with greaseproof paper, in the containers and froze them. On tour the meat would hold up for five days in reasonable weather, three in a hot spell, and we were never more than five days from provisions.

I believed it was imperative to distance ourselves from the coach tour operator's mentality—like having a 'coach captain,' a term invented around that time. They seemed like secondhand airline pilots to me. Then having them talk at people all day long, handing the roving microphone around for passengers to tell unfunny jokes, organising them to stand up and talk about themselves, passing out song sheets for community singing, insisting people wore name badges, some operators even had ridiculous punishments if a punter left their name badge off. They ran a tour like an old people's home.

And that wasn't the end of it. Some companies instructed the punters to set up their tents in uniform rows so that common tent pegs could be used. Just think of two rows of a dozen tents all pegged together, 40-odd people all within an arm's length of one another and two pieces of canvas between them. Walk past in the early hours and the snores and farts could reach a crescendo. Trust me, I've heard it many times.

I knew there were others who felt like I did. They wanted to experience the outback but didn't want to feel regimented, even if they were. They would have preferred to do it themselves, but they couldn't; they didn't know how and had neither time nor gear. We were to be the alternative. If our passengers wanted to scatter their tents all over the place, fine. Why not?

We also preferred to call our crews by their job specifications—'tour leader', 'camp cook', and so on. I believed those to be more pragmatic titles.

Itineraries were the next question, and we offered three arrangements. The first was our 21-day Burke and Wills expedition travelling up through Birdsville to the Gulf and returning through the Centre and the Flinders Ranges; the second was 'To the Desert with Sturt' and the third was our bread and butter, the sixteen-day tour to Alice Springs and Ayers Rock in the Denning.

Distribution was another issue to be addressed and I dearly wanted one of the local airlines to package the tours with holiday airfares. So, armed with nothing more than a few ideas, I went to visit Ansett Airlines' holiday travel office in the 'big building' at the top end of Swanston Street in Melbourne. And that was when I met Geoffrey More and Nick Hill, the guys who put stuff together in the Ansett package holidays department.

We had a long discussion about what we intended to deliver with our concept of outback travel and I was gratified indeed when they enthused about our tours being refreshing and different. We would have our coach tour to Ayers Rock and our Burke and Wills safari, both from Melbourne, packaged as an Ansett holiday and sold through their outlets Australia-wide. It was the beginning of a long and rewarding association with Ansett Airlines and the beginning of a personal friendship that has continued. Geoff and Nick are good blokes. While we have all moved on through various phases of our lives, the three of us still catch up every year or so when we lunch at the Emerald pub in South Melbourne on AFL Grand Final eve.

CHAPTER 7

HIPPIE HEADACHES— THE AGE OF AQUARIUS

THEN ALONG CAME BILL the entrepreneur. We needed some cash flow badly so we came up with this brilliant idea of running a weekend trip to Sydney to see the American tribal rock musical *Hair*. It had opened in Sydney in June 1969, and glorified the culture of the day, the anti-Vietnam movement that was fuelled by drugs, sex and rock 'n' roll. Not your normal night out at the theatre, I might add, but that didn't stop ordinary Australians turning up in their thousands to be outraged by the nudity and goings-on while the flower children swooned in delight. If it worked we could commence operating a regular monthly service, in between outback tours, and more in summer for Melburnians to be outraged with our northern neighbours.

The plan required a trip to Sydney to arrange theatre tickets and accommodation. They were at a premium at the time and I needed tickets now, hence the decision to make a personal appearance rather than send a telex. Rosey had little work on at the time so he hitched a ride with me, saying he wanted to catch up with his mate Bobby Gleeson. Bobby was an artist who shared his time between the Sydney and Eltham 'scenes'. When he wore out his welcome in one scene he would move off to the other to give it a rest. Rosey said he would tee it up so we could camp at Bobby's in Woolloomooloo. I was happy with that; it was handy for what I needed to do, and certainly economical.

Then Val said, 'Why don't you take Bo-Bo for a ride?'

Now I haven't mentioned Bo-Bo before, but he was a very important and noticeable member of our family. A chocolate brown standard poodle, he was a handsome fellow with impeccable manners who conducted himself like a thorough gentleman. That was our Bo-Bo. He was a real head-turner, too—walk him down the street and you could strike up a conversation with a pretty young lady in an instant. Maybe that's why Val always let everybody know he was her dog.

It was pretty late in the day when we arrived in Sydney and what an ordeal it was finding Bobby's place. Cindy, his lady at the time, greeted us with, 'Hey, you guys picked a good time to come, the coffee pot's on and I've baked a batch of cookies.' It certainly sounded nice after our long drive.

We had just settled down in the living room to watch TV when we heard this unholy shriek—'Bo-Bo, you bastard!'

'What's he done?' I asked, leaping up and heading for the kitchen, thinking he'd disgraced himself, but no, the normally polite poodle had hopped up on the table and eaten a plate of cookies, scoffed the lot. 'I'm sorry about the cookies, Cindy, I'll go down to the corner store and get some more,' I said.

'I don't think so,' said Cindy, wringing her hands and wailing loudly. 'They were hash cookies.'

'WHAT?—I'll have to get him to a vet,' I said.

'Might be difficult explaining where the hash came from,' said Bobby, which was true. The authorities took a much dimmer view of all that stuff in those days, and I was in Sydney, out of my comfort zone.

'Val is going to kill me,' was all I could think. I tried squeezing him tight to make him regurgitate. Nothing came out. I tried to get saltwater into him, but he wouldn't have a bar of it. All he wanted was fresh water, litres of it, and I thought that had to be good. I took him out for a pee and to walk it off, but he was all over the place, reeling from one side of the footpath to the other, licking any moisture, then he kept lying down and wanting to go to sleep. He was stoned out of his little brain. 'Val is going to kill me,' I kept thinking. So I walked him and walked him for hours, in between trying to quench his insatiable thirst, but Bo-Bo was still stoned while I was exhausted.

The next morning Rosey and I had to go off to do our business. There was no way I was leaving Bo-Bo with the Gleesons, bloody idiots, and I didn't want him out of my sight because he was still in a daze so we took him with us. At the theatre I was referred to a lady at the ticket box who was in charge of group bookings. Rosey waited with Bo-Bo on the lead in the foyer. That didn't bother Rosey one bit because he soon had a couple of pretty ladies chatting away and making a fuss of Bo-Bo. Until Bo-Bo decided it was a good opportunity to cock his leg and pee on the foyer wall. I could see the look of panic on Rosey's face as he started dragging the reluctant dog, hoppity-kick on three legs while still trying to relieve himself, out through the front door.

I was trying to give the lady in the ticket box my undivided professional attention while this little incident was being played out in the foyer. There was no way I wanted to be associated with the bloke with the disgraceful dog.

I could not get out of Sydney fast enough.

•

We now had tickets and accommodation, but I had forked out pretty hefty deposits and when I arrived home I was starting to feel a bit apprehensive about having to sell the trip.

Hoping to avoid the expense of newspaper ads, I printed some flyers with all the pertinent information for distribution around the town: tour leaves Eltham at 6 p.m. on Friday, arrives Sydney Saturday morning, check into hotel, rest of day free, transfer to *Hair* on the Saturday night, depart Sydney on Sunday 5 p.m., arrive back in Melbourne in time for work on Monday. Cost of package includes all transport, bed and breakfast accommodation and theatre tickets. Deposit required with reservation, balance seven days prior to departure.

Was I kidding? Would our gamble pay off?

Much to my relief I sold half the seats in the first week, and then it started to drag. I had costed the trip on twenty people and I reckoned it was a safe bet to reach that number, but I needed cash flow, so the last nineteen seats after outgoings were the crucial ones for me. Then somebody said, 'Hey, give us some of your flyers. I'll hand them out at the Albion pub in Carlton. I go down there a bit. You'll get plenty of starters out of that mob.' We did, too—we sold out.

Getting the money was a new challenge, however, and only threats of accepting wait list passengers (of which there weren't any) seemed to work, although on departure day three still had not paid. They would pay at departure, I was informed.

When we were sure of a sell-out I decided not to drive the coach. I kept the last two seats and told Val to arrange for a housesitter so she could have a break. We would travel along with the punters. Brian Noakes and Joe Gauci were two of my old man's best coach drivers and they organised their shifts so they could do the job for me. I was looking forward to a great weekend away with my wife.

When planning the trip I'd figured the 6 p.m. Friday departure would allow people to do a day or part of a day's work—silly me. I think a lot of them spent the day at the pub. The Denning was not fitted with a toilet system, and our usual practice while on tour was to stop every two hours. This information was in the documentation the punters received, along with the edict, 'No drinking on the bus'.

Toilet systems in coaches were a comparatively new innovation in the 60s and in those that had them the drivers usually put an 'Out of Order' sign on the door as soon as they left the depot. If somebody did a twinkle that was okay, but if somebody did a twunk it could have a bad effect on the enjoyment of the surrounding passengers.

The drama began when the first couple arrived carrying six-packs. 'No drinking on the bus. There's no toilet,' I informed them. 'Give your grog to Brian and he'll store it in the luggage bins.' They were both half drunk by then anyway and wandered over to Brian to follow instructions.

It didn't take long for the word to get around, however, and not one stubbie or tinnie could be seen: they were all concealed in hand luggage—natural-born smugglers.

We were down to the end of the queue and the unpaid fares were from three young ladies whom I had never seen before. 'Oh, we're pleased to meet you, Bill. We still have to fix you up but we'll do it in Sydney. We're meeting "somebody or other" and they're paying for our trip.'

I just stood there. 'No money, no ride,' I said.

They just stood there, too. 'But we're here now,' one of them said.

'I'm aware of that—I'm looking at you, but no money, no ride.'

I could see a bit of anguish starting to appear and by now a couple of the Albion mob had alighted to see what was going on, and they all started muttering among themselves. The three girls in question were surrounded by the blokes who had got off the bus, and I could see money being passed around. The girls were fluttering their eyelashes at everyone and smiling sweetly. They pulled some dollars out of their handbags, too, little cheats, and suddenly they'd managed to pay up.

It was time to get the show on the road.

Well, my worst fears were soon realised. We reached Greensborough, only about fifteen minutes after departure, and I saw some bloke head down to Noakesy and whisper in his ear. I knew precisely what he wanted and we had to stop. By now the cans were popping and the precedent had been set. The nightmare got worse—we had stopped three times along Mahoneys Road before we even reached the Hume Highway, then there was a stop at Wallan for the females, then again at Kilmore. Noakesy was really angry.

'Mate,' he said to me, 'I don't care what happens, I'm not stopping until Euroa. At this rate the only part of *Hair* they'll see will be the curtain call.'

He was right, of course, and I had been racking my brain for a solution. 'Give me your toolbox out of the locker,' I said.

Years ago we'd had a rear differential problem with the Denning and I knew there was a small removable panel in the floor above the rear axle. Detaching the alloy carpet beading and carpet meant the panel could be lifted out, leaving a hole in the floor about 30 by 30 centimetres square. I set my plan in motion and Noakesy went tap, tap, on the microphone for attention and delivered the ultimatum: 'Next stop Euroa, and if we don't make better time we're never going to get to Sydney. Thank you.'

Well, my improvised toilet worked, sort of, but it was no good when we were travelling down the highway at 100 k's per hour. We discovered the fault when the first customer gave it a try. We had just gone over a hill when this girl visited the opening, organising the passengers on either side to hold up their travelling rugs to give her some privacy. Now that was all well and good, but as we picked up speed so did the wind rushing in through the gap. All of a sudden the travelling rugs and her dress were flying everywhere and so was her pee—which showered those sitting in the back seats and there were shouts of: 'Get away you grubby bugger—oh yuck!' After that toilet breaks were strictly up hill only.

But that was only part of the nightmare resolved; there was more to come. I'm sure most readers would have smelt the pungent odour of marijuana. The atmosphere in the coach had become so laden with secondary smoke that Val and I were getting light-headed. What a shemozzle, I thought, and went down to speak to Noakesy and Gauci. I had visions of the crew getting stoned. Desperate for fresh air Noakesy was driving with the fan on the dashboard going flat out in his face. 'Last bloody time I'll ever do a job like this, Bill, bloody ridiculous,' he said.

I was both naive and foolish in the way I managed that operation. Firstly, I targeted the very people the producers of *Hair* personified—I should have expected them to behave as they normally do. Secondly, I should have been prepared to sacrifice some return on the tour and chartered a coach with a toilet.

At home, I was in even more trouble—it soon became obvious that our previously well-mannered and lovely Bo-Bo had gone through a complete personality change following his unintentional foray into illicit drugs. I was compelled to tell Val what occurred at Bobby Gleeson's place in Sydney. I will go into no detail as to what transpired at the moment of my confession, because repeating a dissertation on my limitations as a human being, interspersed with bad language, would serve no useful purpose.

The first sign of this came on the morning after we returned from Sydney. I went outside and there was Bo-Bo with a chook he'd killed. Our neighbours, the Hawkers, had a poultry farm. Bo-Bo had grown up with chooks and never shown the slightest bit of interest in them—now he had a white leghorn hanging out of his mouth. 'Give it to me,' I said. Dog took position ready to flee. 'Bo-Bo, sit.' Dog wags pom-pom. 'Give it to me, Bo-Bo,' I said, moving forwards with hand outstretched. Dog goes mad.

Round the front of the house he went, down through the horse paddock, then up the gravel drive with puffs of dust squirting out from his flailing paws and a trail of white feathers fluttering out behind him. After running all around the place like a crazy thing, he eventually dropped the chook. I grabbed it and buried it with what tell-tale feathers I could gather up then went to see Frank Hawker.

'I'm sorry, Frank,' I said, 'but Bo-Bo killed one of your chooks.'

'Nah, Bo-Bo wouldn't kill a chook, he comes with me when I gather the eggs. He wouldn't harm a fly,' Frank says. 'It's the bloody foxes. They're a pain in the arse and the sooner they put the bounty back on their bloody tails the better. When there was a dollar in 'em, they weren't a problem. The Wilsons over the road used to be out all the time shooting the bastards . . .' and on and on and on.

'I think I'd better go, Frank,' I said.

'That's okay, Bill, and don't you worry about Bo-Bo now. He don't kill the fowls. It's the bloody foxes kills the fowls.'

Soon after that Bo-Bo disappeared. He had never wandered before. He had always been happy living on our few acres and there was no way we could keep him in anyway, other than lock him up. Off we went to look for him, Val going one way and me the other, driving around the streets of Eltham and Lower Plenty—nothing. The following morning I again went looking and eventually I spotted him, trotting down the road with his beak stuck in the air, surrounded by the scruffiest group of mutts you could ever imagine. All were in pursuit of a little bitch that looked like a cross between a flea and a rat. 'Bo-Bo, get in the car,' I said, and in he hopped, large as life, pom-pom wagging, with a big grin on his face. 'You're not too choosy,' I said, as I started to get a whiff of him. My goodness he was high.

I was off on tour soon after and when I got home Val told me Bo-Bo nicked off twice while I was away. He was gone for four days on the second occasion and she had only got him back that morning. Somebody who knew him saw the ranger pick him up and cart him off to gaol. So Val had to front up to the council office to pay his fine and 'be admonished by some pimply faced little twerp who could hardly see above the counter'.

Rosey happened to be at our place that day and was privy to the goings-on. We were stressed out and the sun was over the yard-arm somewhere so we decided to have a tipple, to welcome Bo-Bo home, probably. It wasn't long before Val and I were both bemoaning our beloved Bo-Bo and his problems. 'He'll have to go, won't he? No, I couldn't do that,' she said, answering her own question. She was beside herself with anguish, interspersed with 'It's entirely your fault. You're responsible. You're going to have to do something about him.'

I didn't know what to do. I'd hoped Bo-Bo would fully recover from his pot-induced personality transformation, but it now appeared his future was touch and go.

'I'll take him,' said Rosey.

'What!' Val and I both exclaimed.

'I'll take Bo-Bo,' Rosey repeated calmly.

And that was the start of the conversation that saw Rosey become the top dog in the kennel, as far as Bo-Bo was concerned anyway, and Val and me became just members of the pack. Rosey drove a Moke, and Bo-Bo became a Moke dog. Where the Moke and Rosey went, Bo-Bo went. The dilemma was solved—the dog needed a constant companion. Things had changed at our house when the previous pack leader, me, started to come and go for long periods at a time. Bo-Bo's world had been disrupted, and it was certainly not helped by his substantial meal of hash cookies. Anybody who says pot is harmless is kidding themselves—that's my opinion, anyway.

The company was still struggling then out of the blue, divine intervention, we got another big job—two busloads of rock hounds wanting to go to the White Cliffs opal fields over Easter. I needed to charter another coach and crew, which I was successful in achieving at a good rate, so I could see dollar signs galore on the cash register.

The residents of Eltham in the 1960s were a unique bunch: you could walk in the village on a Saturday morning and rub shoulders with writers, artists, sculptors, potters, business men and women of note, film directors, actors, musicians, millionaires and paupers, soapbox socialists, academics and arseholes, beatniks and hippies. Over a period of time we would come in contact with them all.

In the late 60s and early 70s, though, Eltham had a large population of itinerant hippies and after I had Bill King's Northern Safaris underway they provided a well of casual employees. Olympia, who hung about the town and did a bit of modelling for life classes at Alan Martin's painting school, was one of these. For whatever reason I was short of a cook for a landscape painting trip we were running in the Flinders Ranges, with Alan as tutor, and Olympia had nothing to do. 'Be here at six tomorrow morning—you've got a job for a week as cook's help,' I told her. She did okay, too. So I trained her up to do things my way, which was easy because she had never done anything in any case. Olympia then did a couple of tours and it worked out well, so I gave her the job on the Easter trip.

HIPPIE HEADACHES—THE AGE OF AQUARIUS

There were 80 people in the group so we needed a crew of five to prepare meals, set up and clean up. It was Saturday afternoon in White Cliffs, lunch over, dinner prepared, so I said to Rosey and Olympia, 'Why don't we walk over to the pub for a couple? All's well here and we deserve a breather.'

Outside the pub was this stock crate, a big Kenworth with two trailers loaded with sheep. Inside the pub was the driver, a young bloke, a real bushie, who'd probably had more to drink than he should if he was heading down to Adelaide. More likely he would only make a couple of k's out of town and take a kip on the side of the road—that's if he left White Cliffs at all.

The bloke, however, had taken Olympia's eye and she was flirting with him, pulling her neckline down lower, while he was buying her drinks that she was consuming too quickly. Before long she walked out the door with him, holding hands and saying, 'I'm going to look at his truck.' After, nearly an hour I was starting to think, 'Where the devil was Oly?' It was time we were back at camp cooking the dinner. I was about to go look for her when she rushed through the door and declared that she'd fallen in love and was going to Adelaide with the young bloke.

What! She'd only met him a couple of hours before! It didn't take much to guess what they'd been doing in the driver's cab of the stock crate. He was just standing there with a dazed look on his face. 'Bullshit you are. He's too drunk to take that rig anywhere, and if you think you're going to roll around all night with him in that sleeper cab while we work our arses off feeding eighty people you've got another think coming.' I was bloody furious, and glared at the young bloke who scuttled off while Olympia and I had a blazing row. I heard him crank up the rig and make his getaway and I dragged Olympia back to work.

Olympia didn't speak to me for a couple of days and when we got home we had a serious talk about the job and decided to call it quits. She was really apologetic by then and as a peace offering she volunteered to do some embroidery on my jeans, a popular mode of attire with the hippies of the day. Olympia was actually quite handy with a needle and thread: she returned the jeans with decorative patches on the threadbare knees, and a couple of beautiful yellow sunflowers embroidered on one side of the crotch and bluebirds of happiness winging their way out of the fly on the other.

CHAPTER 8

THE OLD DAYS OF OUTBACK HOSPITALITY

WE MADE GOOD MONEY out of our Sydney trip and the White Cliffs opal tour, in fact they carried us through the off season, but there was no way you would entice me to run another 'Scrag Tour'—as Val referred to the *Hair* enterprise. I had a good product to sell and a clientele of layabout hippies had no appeal whatsoever.

So, the first job was to create a business plan for the following year. Difficult to do when you don't know what you're doing and there's no model or competitor to take a lead from. I just pencilled in 'survival'.

What about marketing? I set aside what money could be sensibly allocated and when it was gone we stopped. We used the Melbourne *Sun* for advertising and I began seeking out journalists who wished to travel in return for editorial. I also knew that there was going to be no substitute for rubber on the road and leather on the footpath, and that meant visiting travel agents to distribute our brochures, educate them on the content of our tours and provide them with our poster. Then, hopefully, convince them to sell the package. This formidable task became Val's lot. It had been her lot from the day we began in business, actually, but she was coming under more and more pressure to crank it up a notch, plus manage the reservations, process the documentation, maintain the bookwork and raise four kids.

What about our budget? I wouldn't have a clue. People paid us money, we ran a tour. What was left was ours for maintenance, and that was the biggest expense. We were breaking things, and I was yet to discover there was not a vehicle made in the whole wide world that could withstand the work we gave it.

What I did do, though, was to run the business on a cash basis. We required payment in advance from agents or passengers, and we paid our suppliers by cash or cheque as we operated each tour. We soon became known as good payers and I negotiated significant discounts on fuel, food in the supermarkets, tyres, spare parts, and even some entry fees.

Each tour would depart with signed non-negotiable cheques made out to our suppliers, with a couple of spares—the tour leaders would fill in the amount. Our bookwork was completed tour by tour and was a simple process.

I never altered that policy. From the day we started the business until the day we sold it we ran our tours on a cash basis. There were those who said it was an odd way to run a business. Well, we were in an odd business. We sailed close to the wind on several occasions, but by maintaining that policy we survived. There were operators going down the tube from time to time for various reasons, such as pilots' disputes, operational conditions such as bad weather and impassable roads causing cancellations, or slowdowns in the economy. Put all three of them together and it could be bye-bye, Bill. We had all of those challenges on one occasion in 1977, but because we had no debt that couldn't be managed, we survived—just.

When the coach operator Centralian Tours went belly-up in the 1970s, it was a nightmare. They had tours all over the country at the time. Crews were stranded with coachloads of passengers and no money and no credit, and the bank had shut the door. Some of their drivers fuelled vehicles with their own money to get back to base. Some passengers found their own way home. I was on tour in the Denning and we had five spare seats so we picked up five

WANTED

TOURISTS, if there are any left in the world with a spirit of Adventure.

WE DO NOT OFFER the beautiful buildings, parks and gardens, or luxury Hotels, swinging Night Spots and the fine food prepared by Continental Chefs that you will find in our big cities.

ALL WE CAN OFFER is to show you the 'Outback' on a personalised 4-Wheel-Drive Safari.

OUR BUILDINGS are the mountains in this prehistoric land sculptured by weather and time before the Americas and Europe were thrust from the bowels of the earth.

OUR PARKS are the deserts, a carpet of wildflowers and sentinels of mulga, sown by nature on a bed of red sand.

OUR AVIARY, our Zoo, nature's realm, hundreds of miles from the cities, inhabited by strange animals, Kangaroos, Euros and Frill Neck Lizards, beautiful Birds by the thousand, singing their songs of freedom.

OUR HOTEL, a roof of canvas, a roof of stars, a spring camp bed and warm sleeping bag.

OUR RESTAURANT, a campfire grilling juicy beefsteaks, coal-roasted potatoes and perhaps a salad, washed down with red wine, followed by camp oven damper smothered in honey.

LIVING in denims, following century-old Camel Train paths, sipping billy tea while swapping tales around the evening camp fire.

IF these things make you yearn for London, Paris or New York, forget us.

WE are still trying to find somebody in the World with a spirit of Adventure.

Signed *Bill King*

BILL KING

stranded people and took them back to Melbourne. Other operators pitched in, too.

We released our program just after Christmas to begin in March 1970 and continue through 1971. We also produced a poster to be displayed in travel agencies. I advertised in the *Age* newspaper for a person to train as tour leader on outback expeditions and attracted heaps of respondents. Most of them you wouldn't feed, but one stood out. Brian Shaddick was a young Pommy bloke who had worked in the outback with a mapping survey crew. He had a heavy-vehicle driver's licence, was well mannered and neatly attired, and gave the impression of being a nice bloke.

We had our problems with fools over the years, but Brian was not one of them. He was the only person we employed full-time in the early days; the others were seasonal. I bought an ex-Commonwealth Holden Kingswood at an auction for him to use in the off season, servicing travel agents, delivering brochures and posters. Brian became a jack of all trades, the same as me, and he did a good job. In later years it also became Brian's responsibility to train crews in our style of operation—he really was an asset. Unfortunately he fell by the wayside when he succumbed to the charms of one of his passengers and left to get married. (This, I would discover, was a common way to lose a tour leader.)

I had another interesting bloke apply: Dusty Wolfe had done a bit of courier work (tour escort) for Centralian Tours, owned a four-wheel drive and had taken a couple of punters on trips. I heard via the grapevine in later years that on his tours he would never pass a fresh road kill without stopping to check the carcass for undamaged meat. 'Waste not, want not' was his motto. When I heard that rumour I was positively appalled, but nobody on our tours ever complained. Dusty also had a bush camp out of Borroloola, where he spent time living with the Yanyuwa people and writing books. He left the impression that he could be useful, so I filed him away.

We began operating tours in the mid 70s around the Gulf of Carpentaria, through Borroloola. It was at that time I began researching the history of the region and what I discovered was positively horrifying. I had no idea that when the cattlemen began taking up land and moving stock between the Northern Territory and Queensland, their treatment of the Indigenous people was so barbaric and inhumane. They had lived in total isolation from Europeans until the 1870s but within a few years they had been totally decimated. 'Dispersing of the Natives', the policy was known as, and stockmen, landowners and police were all responsible for the bloodshed. It is a pretty dark passage in our history that has been either disregarded or conveniently forgotten.

•

March to October was when it all had to happen, and we allocated Brian to the sixteen-day Alice Springs–Ayers Rock tours in the Denning. It was repetitive and would allow him to get the feel of the job. I still had to take him on a familiarisation tour, and I hoped my judgement of him was correct; otherwise I was in the shit.

I was to discover that the old cliché of always being in the shit and it was only the depth that varied would be par for the course over the coming years. Like having a vehicle in some faraway location hopelessly bogged or broken down, or being in the middle of an airline dispute with passengers scattered all over the country, or a problem with a crew member or a punter or a travel agent.

We got going in March with a full deck on 'Gertrude', the name the Denning inherited from somewhere, and Brian and me at the helm. We had a Burke and Wills expedition booked as well, so Rosey took that tour. Our itinerary took us through the Flinders Ranges and up the Oodnadatta Track, and Brian took to the job like a professional. He was a steady and careful driver, understood equipment and never cranked up the coach in the morning without first checking the oil and water and kicking the tyres. I like my tucker and fancied myself as a good bush cook, and I was to find that Brian was also a fair hand with the pots and pans.

The tour was a real eye-opener for Brian. As tour operators we did not have the red carpet rolled out wherever we went. There were still towns and communities that were yet to learn the full economic value of the tourist dollar. We had to travel with a lot of diplomacy to deal with situations that could manifest themselves into unwanted problems.

One day I was walking past the Stuart Arms Hotel in Alice Springs with some of my punters and as we passed the entrance we had to step aside as three young females stumbled out. They looked us up and down, then one of them spat at us and snarled, 'Bloody tourists'. It's no wonder it was commonly called the Stupid Arms in those early days.

On another tour we were in Gertrude and had a large proportion of females on board. We pulled into Kulgera, the first bit of habitation you reach in the Northern Territory when coming from the south, and I have never felt more uncomfortable in my whole life—so I could only imagine how the women felt. The barman was playing pool with a bloke and there were a few truckies and road workers in the bar who were openly salivating at the girls, and their smutty remarks were meant to be overheard. In addition they were glaring at Brian and me, daring us to say something. I'm not bloody silly. We couldn't get out of the place fast enough, and I was really pissed off with the bloke who appeared to be in charge; he never uttered a word.

We never stopped at Kulgera after that and as our business grew we recorded it in our instruction manual—Kulgera was banned. I tell a fib, I did stop there on another occasion, but not by choice. We were churning our way down the South Road in heavy rain, and as we got abreast of the Kulgera pub I slid into a monster bog hole. We were stuck there with mud up to the floor; we were going nowhere. They had only that day dragged a road train out of the trench with a bulldozer and nobody had thought to jam a stick in the hole as a warning. What's more, the dozer had taken off to rescue some other poor buggers who were bogged down the road.

The shearers arrive at Exmouth Gulf Station in the 13-passenger 'bus' in 1924.

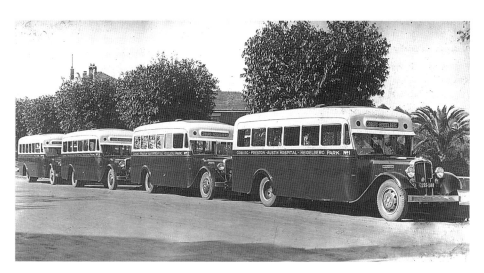

'The First Fleet' in December 1938. The Coburg Heidelberg Omnibus Company vehicles were built on extended American Federal truck chassis by coach builders Cheetham and Borwick. They gave honest and reliable service for over 30 years.

The Bangemall pub in the Gascoyne goldfields, WA, in 1928, where I had my beginnings.

Our Eltham abode, the replica of the Bangemall pub where Bill King's Northern Safaris had its beginnings.

Yours truly at Burke and Wills' Camp 76 on the Diamantina River near Birdsville in 1969.

Alan Martin, demonstrating for the class at the Cooper Creek painting school.

Clifton Pugh's *Bacchus* mural, on the bar wall of the Family Hotel in Tibooburra.

Gertrude, the punters and me. Sometimes we got there, sometimes we didn't.

My old man, second from left, was a 'bogologist' from way back when he was taking Charles Kingsford Smith's Gascoyne Trading Company rigs from Carnarvon to all settlements north in the 1920s.

The Gascoyne supply truck with Lindsay Skipworth (left, and my old man, right) was the first motor vehicle to reach the North West Cape of WA in 1925.

We became 'bogologists' in our own right when the 15-year drought broke in 1973.

Dig it out, push it out, winch it out—or all three.

Little Ben, in Palm Valley with the 'Frolics'. It was one of the first custom-built 'Desert Cruisers' that we put into service.

Where there was a will there was a way—the Land Rover 6 en route to Alice Springs along the old Ghan track.

THE OLD DAYS OF OUTBACK HOSPITALITY

So we had a couple of days at Kulgera while we waited for it to return, and the hospitality had not improved.

Quick thinking can sometimes divert trouble, like the time we pulled into West Wyalong to camp for the night with a group from a teachers college. The campground was on the edge of town in those days, and there was no fence around the area where they put bus tours. It was just on dusk when we heard the roar of motorbikes coming up the road and in they came, about a dozen of them, and started circling our camp—nothing to do in a country town in the middle of New South Wales, so let's piss off the tourists. We weren't camped on grass either, so you can imagine the dust they were stirring up.

Some of the girls were getting frightened, and John Knox, my co-driver, asked, 'What are we going to do?'

I walked out and stood in their path. A couple of riders swerved around me, then this bloke on a big black Matchless 500 rode straight at me and skidded to a halt in a cloud of dust. 'Nice bike,' I said. 'Buy it new?'

'Nah. I bought it off Bluey over there when he bought his Norton.'

And so it went on. The others started gathering around and we went on about bikes for a bit until they got bored and started drifting away.

On another occasion Knoxy and I were heading across the Barkly Tableland intending to make a camp near Three Ways at the junction of the South Road. We were behind schedule and it was pretty evident we weren't going to make it, so we pulled into Frewena Roadhouse, about 100 kilometres short of our destination. (Frewena is no longer shown on some maps, but it was near the turn-off to Rockhampton Downs Station.) The publican, a bloke named Joe, said, 'No worries, mate. Camp out the back—there's a shower and toilet.'

So we set up camp, got the grub out of the way and while we were tidying up, our punters started wandering over to the roadhouse to see what adventures awaited them in the Northern

Territory outback. We joined them in due course and apart from our mob there were about twenty or so blokes in the place. Half of them were jackaroos from Rockhampton Downs, the others were from a road crew camped a few hundred metres down the road. The roadies obviously had a pretty big job on, as their base was surrounded by trucks, rollers, graders and the like.

It was a pleasant evening until a few of the young bucks got a skinful and started to do chin-ups, seeing how many times they could touch their chins on the exposed beams in the bar. That was all well and good until they started challenging people to a contest. One of them started on me, and I said, 'Mate, with my avoirdupois problem I would have no hope.' I saw a vacant look come over his face—he had no idea what I'd said, so he turned surly.

'Hey, settle down!' Joe the publican told him.

Time to go to bed, I thought, and sidled off when nobody was looking. I never bid anybody goodnight on tours—it takes too long. Shortly after that the rest of our mob wandered back in dribs and drabs and were soon settled down.

It was a beautiful night, and I was dead to the world in my swag under the stars when in the early hours I heard this machine. It was one of the roadies on the grader and he was heading for our camp. Then he started doing a slalom through the tents, before coming straight at me. The night was pitch black by then and I was totally blinded by his lights, and I can tell you he had my undivided attention. I had no hope of extracting myself from the swag before he got to me, and the thought flashed through my mind that I was a goner.

But at the last second he dropped it on full lock, and that bloody big front wheel, about a metre and a half across, missed my head by 30 centimetres. Thank goodness he had the blade elevated, because the edge of it went over the top of me as he swerved around for the return run to his camp. I know he never saw me on the ground, he was just looking at the tents, and to this day I believe my survival was pure luck.

It was not my time to go to that other place, but it was certainly my time to get some help, because I could see him wheeling around down near the roadies' camp and I could hear him revving the throttle as his headlights settled on our camp, preparing to come back for another run. I took off in bare feet and underpants and experienced extreme pain as I ran through a patch of bindi-eyes on my way to the pub to wake up Joe while yelling at Knoxy to get the punters out of the tents.

'What the fuck is going on?' Joe said as he stumbled out the back door.

'That bloody idiot on the grader is doing slaloms through the tents!'

'Jesus Christ!' he said, as he ran straight through the middle of the camp, yelling at people to get out of the way, as most of my punters had emptied out of their tents and started running in all directions when they saw the grader driver backing up for his second run.

By this time the grader was boring down on our camp again, but Joe marched out directly into the headlights. I could see his silhouette as he put both palms out in front of his body and commanded the machine to stop. With that the grader deviated to the side a little, with Joe following suit, then to the other side a bit, and Joe followed again. By now, though, Joe had a captive audience, and slowly the thing came to a halt. 'What the fuck do you think you're doing?' Joe screamed at the driver. I didn't hear the answer, but I could see the roadie was pissing himself laughing. 'Get down out of there, you fuckin' moron!' The culprit started extracting himself from the cab, still killing himself laughing, but missed his grip on the step handle and flopped on the ground, rolling over spreadeagled in the dirt. He was absolutely whacked out of his brain.

Now we all know there's an old saying that when someone is full of alcohol they feel no pain. Well, that was about to change. While I was still barefoot, Joe had pulled on his boots and as he said, 'You useless piece of shit,' he gave the fool an almighty kick right in the fork.

I have no idea if that action had any sobering effect, but obviously the figure on the ground still had responsive reflexes, because it immediately contracted into the foetal position, where it remained all hunched up, letting out long whimpering moans.

By this time some of the audience from the roadies' camp, who had been encouraging the fool, arrived at the scene, so Joe gave the curled up figure another roost in the ribs with the R.M. Williams and as it rolled over another one up the backside. 'Get this bloody idiot outta here!' he yelled at the roadies, who were still laughing their heads off, but now the amusement was sparked by the pain being inflicted on their dopey mate.

They didn't bother to pick him up, either. The last I saw a couple of blokes were dragging him off into the night by his feet. Joe was really annoyed and I discovered later that the same bloke had got into a fracas in the bar with some of the crew from Brunette Downs Station a couple of nights before, so there was a bit of payback in it.

I should add that it was the last thing we needed on that tour—up half the night, no sleep, and we still had to catch up time the following day.

In the mid 60s my brother Alan stopped over in Mount Isa with two coachloads of college girls. When the word got around about the bevy of beauties down at the camping park, a few of the local lads arrived to 'chat up a sheila'. Now that was okay, just a bit of fun, until later in the night a mob of over-refreshed yobbos arrived in camp and began harassing the girls. Alan wasn't getting involved in that lot, so he rang the cops, who duly arrived, and the boozed-up mob then became more interested in whacking a cop than picking up girls. The cops in turn called for reinforcements and told the crew to pack up and get out of Mount Isa while the fracas was in progress.

Alan says that was the fastest pack-up of all time—they were out of there in 30 minutes flat. Not alone, though. The lads jumped in their cars and set off in hot pursuit. Alan reckoned there was a kilometre of headlights winking in the rear-view mirrors.

The pursuers obviously assumed the tour would pull over to camp somewhere down the road, but with 700 kilometres' worth of fuel on board the coaches, there was no way that would happen. Alan said they had travelled well over 200 k's before the last pair of headlights dropped off; they either ran out of fuel or got to the point of no return.

Some time later I relayed the story to playwright John Powers. He had successfully staged *The Last of the Knucklemen* at about that time, and was travelling with his wife, actor Carmel Dunn, on one of our camping tours to Lightning Ridge opal fields. I also related another story that occurred some years before: it concerned a pair of male and female school teachers who were in charge of a group of co-ed students, hence the escort of both sexes.

Let me tell you, we weren't into that tour for more than a couple of days when it became perfectly obvious that the female teacher was receiving 95 per cent of the male teacher's attention and vice versa.

Now, boys will be boys and girls will be girls and it didn't take long for the kids to take advantage of the situation. After dark their silhouettes could be observed flitting between tents, the glow of cigarettes lit the camp like fairylights and the giggles coming from the tents became louder with the popping of the cans. All that passed Romeo and Juliet by; they just remained starry-eyed and disappeared early at night.

As a result the kids had a ball on that tour. They were let loose for sixteen days with only a cook and a bus driver to manage their affairs, and frankly we didn't care what they did as long as it didn't affect other people or the equipment. Normally, the teachers in the party rostered kids for varying duties such as pack-up team, kitchen chores, firewood gathering and the like. We just delegated the responsibility to a couple of the obviously smarter kids. They organised the others and it went like clockwork.

John Powers was good company and we did enjoy many campfire chinwags. In 1975 he staged the play *Shindig* that alluded to the former stories and I read an interview with journalist Peter Haddow many years later, in which John said he got the seed for that play from a bus driver on a tour to Lightning Ridge.

•

December 1972 was hot—bloody hot, more to the point. We left Melbourne on Boxing Day with Gertrude fully packed with punters, heading for Alice and the Rock. We stayed the first night in Mildura and the second in Wilpena Pound and were heading for a bush camp somewhere on the Oodnadatta Track. The third night was always flexible, the distance being governed by the time we left the Flinders Ranges after a walk in the Pound. But the weather didn't improve and December 28 was an absolute scorcher.

Inland Australia to all appearances at that moment was dead. The few leaves left on the mulga trees after years of drought had curled inwards to shade themselves from the relentless rays of the sun and conserve what little moisture they had left from evaporating into nowhere. Even the usually resilient birds and animals found it difficult to cope.

I remembered my old man telling me that when he was working on the North West Cape in the 1920s he had seen birds fall out of trees stone dead in stinking hot weather. I occasionally saw rows of galahs hanging upside down on the telegraph wires along the Oodnadatta Track, with their wings and beaks wide open, as if they just didn't have the strength to stay upright. One day I saw a couple fall off, flutter to the ground, then lay still. I stopped, picked one up and considered blowing in its beak to try and revive it, but then a vision of success manifested itself in my mind. I could see my little feathered friend waking up and thinking, 'What the bloody hell does he think he's doing?' and putting its needle-sharp beak through my lip. Bugger that, I thought, and dropped it.

Gertrude, I might add, was not air-conditioned. There was not much point when as much time was spent out of the vehicle than in it, more in fact, and hopping in and out of an air-conditioned

THE OLD DAYS OF OUTBACK HOSPITALITY

atmosphere wearing sweaty clothes can make people crook. However, on that day I would have dearly loved to have that air-con switch on my control panel.

We were on track to make a bush camp that night in the vicinity of Coward Springs, but at lunchtime I put it to the punters that we reduce breaks to the minimum during the afternoon and push on to William Creek pub. We would arrive about 7 p.m. and have cold drinks at the end of it. The suggestion was not a hard sell.

The William Creek pub in those days survived on the Ghan railway maintenance crew that had their dongas over the road. Now where do you spend your wages way out there? There was nowhere but Fergie's William Creek pub. Some of those blokes gave their pay packet to Fergie and when all that had gone he kept their drinks on the slate, so 100 per cent of their income went to the pub. Dick Nunn and his crew from Anna Creek Station and the odd passer-by also supplemented his income.

Mind you, there was a fair mob of workers on Anna Creek. It was, and maybe still is, one of the world's largest cattle-raising properties, covering an area of some 24 000 square kilometres, with up to 16 000 head of cattle. To put that in perspective, Belgium is of similar size and is home to some 10 million people, so that gives you some idea of the vastness of the enterprise. Fergie did pretty well with his captive audience, thank you very much. He had his airstrip next door and his aeroplane parked at the front door of the pub.

Nevertheless, with the pub's limited clientele, you would have thought the tourists would be welcome, but no, Fergie was a rude bastard and had a bad attitude: 'Oh, do come—but chuck your money out the window as you drive past. For Christ's sake don't stop.'

We pulled into William Creek about seven and our mob needed no encouragement. They were all young folk and about half of them were American school teachers still being sponsored by the Victorian government. They were standing in the aisle waiting for the door to open and their tongues were hanging out as they spilled from the coach and fled across the road with visions of their first cold stubbie or Coke.

By the time I disembarked I could see them all milling around at the front door. 'What's wrong?' I asked, as I pushed my way through the throng.

What's wrong was that Fergie had slammed the door in their faces and said through the flywire screen, 'I'm going for my tea. Come back in an hour.'

'Fair enough,' I said. 'Sell me some slabs and we'll be on our way.'

'No, come back later,' he said, and walked off, all this while there were a dozen or so railway workers still drinking in the bar.

The miserable bugger obviously thought I would pitch camp down at the racetrack near the end of his airstrip and in due course everybody would wander back and he could begin emptying their pockets at his convenience. 'Well, stuff you,' I thought, as I loaded my gasping flock back onto the bus. The sun was gone and it was cooling down, so we headed off to a dry creek bed a few kilometres up the road, where there was a bit of firewood about.

We had plenty of beer and soft drink in the coach, but it was warm, so I did the old trick of putting the cans in sugar bags, hanging them under a tree and throwing a bucket of water over them. 'Let's get camp set up, a campfire going and the tucker underway. By that time the drinks will be good.' It is amazing how well the old Coolgardie-style cooling system works.

Another time we were heading north in the Land Rover and I stopped at William Creek for the punters to buy drinks, lollies and whatever. I was sitting in the car waiting: I wouldn't set foot in the joint after the 'come back later' episode. I see this vehicle heading south and it was 'Saltbush Bill's Safaris'. Saltbush Bill was a 'mushroom'—I called them mushrooms because they came and went seasonally. Many advertised their tours using our itineraries and ran them backwards, charging less. Competition was beginning to evolve.

Anyway, I knew as much about this bloke as he knew about himself, although it was the first time I'd laid eyes on him. I had put my feelers out after I saw his advertisement in a newspaper: after a few years in the job I had a good network of spies. All the operators went to the same places and dealt with the same people. The story goes that he had worked as a technician on a couple of documentaries in the outback with the ABC. Captivated by what the inland had to offer, he then decided his future lay in being a tour operator. The consensus was that he should have stuck with docos. I was doing my sums by then and with his fare structure he wasn't making any money. Good.

Saltbush Bill didn't know the rules. He had three females on board and had just stopped for them to have a pee, and obviously he was in a hurry because he sat in his vehicle with the engine running.

Now Fergie had a rule that you only leave at his place what you put in at his place. So the three women, who literally bolted for the dunny at the back of the pub, found it locked. The urgency of their problem then became even greater as they ran into the pub and asked Fergie for the key. They still hadn't bought anything and Fergie had no compassion for anybody no matter what their plight. According to my punters who enlightened me later about the scene, Fergie shouted at the unfortunate visitors, 'No, I've just had the bloody septic tank pumped out. Use the one out the front.'

Now the dunny out the front was a 'five-sider'. They were quite common around bush pubs, country racetracks and the like, and are designed for blokes. If you make a square with one short side and a panel running back from the short side into the square it acts as a screen and you can't see through the opening. Fergie's five-sider was six posts stuck in the ground with sheets of rusty galvanised iron nailed to them. A piece of roof gutter that had fallen off somewhere was wired lopsidedly across the wall inside for blokes to pee into and that drained into a hole filled with rocks. I saw the ladies hurry into the dunny with cries of 'Oh no, yuck!' while Saltbush Bill gave the engine a couple of revs as a hurry-up signal.

Just then one of the railway workers from the fettlers' camp down the road came out of the pub. He was well and truly sloshed and was making a bee-line for the dunny—his need was obviously very great as he had already begun undoing his pants to save time. Saltbush Bill put his head out the window and yelled something at him that the bloke totally ignored as he swung around the corner and into the five-sider. Well, there was this unholy shriek as he flew out backwards with a look of shock on his face and fell flat on his bum. The women scurried out, trampling all over him in their fright, while still trying to adjust their dresses as they fled towards their vehicle. I almost felt sorry for Saltbush Bill; I could hear the three of them giving him an earful for telling them they could use the facilities at William Creek. So much for Fergie's outback hospitality.

Fast forward a few years and I read in the daily that a light aircraft had crashed in the South Australian outback and the pilot was killed. It was Fergie. Shit happens.

I probably should point out that in writing these recollections I could understand if folk might think that Bill King's Northern Safaris were just a progressive pub crawl, and indeed I did have punters from time to time accuse me of operating precisely that. However, the majority would understand that places marked on a map were not necessarily towns or settlements—they were more likely to be just a pub and a petrol pump. Not to stop would be to disregard the need for fuel, entail a trip through the outback without contact with another human being, and even more importantly without contact with the characters and the way of life enjoyed by the folk living in that environment. And besides, from my experience, females much prefer to use a toilet seat than squat in the bush.

•

While I'm writing about outback hospitality I cannot let park rangers go by without a mention, as they were an incongruous lot. One would think that the job specification was to manage the environment in which they had responsibility and ensure that visitors left with memories of a rewarding experience. Pretty simple really, but some of them found that a complicated task.

When we began taking paying passengers into national parks, I had many varied reactions. There were those rangers who saw any visitor as a nuisance, like an intrusion into their own home, and the park as their backyard—guests not welcome. Others saw us as the great polluters of the nation, as if every can or stubbie that had been chucked out of a vehicle window was the work of those mongrels in tour buses. Bloody tourists!

It was true there were tourists who were polluters, but the real problem came from locals. The point was that we, as organised tour operators, were easily identifiable with sign-written vehicles, so it was convenient to drop all of the sins of mankind on us. The fact was we were the reverse. 'Take nothing but photographs, leave nothing but footprints,' was our philosophy. Why would we destroy the very thing we are trying to sell, the pristine Australian experience? That would be foolish.

Some rangers took offence at tour operators because they were making money out of 'their' park. How dare private enterprise exploit the people and profit from national parks? How dare you give the public what they want? Weird mentality, I tell you. They had no qualms about putting their hands out for entry fees, which is fair enough. I have no problem with the user-pays system either, as long as the quality of the experience is equal to the amount of the fee.

On the other side of the coin there were parks and attractions that were managed in a highly professional way. John Gerritsen, the chief ranger at the New South Wales Parks and Wildlife site at Mootwingee in the 1960s, was a fantastic bloke. John would go to any lengths and offer whatever time was required to ensure that every point of interest in his park was identified and explained so that tour operators could interpret the features accurately to their clients. He also did a lot of research and published his findings on the Mootwingee rock peckings and also the rare yellow-footed rock wallaby, of which there are small colonies in western New South Wales. Ted, the ranger at Ormiston Gorge, was also a good bloke; a bit wary of us at first, but in time I know he looked forward to our visits.

So that was the environment in inland Australia when we began in the job. Outback hospitality was not everywhere. There were both 'tourists welcome' and 'tourists keep out' signs to greet the visitor.

Still, this was tourism in its infancy and a learning experience for all involved. These days we know that outback towns and national parks are very much geared to the visitor experience and have benefited from the lessons in people management during those earlier times.

CHAPTER 9

THE PAINTING SCHOOLS

'When travelling to distant places, open the eyes of the soul.' So advises an ancient oriental proverb, and that was the introduction to our 1973–74 tour brochures. I had changed the concept dramatically, marketing our product under the 'special interest' banner to introduce a whole new program of painting and photography safaris. In those days it was a very innovative concept and we had already operated two schools at Milparinka and Mootwingee, with students from Alan Martin's classes, topped up with a few from advertising in *The Age*. Now it was time to expand the concept. We cranked our departures up another notch with 574 days of operation and we were looking for 800 passengers.

'How did I get myself into all this?' I thought at the time. We were starting our fourth season in business and were making money, but I hadn't worked out how to make some of it stick to the fingers as it went past.

Today you will find painting trips to exotic locations advertised frequently in many forms of media, but in the year of our Lord 1973 the only place you would find them was in the arts section of *The Age* on a Saturday:

> Bill King's Northern Safaris will take you to faraway places with an accomplished artist who will teach you to paint, expand your awareness of the real Australia and introduce you to experiences that will remain with you for all time.

We had put together a stable of well known Melbourne tutors. In addition to Alan Martin they included Karlis Mednis, who studied at the Riga School of Art in Latvia and migrated to Australia from Russia in 1949; Lesbia Thorpe, a graphic artist who studied with Dattilo Rubbo in Sydney before moving to London to study under Gertrude Hermes; Alfred Calkoen, who was born in Amsterdam, where he studied art; John Yule from the National Gallery Art School; and Bill Caldwell, a multi-award-winning tonal realist painter who studied under Doug Miller.

These were our tutors, and in consultation with them we selected a variety of locations for our classes, such as Omeo in Victoria's High Country, Mount Buffalo, Merimbula on the south coast of New South Wales and Peri Lake.

Peri Lake in the Paroo Channel is typical of the locations for which that part of central inland Australia is renowned—a vast stretch of water about 20 kilometres long and 10 kilometres wide, the lake is a link in the chain that forms the Paroo Channel. It is surrounded by pure white sand that is strewn with ancient Aboriginal cooking fires and stone artefacts. There is also a group of smaller lakes to the south and an abundance of native fish that provide the perfect habitat for the pelicans that have been breeding there forever. The fascinating thing about the pelicans is that if you swim out to their islands and crawl about in between their nests of sticks on your hands and knees, the birds think you're a pelican. Even if there are eggs and chicks in the nest they'll take no notice at all. Stand up, however, and the whole island will fly into a panic.

Each morning the pelicans flew off in a southerly direction to feed in lakes to the south of Peri. When they returned in the late afternoon the little specks far in the distance slowly grew in size as they came towards you, sometimes high in the sky riding thermals

THE PAINTING SCHOOLS

and sometimes low over the water, just gliding, exploiting the wind, not even flapping their wings. Then as they neared home they would tilt the wings up, put the feet forward and skim the heels along the top of the water until they gracefully settled down to a stop. To see a big flock coming in to land is truly a beautiful sight.

As part of our painting school expansion, we ran a tour in June with Alan Martin to the island of Bali, a pretty adventurous excursion almost 40 years ago. The painting school was at Ubud, high in the mountains, an area of lush green hills, cool waterfalls and terraced rice paddies. The group stayed at the Tjampuhan, which is situated on a hill overlooking the confluence of two holy rivers. Owned by a local prince and set in several acres of manicured flower gardens in which all manner of tropical vegetation flourished, the Balinese-style bungalows had one or two bedrooms each and were fully self-contained. It was indeed a little piece of paradise.

Apart from the painting classes we had also organised a lecture on Balinese art traditions by the famous local artist I Gusti Sobrat. Another day the tour group walked through the paddy fields to the nearby village of Penestanen, to be rewarded with a lecture by I Njoman Tjakra, founder of Bali's 'primitive art' school. It was an opportunity to join his class and exchange techniques with the locals, even if it was in sign language, although they did have an interpreter with them.

They had a great stroke of good fortune on that tour. While visiting the museum in Ubud to view the works of Lempad, the world-renowned Balinese artist and friend of Pablo Picasso, they met the man himself. He was then well into his 90s and working in the museum, restoring his own work.

Back at home, in late June we headed off to Tibooburra with Karlis Mednis. We were camped at the racetrack, which was good—there was a shelter for us to set up our kitchen and dining area, a toilet and a bush shower. To give the punters a treat I had organised a barbecue at Barney Davies's pub. He had gone out at the appropriate time prior to our arrival and shot a 'killer' (a nice young fat steer ready for the table), to have it hung just right for the big event. Barney and Jos Davies had spent most of their lives on cattle stations and 'retired' to the pub in Tibooburra. They were gregarious folk and just loved having guests.

So we all arrived to enjoy an aperitif and Barney had some pre-dinner nibbles— succulent little cubes of meat on toothpicks— sizzling away on the hotplate for us to eat while the spit roast was coming along.

'Bloody delicious. What cut of the meat is that?' I said to Barney.

'Little pieces of offal,' he replied.

'What offal?' I asked.

'Bull's ring.'

I didn't believe what he said, 'What! You actually mean bull's ring? You're kidding me.'

'Nope, no sweeter part of the beast,' he said.

'Don't you dare tell my punters,' I warned him. I could visualise any dislike being directed at me, not him.

The next painting school in September took us to Cooper Creek with Alan Martin, and when I think about that now it was also a pretty adventurous trip in a 1968 model, single-axle Denning. We set up camp on the northern side of the crossing about a kilometre downstream in a lovely clearing situated on an enormous waterhole. We had camped in the bush between Tibooburra and the Cooper in a dry location the previous night, so the luxury of a bucket of water for a 'scrub up' and change of clothes was seen as an excuse for a night out and a chance to visit the pub on the southern side of the crossing. It was too far to walk, so I loaded the folk aboard Gertrude and chauffeured them into 'town'.

You will recall that on our first painting trip we had a group of folk, predominantly female, in a similar situation at Milparinka when the shearers from Theldarpa Station arrived to check out the talent. This time it was the workers preparing to construct the pipeline from the gas field at Moomba to Sydney, and a rough and tumble group of characters they were, too.

Not to be denied, a few of the truckies who carted the pipes from the rail siding down near Lyndhurst managed to get wind of the event and they lined up out the front of the pub with these huge pipes still on the back of their rigs. And if the pipeline workers were a rough and tumble lot, those truckies were to be avoided at all costs. They were as rugged as their trucks (old Macks and Kenworths). A couple of them were well past their use-by date, and this applied to the drivers as well. It was the same story as the shearers, just a different cast.

One drunken fool arrived at our camp in the early hours of the morning. He had driven this monster truck with one enormous pipe on the back down this skinny little track beside the Cooper to (hopefully) entertain one of the ladies he met in the pub. His mission was thwarted when the pipe snapped a huge branch off a eucalypt that landed under the front wheels, bringing the thing to a grinding halt. He got his comeuppance, though. He had to back the thing out the following day—it took him hours.

•

We added some new destinations the following year, distributed our brochures to agents, booked our first couple of months of advertising space, secured all our camp sites and accommodation bookings, prepared our vehicles and briefed our crews. We were underway with the new concept: special interest tours with Bill King's Northern Safaris. We ran ads in the Melbourne *Age*, *Sydney Morning Herald*, *The Australian*, Melbourne *Sun* and Melbourne *Herald*. We featured headings like: 'Outback Painting Safaris Go Outback' and 'Summer Art Vacations—on a personalised four-wheel-drive safari'.

I felt pretty good about all that until one Saturday morning Terry Watts, a good friend who'd been an executive with an advertising agency, called into our home for a chat and a coffee. He passed the remark that my advertising was a non-event. 'What do you mean, a non-event?' I bristled.

'It's bloody awful,' Terry said. 'It's just jumbles of words. There's no theme, no uniformity. You phone the newspaper with your unmemorable little words and some typesetter lays it out and sticks it in the appropriate section, and I'll bet if you looked at your last twenty ads there wouldn't be any two that would resemble one another, or be recognisable as a Bill King ad. As I said, it's just crap.'

I knew he was right and I'm sure he knew that I would know he was right, because he opened a presentation folder, and there was a series of display advertisements, all taken from my 'non-event' insertions in newspapers and laid out by an art director. They were really eye-catching, although I said to Terry I wasn't keen on my head being featured in every ad.

Val then put in her six cents' worth and said, 'There's no way he can have his head in every ad we run. Everyone will think he's onto himself.'

'Well, he is, isn't he?' Terry replied. I was about to defend myself but then Terry explained: 'That's it, you silly buggers. That's the identifying BRAND. That's the consistency. Get it? Hey, you're being featured in all manner of magazines and newspapers with photographs anyway. It would be dopey not to spin off that. You're it. You're selling your tours as Bill King's Northern Safaris. Well, who the bloody hell is Bill King? You might as well introduce yourself to prospective clients, and it's got nothing to do with being up yourself—it's just sound business practice.'

So I had myself an advertising agent. Terry had set up his own agency, and I was one of his first customers. What's more, he remained my agent for the entire time I was in business.

We had worked really hard at seeking editorial and our PR had started to bring results. Stories in magazines that hang about in racks or sit on coffee tables are great value with their longevity. Rennie Ellis wrote a story about our Burke and Wills survey expedition on which we made our movie and submitted it to *Walkabout*, the now defunct Australian travel magazine. Published by the Australian National Travel Association since the mid 1930s, it had worldwide distribution.

The story was featured under the heading, 'Follow the Fence: Follow Your Nose', which alluded to the 5614-kilometre dog fence stretching from the Great Divide in Queensland to the Great

THE PAINTING SCHOOLS

Australian Bight in South Australia. The story covered nine pages and we did get a great number of enquiries and a couple of bookings from Australia and the US. Rennie was a talented wordsmith and had a great insight into the 'feel' of the bush. His work was summed up by his editor, John Ross, who said: 'Rennie Ellis goes on safari and returns with a luminous narrative of life on the track, a glorious collection of characters and a city man's wondrous first vision of inland Australia.'

We got another run in an issue of *New Idea* magazine. Titled 'Swinging Safari', it was a story about Helen Homewood, a former Hartnell of London model who at that time ran her own agency in Melbourne, and two other girls, sisters Diane and Caroline Dawson. On return from one of our tours Helen told her story to Alix MacDonald, who in turn had it published by the magazine. It was a two-page article written from a female point of view and we ran an ad in the same issue with a return coupon headed: 'It used to be male stuff—But we have changed all that. Helen Homewood, Diane and Caroline Lawson have just returned from the rugged outback—See their story on page 7.'

We were inundated with requests for brochures—our tours did appeal to females.

Derek Ballantine from the Melbourne *Sun* did some good spreads. We took him away and he called the journey the 'Bush Walkabout Safari', filing stories during the trip, nine articles in all, which included half-page spreads about people like Don Maxwell. Don drove his van around the outback stations selling all manner of goods such as men's and ladies' clothing, musical instruments, cigarettes, firearms, ammunition, knives and cooking pots. You name it, Don had it. On the road for a month to six weeks at a time, he could finish up 2000 kilometres from home before returning to load up and head off again.

Derek also wrote about Trevor Hampel, the school teacher at the Parachilna Primary School, which sits between a few houses and a pub on the track to Marree. There were fourteen students in the school, ranging in age from five to twelve, and the kids comprised about half of the town's population. Trevor found romance in the bush, too, with his colleague Corrine Mills, who was posted to another little school at Blinman, 30 kilometres to the east.

Dick Nunn from Anna Creek Station also featured in Derek's articles. Dick had a string of working camels, four of them harnessed to the chuck wagon, in support of the eight stockmen who were rounding up cattle to be sent off to market. Derek wrote about the romance of the drovers' camp, so often the subject of bush ballads and stories from great Australian writers like C.J. Dennis and Henry Lawson.

A worthy subject was Gus Williams, who I knew well. He was an Indigenous elder from the Lutheran Mission at Hermannsburg, about 100 kilometres west of the Alice. It is situated near the ancient riverbed of the Finke River, where it forms the access route to Palm Valley. The valley is a very rare environment where cycads and *Livistona mariae* palms flourish in an isolated microclimate, relic plants from another age when the centre of Australia was lush and tropical. Gus decided to pursue a business career in tourism and launched his Western Aranda Tours, specialising in Palm Valley day tours. It was a good initiative.

I thought Derek's best story, though, was about Sergeant Owen Perks, the cop at Marree, at the southern end of what in those days was the infamous and quite dangerous Birdsville Track. Derek outlined the country cop's duties: everything from first aid provider, ambulance driver and undertaker, to motor mechanic and airport operations supervisor. All of this was in addition to managing a regularly patronised lock-up. On top of all that Marree had recently lost the last of its clergymen, so the reading of services at funerals also became the lot of Sergeant Perks.

CHAPTER 10

AND THE RAINS CAME

DID THEY EVER! In 1973 Lake Eyre flooded and would be regularly topped up for the next three years. Lake Eyre is fed by the Finke and Macumba river systems from the northwest, the Neales from the west, the Barcoo–Cooper Creek channels from the east, and the Diamantina–Warburton channels from the northeast—and it wasn't common to have all of those catchments receive flood rains at the same time. Lake Eyre, being 15 metres below sea level and nearly 150 kilometres long and 100 kilometres wide, certainly holds a lot of water.

We became 'bogologists': dig it out, tow it out, winch it out, push it out. On nearly every trip we were churning through mud, and was that stressful! And did it play havoc with the vehicles. Brakes and brake drums had to be relined and turned out after each trip. Universal joints lasted no time. Water in differentials and transmissions was a hazard. Roadhouses had their problems, too, with water getting into their fuel tanks and then into mine. There was mud in every nook and cranny of the vehicle. But we didn't cancel one trip. We took the punters to places they never dreamed of, and neither had we. We never gave up trying to get to destinations. Sometimes we made it, sometimes we didn't.

My old man inspired me to keep going at a time when it would have been easy to walk away and just say, 'It's all too hard'. The photos on the wall in my study reminded me of what he and his mate Lindsay Skipworth achieved in the 1920s, pushing those old single-axle trucks belonging to Charles Kingsford Smith's Gascoyne Trading Company through the harsh terrain of the North West, from Carnarvon to Marble Bar. 'Don't be a bloody sook,' he would have said, if I had taken one backward step. I was too frightened to give up.

Dusty Wolfe and I took off on a journey that was to take us to Ayers Rock and Alice Springs with the two Land Rovers, one of which was pulling a trailer, with a complement of nine passengers and the two of us as crew. We left Melbourne in bright sunshine, little knowing that there was weather and lots of it happening in the top of South Australia. We went north through Mildura, then on to the Flinders Ranges, the plan being to reach the Alice from the Oodnadatta Track. The weather was a bit ordinary on the second day, but not beyond some heavy showers, so we stayed in Brachina Gorge. The creek was running and was quite spectacular.

We headed north again the following morning towards Blinman, where we intended to leave the Ranges and reach Parachilna before continuing north to Marree, and that's where we got the bad news. 'No way north,' the cops said. 'Birdsville Track's shut and the Oodnadatta Track's shut beyond William Creek.'

'We'll have to go back to Port Augusta and head up the South Road,' I said, as I turned to Dusty, but the cop wasn't finished.

'No good doing that either, son. They've shut the South Road at Port Augusta.'

Bloody hell! I turned pale. I had no money left to be abandoning the trip and paying refunds. 'It's getting late,' I said to Dusty. 'We'd better go and make a camp up the road.'

'Never turn back until you are compelled to. Keep going until there is nowhere to go.' I had adopted that policy and it was surprising how often something happened that allowed you to go that little bit further. The cop had said the Oodnadatta Track was closed beyond William Creek. Well, Anna Creek Station was only about 20 kilometres up the road from William Creek, and I knew there was a little-used track from there to Coober Pedy, so all was not lost—not yet, anyway.

We were in low-range high gear most of the way, slipping and sliding, then the rain started to get heavier and we began ploughing the road up. If the powers that be in Marree had known it was this bad, they would have shut the gate there. We struggled to make the floodway crossing at Strangways, so it was time for a stop and a think; a stubbie, in fact, as this thing might be coming to a close. 'I think we're stuffed, Bill,' Dusty said.

'I think you may be right,' was my reluctant reply. We had pulled up at the railway crossing just short of Irrapatana Siding. As I looked at the old Ghan track disappearing out of sight to the north, I noticed two faint wheel tracks running off along the side of the line where the occasional fettler crew had used motor vehicles instead of a rail car to get to somewhere or other.

Then I had a brilliant idea. 'We'll see how far we get up the railway line. Load up—we're off,' I said to Dusty.

And so the long slow journey along the railway line began, not on the Ghan, unfortunately, which was a trip I always wanted to do, though I can truthfully say I have been to Alice Springs by rail.

The storms had really buggered the railway line. There were washaways and more washaways. I began to think about food. We had five days' supplies on board, seven at a pinch, water wasn't a problem, so we could do no more than cross our fingers and hope for the best. There would be nobody going where we were going. We were on our own.

It would be a long time before the train would run again. Sometimes we would travel for kilometres along the track itself or over the trestle bridges. In some places the railway line was the only bit of dry land for miles because it was elevated. The number of days it took I can no longer remember. It was quite a few, seven maybe. I know we were almost out of tucker by the time we got to Finke, but we managed, just. We only had to 'keep 'em alive, not make 'em fat'.

At Finke I got a big lump of meat and some other supplies from the bloke at the pub, so we cooked up a hearty barbecue. The meat had a strange gamey flavour. It was okay, but different. I discovered why later on. There were brumby hunters working that country at the time and they used to sell prime cuts to the bloke at the pub, who in turn sold it to the Indigenous locals. My punters would never know unless any of them read this yarn.

We followed the Ghan line until we reached Maryvale Station, where the country had noticeably begun to dry out, so we turned off and drove into the station. 'Where did you come from?' a bloke asked, seeing us coming from the east.

'Up the railway line,' I said.

'Bullshit.'

'No, it's ridgy-didge. I kid you not.'

'We did, we did,' chorused the punters.

The station hand looked at his mates, all shaking their heads, and said, 'Well, bugger me.'

'What's the track north to Alice like?' I asked him.

'Wouldn't have a clue, mate. Never been that way. We cut across to the South Road to get to Alice. There's some pretty tough country north of here.'

'Is the South Road open?' I asked him.

'Dunno, mate.'

So that was it; do what we were doing, just keep heading north. We arrived in Alice Springs, much to the amazement of the locals, as no vehicle had been in or out of the town from the south for well over a week, and with everything covered in red mud we had obviously come through some tough country. 'How the bloody hell did you get here with all the roads closed?' was the question.

'Ah, we have a secret route,' was the reply. I had sworn the punters to secrecy, as I had no idea whether travelling up the railway line was permissible or not. There is always a small bureaucrat looking for somebody to punish.

There was not one of us who had any clean clothes left after our journey along the Ghan track and we hadn't had more than a bird bath in a puddle for days. We were a grubby lot, I can tell you, but then to be able to stand under a hot shower and watch all that dirt run down the plughole is one of the great pleasures in life.

On the subject of washing, Dusty was a funny bugger with his laundry habits, too. He just chucked everything in the machine and I was always amused by his washing hanging on a clothesline, consisting of underdaks, shirts, socks, shorts, handkerchiefs and his desert boots. Never before or since have I seen boots hanging on a clothesline.

•

The Ghan being out of action was not an unusual phenomenon. It was renowned for its unreliability; not surprising, really, as the greater part of the track was supported by sleepers laid on sand, and any semblance of bad weather would see the track 'out'.

Len Tuit, the guy who began tours from Alice Springs to the Rock in the late 1950s, using an ex-WWII four-wheel-drive Blitz Buggy truck, relied on the Ghan to transport his passengers from Adelaide, and this unreliability was the bane of his life. He would be waiting in Alice Springs, his vehicle laden with provisions and ready to depart on tour, unaware whether his punters were on time or not. In those days there was no portable refrigeration. Any delay could have disastrous consequences on the supplies, and reprovisioning was extremely expensive.

So Len had a brainwave—fresh food all the way. He built cages along the side of his truck to house chooks, ducks and a piglet. With fresh eggs and roasted chicken, duck and pork, they would live like kings. He was soon to discover, however, that the best laid plans can go awry. His punters were positively horrified when they discovered the little 'pets' were to be slaughtered to provide food for the table, so they were forced to survive on porridge, damper and the occasional egg.

Len also told the story about the train that finally arrived in Alice Springs after a long delay and the very pregnant and distressed woman who alighted and immediately began to berate the stationmaster about her plight.

'Well, madam, I am surprised you boarded the train in your condition,' he said.

'Well, sir, I was not in this condition when I boarded your train,' she replied.

•

Not long after the impromptu Ghan tour I was doing a Burke and Wills itinerary, but again had to re-route because of bad weather when we couldn't ford Cooper Creek. 'Want to go to Ayers Rock?' I asked. I was in the Land Rover with four passengers, who were a laidback lot.

'Why not?' came their reply.

However, when we arrived at Marree to enquire about conditions on the Oodnadatta Track, the cops said: 'Wouldn't know, mate. There hasn't been a vehicle come down from there for a week, but there is a bloke at one of the railway camps up the track we'd really like to have a word with, so we'll come with you if you like. Two vehicles are better than one.'

So off we went with our police escort and got to near Curdimurka, about 100 kilometres north of Marree, where we were confronted with a floodway that was really moving, a lot of water, but it was quite shallow. We had a look and a bit of a chat and I decided to give it a go. The cops said they would hang back to see how we went and be on hand if it turned sour. And turn sour it did.

I was going really well until midstream when the Landy dropped into a hole, then—whoosh—we were off. The water picked us up and downstream we went. It was still not that deep, so every now and again I would get a bit of traction. I had the hand throttle keeping the engine revving, so we had power. Not far downstream the water spread out onto a floodplain, so I found some bottom and got the vehicle out and onto dry ground where it stopped. Bloody hell, it was stressful—another lesson to file away.

We were standing around waiting while the electrics dried out and the cops arrived, having made their way along the high ground.

'Are you okay?' one of them asked.

'No worries,' I replied.

'We'll stay with you until you're back on the track. There are some real shitty spots between here and the road. Then we're off back to Marree. If we can't get in to where our man is, he can't get out. He'll keep.'

It was getting late when we got back to the road, so we camped there for the night. In the morning, lo and behold, the floodway, although still running, was quite tame. So off we went again, through William Creek and north to the Neales, but that's when it all came unstuck. There was no way in the wide world we could get through that floodway. What's more, it was starting to rain.

Making our U-turn, I decided to give the track across to Coober Pedy a go. The turn-off was only about 90 kilometres back. And that is the reason the punters and I visited Lake Cadibarrawirracanna, the place with the second longest name in Australia. It means 'stars dancing on water', a name thought to be from the Kuyani dialect. The longest place name is Mamungkukumpurangkuntjunya Hill in the north of South Australia near the Northern Territory border; it is from the Pitjantjara language and means 'where the devil urinates'.

We made Coober Pedy, just. It was pelting down by the time we arrived there and the Landy was slipping and sliding all over the place. We were lucky, too. Faye Nayler had a shed at the Opal Cave vacant, so we had a warm and dry camp for as long as we needed it.

I went to the police station the following morning to check road conditions with the cops. They had got their paddy wagon bogged in the front yard of the police station, which was at that time a domestic dwelling. To complete the 'official' establishment they had built a row of wire cages across the back fence, which served as 'cells'. Obviously they were in demand, because they were full at the time, all Indigenous, men and women. 'Hey, you buggers. Get out here and give us a hand,' the cop yelled, and half a dozen or so of the inmates wandered out, looking very worse for wear.

There were no locks on the cells. There was no point in nicking off, I suppose, as there was nowhere to go. Besides, it was no good being out in the open with shitty weather about, and I'm sure the tucker was delivered on a regular basis.

Anyway, they all got around the back of the paddy wagon with one of the cops and lined up ready. The driver of the wagon said, 'Righto, heave!' and gunned it. The pushers at the back staggered forwards, and suddenly there was this great plume of spray flying out from the fishtailing rear end of the wagon, leaving the cop and inmates stuck up to their ankles in a gluey bog and coated in thick red mud. I'd never heard such shrieks of laughter in all my born days. The women, who had left the cells to form an appreciative audience, thought it was the funniest thing they had ever seen, and I must say it was hard not to agree.

The road was not opened for another two days, and then it was only open to the south, so we never made the Rock, but the punters enjoyed the experience. They were the things we were selling at that time: experiences and cock-ups.

For more than two bloody years the wet conditions went on, but I was lucky in one sense as I only had six tours to Ayers Rock and the Alice planned for Gertrude in the first year, and we did get them all away. We got all the painting schools done as well. It was our four-wheel-drive tours that suffered all the damage.

And when I say we got the sixteen-day Ayers Rock tours away I should mention that on one departure we got rained in at Port Augusta—we were stuck. I had a big awning that we carried as part of our equipment, so we stretched it off the side of the coach where we could all huddle while we cooked up a barbecue. I kept unscrewing the tops off flagons of red so the punters would all become mellow and warm and fuzzy and stick with me.

The next morning the road north was shut indefinitely, but the weather seemed to be clearing so I made all the appropriate phone calls to see where we could go. I should add here that I never phoned a weather bureau. They only gave you general stuff and were sort of non-committal. I always called postmasters. They knew what was going on, and the bloke in Kalgoorlie and the bloke in Esperance both said 'It's clearing'. So I did the hard sell on the punters and it was Western Australia here we come. I'd never been across the Nullarbor before, and neither had Joan Rynia, my cook, so it was all 'follow your nose'.

My goodness, it was a slog across the Nullarbor and back. It was only a dirt track in those days, and in many places it didn't take much water at all to turn it into a bog hole. We got to Kalgoorlie, Boulder and Coolgardie, and then took off around the coast to Esperance, but we never made Perth—we ran out of time. That tour was almost 40 years ago and I bet the punters still dine out on their adventure.

•

A year went by and the only thing that changed was the number of passengers. The more they increased, the harder it got to deliver the services we set out to provide. Vehicle maintenance was horrific, and it was each tour leader's responsibility to have his machine right for departure. We departed our tours on a Saturday and returned on a Sunday, in theory giving us five days to service the equipment, reprovision and front up for the next group.

Sometimes it was not enough, and we started to use terminology like 'black days' and 'white days'—if you worked another eight hours at night, you could squeeze ten days out of a week. I can remember one trip where we finished getting the transfer case back in the vehicle at 2 a.m. one Saturday morning and I was due to be at the pick-up point at 7.30 a.m.

Thank God for Ron Bentley. He had a workshop in Greensborough and did the bulk of our work, but if there was a big list on a vehicle we had to give him a hand to get it finished. He was a top motor engineer, Ron. He built and tuned Peter Brock's cars, the A30 Austin and the Torana, at his Greensborough shop in the early days.

CHAPTER 11

HIPS, TICKS AND UNIONS

It was in 1974 that we had our first major cock-up, one that nearly sent us to the wall. It began with these two old dears from Toorak and another from 'I can't remember' who went on our Merimbula painting school.

We had set up our base camp in the park at Pambula and on the first night everybody was sitting around the kitchen tent prior to dinner, some having a pre-dinner aperitif, some not. Now the two dears from Toorak didn't join the group. They got stuck into a bottle of scotch in their tent, and as I've said before there is no sound insulation in canvas and the voices were getting louder and louder and the laughter almost hysterical.

On arrival I had lectured them all and warned them that in a camp situation one must be alert for hazards like tent pegs, guy ropes, paint cases and easels. If left lying about, these are easy traps to stumble on. Plus, 'You should remember that this part of the south coast is renowned for ticks, so don't sit on the grass, and regularly check your legs.'

Anyway, our two whisky lovers eventually stumbled, and I mean literally stumbled, out of their tent where one went arse over head on the tent peg at their door opening. Lying flat out on the deck she said, 'I'm okay, I'm okay,' probably feeling very embarrassed, so her mate helped her back to their tent and laid her down on her camp bed. Well, she was not okay, and during the night I was woken by the survivor, who said, 'Mrs Toorak needs a doctor.' So I woke up the park manager who organised an ambulance to come and check her out.

The medic didn't like what he saw and took her off to hospital. It turned out that the lady had broken her hip and the following day they chartered an aircraft to fly her back to Melbourne, where she was admitted to one of the big hospitals.

I had a really bad feeling about all of this, because just a few months before I had changed insurance companies and their sales rep, let's call him 'Freddie the fool', had knocked on my door after he sold my old man a new package. The old man in turn sent him to see me, because they offered a better deal than the company we both used previously. But when Freddie sent me all the policies and the account, there was no third party or public risk included. On enquiry he said, 'Don't worry about that. It's all in hand.' But time went by and I heard nothing. Concerned, I gave him a call. It was, coincidentally, only days prior to the Merimbula trip on which we had the drama and he said, 'Don't worry, Bill. It's all in hand.'

I rang Freddie immediately when I got home and asked him to send me out a claim form and filled him in on the problem. There was a long silence on the phone before he said, 'No worries.'

A couple of trips went by and I was trying to run good tours, working black and white days in between, and no way was I getting any sleep, because I had bad vibes and a gut feeling the shit was going to hit the fan. And it did. I returned from a tour and gave Freddie another call. 'You didn't ask me to get you public risk insurance,' he said. Can you believe it? The lousy bastard had screwed up big time and left me to carry the bag.

What actually occurred was, when I gave Freddie all of our policies to renew, his company said 'Oops' when they saw that we operated 'outback expeditions'. That apparently confused them no end and it all got complicated, so they took all the general stuff but refused to take the public risk. So Freddie passed the problem to some underling in the office and said, 'See if you can place this somewhere.' Then, you've guessed it, he promptly forgot and never told me what was going on. He was happy to get his commission on all the other policies, though.

I went to my lawyer Brian Smyth in Eltham and told him my tale of woe. 'What an arsehole!' Brian agreed, because by this time I was being sued by the lady from Toorak for unspecified damages and medical expenses. Brian Smyth in turn started suing the insurance company for giving bad advice to his client, leading to prejudiced litigation or some such technical term. But that was not the end of my worries.

Another woman on the trip, from 'I can't remember', who had travelled with me before, had gone home with a couple of ticks stuck in her leg. During the trip I had observed her sitting on the grass on several occasions and told her to be careful, as there was a tick risk, but no, she knew best. So the litigation society is not a modern-day phenomenon—it was alive and well in the early 70s.

Was there any more fuel for sleepless nights? You bet! I opened my mail and there was this official documentation from the Transport Workers Union in South Australia serving me with a log of claims regarding pay and working conditions for our employees. I immediately had this vision of unions, broken hips, hungry ticks and wall-to-wall lawyers conspiring to give me more sleepless nights.

This log of claims had workers coming on the job for about half the current hours from Monday to Friday at a weekly rate of about double that of the current award, and any intrusion on Saturday or Sunday would generate an income far in excess of what was earned from Monday to Friday. And if anybody in the extended family got sick or carked it, there were weeks of time off on full pay. If it sounds complicated, it was. I tried to work out a worst-scenario situation and I reckoned that if some bloke got all things going wrong in the same year, he would earn double the annual current wage and spend hardly a day at work.

This one had even Brian Smyth stumped: 'It's out of my league, Bill. Better go and see the employers federation.' So in between taking my punters into the wilds of outback Australia, servicing my vehicle, ensuring the other vehicles were properly prepared, paying the bills and planning our program for 1975, I now had a flea in my ear from the Transport Workers Union in South Australia.

I went off to meet with some bloke at the employers federation who had undergone a total and successful charisma bypass and he said something like: 'Oh, this is all par for the course. They serve a log of claims on a small business in another state to make it a seriously expensive and drawn out campaign. It is a situation that will certainly disadvantage the recipient of the log of claims, so it would probably be a good thing for you to join the employers federation to participate in the defence.' With that he picked up the phone to make a call—meeting over.

'In a pig's eye,' I said to myself, as I took my leave from the office of the employers federation and thanked the enthusiastic recruiter of small-business proprietors, who, if they were all like me, would dearly like to just mind their own business, free from small-time bureaucracies, which included unions, employer groups, town councils, transport boards and all those other creep-laden 'official' departments that hound you from cradle to grave.

So then I called the Transport Workers Union and tracked down the bloke responsible for my nightmares. 'My name's Bill King,' I told him, 'and you have served a log of claims on me for employees I do not have, who are driving trucks I do not have on my outback expeditions. There are no employees in our business (I regarded Rosey and Brian as extended family); it is a family affair. My wife runs the office and my sons, Russell and Martin, and I take the tours. We have no use for a union and, what's more, pertaining to your log of claims, I have never read such a load of bullshit in my whole life. There's not a business in the whole wide world that could operate under the conditions you are demanding.'

'Oh, that's only the range of issues we wish to address,' the bloke said, as if that made it okay.

'Well, why not make a claim in which you can arrive at a speedy and reasonable solution?' I said as the dawning came. Silly me—the union organisers have to earn their keep; they're no different from any other small-time bureaucrat. Anyway, I never heard any more about it, yet it still gave me sleepless nights waiting for nothing to happen. It was a very stressful time.

Brian Smyth, thank goodness, made the tick lady go away for a reasonable price, but Mrs Toorak cost me $6000. Brian settled that issue on the steps leading into the court. The insurance company paid out another $12 000 in their settlement, and that also went to Mrs Toorak. The $6000 we lost because of Freddie was serious money in 1974, but we survived. Freddie didn't, though—he got fired. I in turn fired the insurer and retained Barry Johns, a broker, to do our insurance, and we had a long and happy business arrangement.

•

All of this stuff, you could well imagine, was putting a huge strain on Val's and my relationship—in fact, there was no relationship. Because we ran the business from home, there were always people about. The phone rang seven days a week, day and night. There were manifests to prepare, supplies to be ordered and always somebody to be briefed on a tour due for departure. I would return from a tour and immediately go off to service equipment, and when I came home I showered and went to bed. I was completely buggered most of the time and all I could fit in my head were business matters. If Val wanted to discuss kids and family issues I had no time, which was not fair to her, and every conversation ended in an argument.

I came home from a tour one particular day and Val said, 'Our relationship can't go on like this. We're in constant conflict. You have your work that has to be attended to and I have mine, and we can both do it better without the distraction of endless friction.'

At the time it came as a shock to me, but I could see she was very serious and I did understand where she was coming from.

In her mind she was stuck at home with the drudgery while I was off all over the country having a good time. With all of my coming and going I had never given any of that stuff a thought, but I can assure you that having a good time was a myth: it was a job, and a very stressful job, although I admit I was hooked on the challenge and more determined than ever to make it all work. I was prepared to exclude everything from my head that was not to do with the business.

Then I realised there was no way Val could leave the house, the family and her business responsibilities. I would have to move out. It was quite odd. There was no debate, no acrimony; there was just too much work to be done. I found a flat that afternoon in South Yarra. 'Why South Yarra?' you might ask. Well, where else could you go and look at half a dozen or so flats within a kilometre of one another and make a choice in a couple of hours. I got a furnished one-bedroom apartment in a block in Osborne Street, just a couple of hundred metres from Toorak Road, with a car park for my Land Rover 4, and where there were plenty of places to eat nearby.

•

So life went on. I would come home from a tour on a Sunday night and go to work at Ron Bentley's workshop on the Monday to service equipment, then head to the family house to attend to the too-hard basket, then go back to Ron Bentley's or home to South Yarra, doing each day what had to be done, before reprovisioning and loading up on Friday for the Saturday departure.

We were making money but I still hadn't found the solution to getting some of it to stick to the fingers as it went past. I had come to realise that four- and five-seat vehicles were impractical, and to get the necessary return would require a fare structure with too wide a gap between what I charged and what the 'mushrooms'—the new boys on the block—charged, and they were coming and going like yo-yos. We had to be conscious of the coach tour operators as well, because they were starting to follow our tracks and they would always be much cheaper than a small group in a four-wheel drive.

We were getting good bookings, but that wasn't the problem. Having small vehicles in convoy was the problem. We had plenty of tours where we had the International 1300 and the two Land Rovers fully booked. Three wages, three fuel bills, twelve tyres, and on it went—there was our problem. Imagine an eighteen-seat four-wheel drive with a driver and a cook. We could operate in our current fare structure and make serious money. We needed a vehicle that wasn't available in the marketplace; we needed a solution to that problem and we needed it fast.

Driving for long periods gives one a lot of time to reflect on things, and I used to dream about the perfect four-wheel-drive vehicle to do the job. It would have locker space designed for equipment like tents, tables, stools, food, racks for people's luggage, a cool store, and a kitchen section with built-in barbecue and gas bottle locker.

Eventually I faced the reality that if I didn't make it happen, it never would, and if we were really going to make this thing work, the time had come to take the big step forward and build our own vehicles. The challenge was to build a machine that could withstand the hard life it was going to have, a machine that retained the rugged appearance that reflected the business we were in and also offered passenger comfort similar to the coach tours.

I met with my bank manager and arranged a line of credit to obtain an appropriate chassis and commence my project. After some research I bought a 3-tonne International D1410 chassis. I designed a body with the required locker space and a seating capacity for fifteen passengers. I called it the 'Desert Cruiser', and somebody else nicknamed it 'Olga'.

I gave the plans to Russell Mee in West Heidelberg and he built it. When it was finished it looked like a giant Land Rover. I had decided on a livery of Land Rover grey, with a white roof, a thick black stripe around the vehicle at eye level and 'Bill King's Northern

Safaris' in big orange writing on the sides. It looked bloody terrific, even though I say so myself. It really looked the part.

Then I proceeded to wreck it. Two seasons and it was stuffed, before I had even finished paying for the bloody thing, but I was so lucky I bought only one. My goodness, it was a failure—much too light for our work. We were operating at its load capacity every time we took it out and I reckon the load capacity was grossly overstated. The lightweight chassis flexed and twisted along with the body frame, causing it to keep breaking away from its mounts and pop rivets out of the panels, and it broke springs, shackles, shackle pins and spring hangers as well; in fact there was very little on it that did not break. It fell to bits and was a very expensive educational experience.

From a passenger point of view, though, it was a success. Fifteen people is a much more compatible group than four or five, and easier to manage. In a five-seat vehicle you can have an obnoxious loud-mouth and there is no escape. You have to wear him or her like a dirty shirt until it is all over. Strangely, in the larger group they disappeared—they found a soul mate, I suppose. So I knew I had reached the solution, but my implementation left a lot to be desired. I needed more robust equipment.

W&P Machinery in Campbellfield advertised a lot of ex-government trucks and equipment and had a 5-tonne AB160 short-wheelbase International for sale. It was ex–Australian Army and had been repatriated from Vietnam. It had a tipper body with a heavy-duty winch attached, and had done little work. They also had a 5-tonne C1600 long-wheelbase International that had been a State Electricity Commission truck. It had a cherry picker on the back and minimal miles on the speedometer. I had no use for tipper bodies and cherry pickers, so they kept the appliances and I did a deal on the chassis and cabs.

Harley Evenden, who once worked for Russell Mee, had set up a workshop behind his house in Greensborough. He gave me a very good price to build the two bodies, so, with modifications to my drawings solving the shortcomings of Olga, we got underway, building two new Desert Cruisers each with seating for sixteen passengers. The C1600 became Big Ben and the AB160 Little Ben.

•

There was a lot going on, I can tell you, and if you were to ask me how I drove safaris, serviced vehicles, planned itineraries and departures for the following year, managed the too-hard basket, and designed and built our own equipment, I would say I do not have a clue. It was seven days a week, sixteen hours a day, and when things went wrong you fixed it and got on with the job. And my old man was never far away either, forever looking over my shoulder.

The worst part of it all was being alone. I had never been alone in my whole life before, and to be away on a tour with a group of people who are all enjoying their holiday, and it is your job to see that they do just that, while you're feeling totally isolated with not a person in the world you can really talk to is bloody soul destroying.

On departure day I used to head down to our pick-up point via Russell Street, and as I went down the hill past the State Theatre to the traffic lights at Flinders Street, I used to recite my little poem (with apologies to William Wordsworth):

> I wandered lonely as a cloud
> That floats on high o'er vales and hills,
> When all at once I saw a crowd,
> But not of Wordsworth's daffodils;
> It was another mob of Jack and Jills.

By the time I had recited that little lot to myself I was pulling into the kerb and greeting my punters with the biggest smile in the world. 'Good morning all. My name is Bill King, and I am your tour leader for the next sixteen days.' And so another journey would begin. I had got to the stage where I looked forward to one moment on a trip and that milestone was the point at which I turned south. From that day on I was heading home, and quite oddly it always felt like a downhill journey.

Then the inevitable happened. I found some rapport with a girl who was on one of our tours to Alice Springs and Ayers Rock. Ruth Goldman was a very smart young woman who was employed as personal assistant to the CEO of a multinational. A single person with no tie, she was very much the professional and dedicated to her job. We found we had a lot in common with likes and dislikes, attitude to events and society in general, and what's more she lived in South Yarra, not five minutes from my apartment.

We went to the Toorak Hotel for a couple of drinks and then to a restaurant on the night the tour returned, and I felt most uncomfortable. Guilt, I suppose, and the fact that she was much younger than I was.

I said I would contact her when I returned from the next tour, but that was three weeks away, so I didn't really expect her to be waiting for my call, but she was. Catching up with Ruth between tours became a regular thing. It was a relationship that we both enjoyed. She knew of my marital situation and beyond that it was never discussed; she was a good person and probably ensured I didn't unravel.

CHAPTER 12

SPREADING OUR WINGS

Planning our programs for 1975 with six vehicles and the two Land Rovers as back-ups became a new challenge, attracting more people to ride in them was another, and getting somebody to drive them was yet another. At least there were three of us now capable of training crew. Brian Shaddick was a first-class operator. There was none better in the business, and I had seen them all. Number-one son Russell, who had been on the job for a season, had got his wings, too.

We had been operating for six years when our first departure for the year took off on 18 January 1975. It was the beginning of a new era, and well it needed to be, as we still had not sighted the light at the end of the tunnel; it was a black hole. Although I had a gut feeling the time was right to bring it all together, we had experimented with our positioning in the market by promoting our tours under the special interest banner for two years, but in doing so I believe we took our eyes off the ball. I now knew that the outback was the key to the success of Bill King's Northern Safaris, and the further we took people into the Never-Never, the more they liked it.

My last tour of 1974 actually finished in 1975, as we departed on Boxing Day, the day after Cyclone Tracy devastated Darwin. When we left Melbourne the true impact of the damage had not filtered through to us, because we were on the road travelling. We were halfway up the South Road heading for Alice Springs when we were confronted by some of the aftermath of that terrible disaster.

That was when we saw the first car loads of refugees heading south. I have never been so shaken in all my life. The survivors were in shock, traumatised, with dazed looks on their faces, driving cars that had been so mangled you had to look hard to identify the make. Some of the poor buggers had no food or water; others didn't even have enough money to buy fuel to get to Adelaide, where they were heading. Some had their 'olds' with them, and their kids of varying ages; a couple of women even had tiny babies. There were others who had people in their car they had never seen before, hitchhikers trying to walk out of the place. All were trying to escape with their cars full of whatever could be salvaged from the remnants of their homes. These were the people who had just fled, panicked, I suppose, because it took the authorities some time to restore some semblance of order.

We gave them the bulk of the food we were carrying, because we could replenish our supplies in Alice Springs, and some money to those who had none. Alice was jammed with refugees when we arrived and the authorities were endeavouring to set up an emergency station. The people we encountered on the South Road had slipped through the net.

It was a horror story. Cyclone Tracy was identified as a category 4 event when Darwin was warned of the impending storm, but there is evidence that it had become a category 5 by the time it reached land. There were 71 people killed and more than 500 were treated at Darwin Hospital on Boxing Day, and that was only the start of the human cost. The bill for damage to infrastructure was just on a billion dollars, and 70 per cent of the city's buildings were destroyed. Twenty thousand people out of 48 000 were left homeless and 30 000 were eventually evacuated. That was a very sombre tour, one totally overshadowed by the event perpetrated by Mother Nature that Christmas Day.

•

I said 1975 was the beginning of a new era; well, it was, in more ways than one.

I arrived home on 10 January and received a phone call from Val inviting me to lunch on the following Saturday. It was a beautiful day and she had set a table out by the pool and prepared a special lunch. I cannot remember what it was, but I knew she had gone to a lot of trouble. I didn't even bring anything to drink, because I expected a sandwich or something, but that didn't matter. She had opened an equally good bottle of wine.

We began our meal and something was said, so I stood up and said I had better go, and then she said, 'I'm sorry, I don't want you to go.' So I didn't. I stayed and we talked about what had gone wrong, and it was perfectly obvious to both of us that running the business from home meant that there was no home, no escape or sanctuary from the intense pressure our business dictated. It had even got to the stage where crews were camping in our barn between tours and using our kids' bathroom. Val and the kids lived in a business premises.

It was a frank and honest discussion, the first analysis of our relationship we had ever had, actually, and it was probably about time. And speaking of our kids, I knew I needed to ease up on the business obsession, participate in being part of the family unit and accept my share of the responsibility. I had a great feeling of guilt over that issue, and still do.

We agreed from that moment on the first priority was to obtain a business premises. We would battle it out together and work to reach that common goal. It was not going to happen in 1975, of course, because we had too many financial commitments, but we would work towards that end. It felt so good to get rid of 1974 and live again in a family environment; it had been the worst year of my life.

Back at work it was time to bite the bullet. The planning had to be done and the program for the coming two seasons set in concrete. As I mentioned I had a milestone that occurred when I turned to head for home, and chatting with my punters I found it was not an uncommon feeling for them either. After visiting all the highlights up north, they sort of felt the last few days of travel were just going home. Which raised the question: were there more options for fly-in, fly-out expeditions, changing over in Alice Springs and Darwin, offering seven-, nine-, and twelve-day tours in addition to those we already had, a new market, if you wish?

I had been getting a gut feeling that it would be the way the market moved in the future. In fact I could see the day coming when sixteen-day tours departing from a capital city to travel to, say, Ayers Rock and Alice Springs then returning to that same city would be the exception rather than the rule. But was now the time to test the water? We were the guinea pigs, remember. There were no other operators to compare us with; the 'mushrooms' just followed what we did and charged a little less.

From our point of view our four-wheel-drive vehicles were not being used as the manufacturer intended. There was not one built that could manage long high-speed journeys on the blacktop, long moderate-speed journeys on bone-shaking corrugations, followed by low-range stuff churning through sand or mud, and that is what we demanded of our vehicles on every trip. The day was coming when we would be forced to move the whole business to Alice Springs; to eliminate the long high-speed road journeys would represent a huge saving in costs to us, but would the airfares make our arrangements too expensive?

I decided to give it a go. So I split our tours and introduced a new four-wheel-drive sixteen-day expedition that went through Alice Springs and the back country of the Western Macdonnell Ranges to Ayers Rock. This gave us three different itineraries, of nine, twelve, and sixteen days travelling on the same vehicle. The downside of splitting the tours, though, was that only one half of the journey went to Ayers Rock—we couldn't take the sixteen-day riders there twice. So, to solve that problem I chartered a light aircraft from an Adelaide company, SAATAS Air, and we began operating 'Ayers Rock Air Safaris' out of Alice Springs, a three-day option with motel accommodation. We packaged the six-day forward journey to Alice Springs along the Oodnadatta Track with the three-day air safari and, along with the twelve-day option, they became two of our bestsellers.

The twelve-day journey to Melbourne began with a tour of Alice Springs and surrounds where we visited the gorges and chasms in the Western MacDonnell Ranges and stayed overnight at Glen Helen. The following morning we visited Ormiston Gorge reserve and Redbank Gorge before driving through Tylers Pass to visit Gosse Bluff. The bluff is like science fiction stuff, where around 140 million years ago a mighty object, probably a kilometre or so wide, hit the earth with such a deep impact it left a crater some 20 kilometres across and satellite photos show circles of ripples in the landscape that travel for many kilometres beyond that.

The Indigenous people call it *Tnorala*. The story goes that way back in the Dreamtime a mother spirit in the Milky Way dropped her child from a coolamon and the child fell all the way to earth, where it landed at *Tnorala*. They had worked out the falling object theory, too. How did they do that?

From there we went across to the Hermannsburg Lutheran Mission for a visit before negotiating our way along the bed of the Finke River to Palm Valley and Cycad Gorge. From Palm Valley we really got into the expedition stuff, making our way down the Finke River through Cocky's Camp and Boggy Hole to Kings Canyon and Ayers Rock before heading back through Coober Pedy to Melbourne.

The next new adventure we timetabled was the fly/road sixteen-day 'Gunbarrel Safari' that began in Alice Springs, then traversed the Western MacDonnell Ranges to Ayers Rock and the Olgas before heading out to the Petermann Ranges to visit Lasseter's Cave.

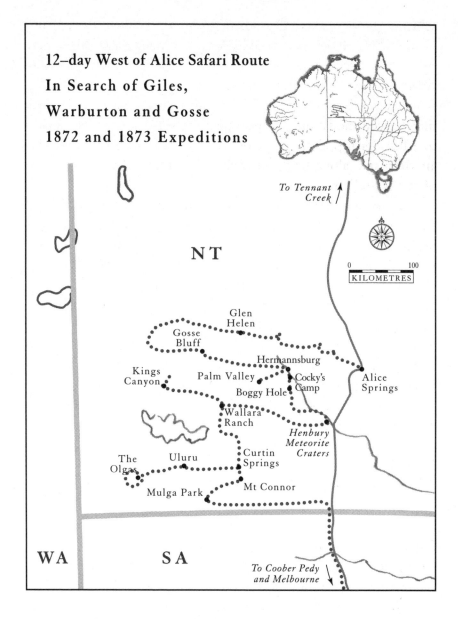

The tour then continued through Docker River and Warburton Aboriginal settlements to Mount Shenton Outcamp, Laverton and Kalgoorlie. From there we headed down to the coast to stay at Twilight Cove and other points on the coast before returning home across the Nullarbor.

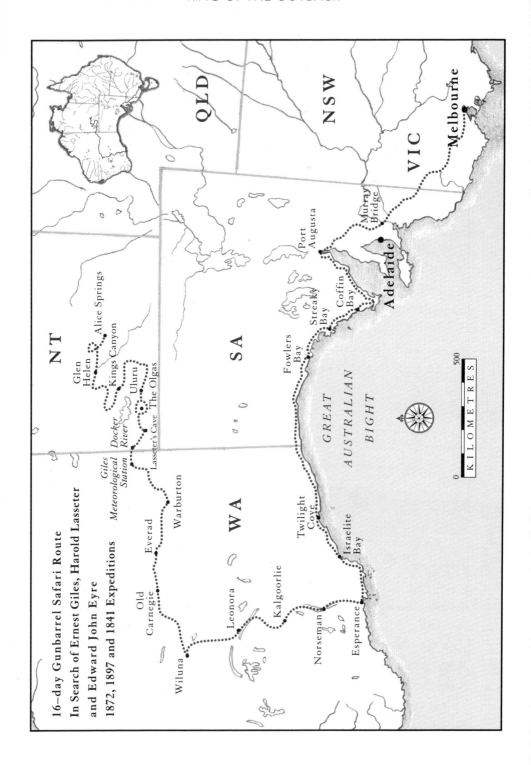

SPREADING OUR WINGS

•

We also decided it was time to test the Sydney market and to do so with the launch the 23-day Leichhardt Safari. There were no outback operators in the Harbour City promoting expeditions in four-wheel-drive equipment at that time, so we relocated Dennis Conroy and the C1300 International to operate the program.

We struggled for two years to foster that market with very little success; Sydneysiders, for whatever reason, were no big fans of the Australian Outback. We put a lot of resources behind the project, too, with travel agency promotions and advertisements in both the *Sydney Morning Herald* and *Daily Telegraph*.

The itinerary travelled through Western Queensland Channel Country, then across the top of the Simpson Desert to Alice Springs and Ayers Rock before heading south to Coober Pedy. From there it headed via Lake Cadibarrawirracanna through William Creek, up the Birdsville Track to Birdsville, then south to Cooper Creek and the Dig Tree before returning to Sydney via Tibooburra and Broken Hill.

It was a fantastic journey through some of the inland's most interesting and scenic country, and, if any Grey Nomads who read this yarn are looking for their next big adventure, try this one.

•

These were bloody good tours and they worked, reinforcing our rewarding relationship with Ansett Airlines. We had put together a more extensive program of tours and departures in conjunction with the airline and included airfares with pre- and post-tour accommodation in the price. It was a joint and groundbreaking effort, as no other operator had split their itineraries or produced holidays of that type in conjunction with an airline.

The next task was to produce a high-quality brochure as our point-of-sale piece. I was introduced to a graphic artist named

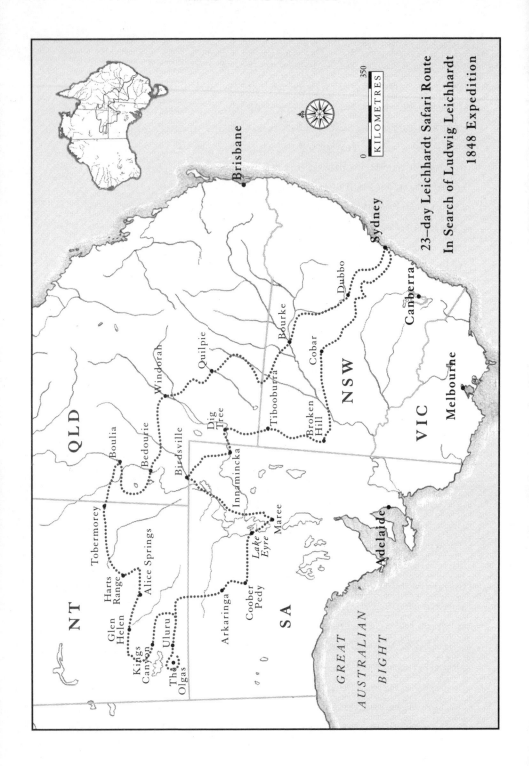

Leon Bouchaud by Rennie Ellis, who had worked with him from time to time. He showed me some of his work, which was really top class, and he also had a good feeling about the project. It had always been one of Leon's ambitions to go 'off the beaten track', so he reckoned he was getting closer. We came to a commercial agreement in which we had the pick of Rennie's Scoopix library for photo material and Leon's artistic skills. I wrote the copy because I had been there.

The finished article was a stunning pictorial of the Northern Territory, with a legible route map on every tour, clear pricing and departure dates. The front cover featured a brilliant Rennie Ellis shot of a Land Rover framed in the broken window of an outback ruin: it was titled 'Bill King's Northern Safaris' with a caption, 'Outback Australia 75–76', at the bottom. Ansett had the back cover, a great shot of a Boeing 727 aircraft in flight, with the deepest blue sky as a background. It said, 'ANSETT Airlines of Australia, a Million Holiday Ideas', and listed all of their Australian and overseas offices.

Bob Doyle was manager of the Northern Territory Tourist Bureau in Collins Street, Melbourne, at the time, so I took him a box of brochures and ran through all the new programs with him. He was impressed, and said, 'Hey, why don't you enter this in the Travel Trade Brochure of the Year Award? It's the best thing that's ever been done on the Territory.' So I did, and promptly forgot about it. Months later I got a call from Bob: 'You've got forty-five minutes to get to the AFTA [Australian Federation of Travel Agents] conference. There's something going to happen.'

'Bob, I'm under a truck covered in dirt and grease, and what's more we have to have it fixed by tonight. If there's something going to happen, you be me.'

'No worries,' he said.

Later that evening I got another call from Bob. 'Mate, you just won the Travel Trade Brochure of the Year Award, and—'

'What?'

'You also won the Travel Trade Award for best brochure on a limited budget.' I'd forgotten I had entered our brochure for

'Painting, Photography and Nature Lovers' Tours', which was a six-page fold-out black and white A4 piece that we had produced around a couple of Rennie's photos. We were obviously a good team.

With the addition of several new holiday arrangements, and by splitting tours, we increased the number of departures dramatically and I needed a vehicle to do the Darwin run. I was fortunate that there had been a lot of movement in the industry about that time and my brother Ron had taken up the Greyhound Express franchise in Melbourne. He had purchased some seriously good equipment and had surplus capacity, so I chartered one of his vehicles to do the 23-day 'Highlights of the Centre and Top End Safari'.

So, with 127 outback departures and eleven painting schools, we had not let grass grow under our feet since Val and I first sat looking at our Land Rover 6 with a couple of burnt-out valves and old Gertrude parked outside our house, thinking, 'Bloody hell. Do we know what we're getting ourselves into?' And it really seemed a lifetime since I took that first tour with the colonel and the three ladies, retracing the journey of Burke and Wills.

It soon came back to me through agents and industry people that many of my competitors, let's call them the 'song book brigade', said breaking up the tours wouldn't work—there were too many dead legs (people who buy half a tour) blocking out people who *might* buy a full tour, with the cost of airfares included the tours were too expensive, and so on. Why would anybody pay $235 to fly to Alice Springs for an eleven-day tour when you can buy the whole sixteen-day tour for $199? 'Kingy will go broke,' they crowed. Well, they missed the whole point. It was all a matter of offering *choices*, and we had more choices in the marketplace than any other operator—25 different holiday ideas, to be precise.

•

My next tour was not until early March when I left Melbourne in Little Ben. I had claimed the AB160 International as my carriage into the outback and had taken off with my complement of twelve travellers on this very hot Saturday, heading for Mildura. The group was made up of three males, including me, and ten females, quite an imbalance, which I hoped was not to be the norm. Not that I don't like female company or working with women; I just thought there would be more social interaction with a more balanced group.

When I first saw the manifest it was even more out of whack—there was only one bloke, Bill Richards, an American freelance photojournalist touring around Australia who had been referred to us by the Australian Tourist Commission. So I gave Leon 'Beau' Bouchaud a call and said, 'Hey, Beau, I've got a vacant seat on my tour to the Centre this coming Saturday. Do you want it?'

The women were all in their twenties apart from one, which was most unusual; we usually had more mature-aged women on our tours. Anyway, 'the one' was very special. When I arrived at the pick-up point in Flinders Street, there was this lady, smallish, dressed in a dark beige tweed suit with a mid-calf skirt, dark stockings and tan leather brogue walking shoes which were polished to the limit. On her head was a matching tweed hat with a small brim and I could see her hair was tied back in a chignon. She was also wearing tortoiseshell-rimmed thick glasses and was sitting on a shooting stick.

'I hope she can put up with these youngies,' I immediatly thought, but I need not have worried. Miss Edna Durrell, a Scot with the broadest accent imaginable, was a lecturer at Edinburgh University, and she knew how to handle young people. Miss Marple, the girls called her.

The tour started well. They were an easy group to work with. Four of the girls were Kiwi friends who had come to Australia for work and two other girls were Aussie friends, which left Edna and three other girls as single bookings. One of the three singles was Debbie Winter. She was a tall blonde lass with an outstanding figure, really noticeable, and it became very obvious that Bill Richards noticed also. It wasn't long before Bill and Debbie would wander off into the bush each evening after pitching camp, before the sun set, with him laden with all his camera gear to do 'life studies'. Well, it kept them occupied.

As we trundled along bush tracks there was always something fun going on in the truck. They were a happy lot and certainly intent on having a good time, although some of the girls when chatting away were inclined to say things that could be deemed to be a little 'off'—it just depended on how your mind interpreted what was said—and Beau at times was positively gross. I used to glance at Edna in the rearview mirror when some of these moments made me cringe and all I ever saw was the wisp of a smile in the corners of her mouth. There were no flies on Edna.

It was bloody hot that March, with lots of big storms about and Hughie the rain god was dropping big buckets of water all over the place. We were very lucky to get into Palm Valley. The route in is along the bed of the Finke River and it had flooded the week before. It was still running high but was manageable. It wasn't the usual Central Australian weather either. Apart from the temperature reaching the high 30s, the humidity was almost unbearable. But then it hadn't been the usual weather for the past three years. The drought was well and truly over and it would appear that the 'wet' was never going to end. It was the weather our early Australian explorers who traversed the Red Centre would have dreamed about. John McDouall Stuart, Ernest Giles and E.W. Gosse would have loved having the constant replenishment of waterholes.

The regrowth of plant life between the late 1960s and early 70s was nothing short of miraculous. I wrote earlier that before the rains the outback appeared dead. Now the growth was lush. Botanists working out near the Rock were discovering plants that had never been named. Then there were the native poplars. They had been dormant for ages and I had never seen them in all the years that I travelled the outback. After the rains had come there were forests of them. Nature knew it was time and got really busy. All those little seeds that for years had blown about in the desert, the sand wearing their shells thin before the wind lodged them against or under some fallen limb or object, had burst into life. It was truly a most beautiful passage of time.

Anyway, it was stinking hot and humid making our way along the riverbed to get to Palm Valley, with not the semblance of a breeze to give us relief, but when we got there it was really a picture to behold. The waterholes were all full to overflowing and the livistona palms and cycads were just so green against the vivid red rock of the canyon. The cycads, with several years of regular rain, had flourished in the crevasses and rock shelves that scarred the walls of the canyon from the floor to the rim, and it looked for the entire world like the Hanging Gardens of Babylon. They were magnificent nesting sites for the birds of prey, rock wallabies and other wildlife that had taken up residence in the valley.

We had no sooner stopped the truck next to this huge waterhole when Beau leapt out, tearing off his clothes as he went. 'Skinny dip! C'mon, skinny dip!' he shouted as he ran then did a big bomb into the waterhole. When he was followed by a flock of screeching females doing similar in varying degrees of undress, with a couple in the 'altogether', I was more than surprised, I was completely bowled over.

I ignored the shouts of 'Get your gear off, Bill!' and Beau soon had them organised into a water ballet. He was in the middle as a centrepiece surrounded by a circle of beauties with their arms linked across one another's shoulders and one leg stuck straight up in the air, then each girl did a little spin and put the other leg in the air. He was a creative bugger, was our Beau.

Meanwhile Edna had asked me if I could get her suitcase out of the locker and allow her the privacy of the truck to change into her swimming costume. She eventually emerged in a burgundy one-piece with skirt back and front, and she was wearing one of those rubber bathing caps covered in little rubber flowers. She said, 'Bill, I'm going around the corner to bathe. Just keep out of the way—you know.'

The Palm Valley water ballet, the 'Frolics' as they were quickly named, was well underway, and Beau's choreography was drawing high praise from the participants, when suddenly there was an abrupt stop. Bill Richards, who had been snapping off shots galore with his camera, had stripped off and was standing stark naked on a rock in all his glory preparing to dive into the pool. Now there is an old saying that 'all men are born equal'. For the benefit of those who have led sheltered lives, that is not quite true when referring to a certain portion of the male anatomy, and Bill Richards was an outstanding example of that fallacy—and I do mean outstanding.

You could've heard a pin drop. The cast of the ballet were speechless, just floating there with their mouths agape. But Debbie Winter, who had disrobed entirely and was sitting in the shallows rinsing out an armful of 'smalls' she had taken from the truck, merely glanced over her shoulder and went on with her washing as if it were an everyday occurrence, which perhaps it was for her, and had something to do with 'life studies'.

Just at that moment around the corner came Edna, breast-stroking her way towards the rock Bill was standing on. There was an audible intake of breath from the 'Frolics' while I stood frozen with dread. Edna stopped swimming, looked up at Bill, then adjusted her eyewear and said, 'My word! I am so glad I wore my spectacles.'

CHAPTER 13

AMERICA—HERE WE COME

It was shortly after mid-year when I read an article in *Truck and Bus* magazine about the Bedford M series four-wheel-drive truck chassis with a 330 cubic inch diesel engine that S.A. Cheney, the Bedford distributors, were importing. Originally designed for the British army to use in their North African bases, it had been found to withstand Australian conditions. Was this the answer to my problems?

As soon as I could I went to the distributors' showroom for a look. It was more robust than the Internationals in every way: the chassis rails and cross members, suspension and axles were all much stronger and most of all it was forward control, the driver positioned in the foremost position in the vehicle to gain maximum floor space. I put my tape over it and did some mental arithmetic and there was no doubt it was the solution. It could carry twenty people: eighteen punters and two crew members. To carry a crew of two—tour leader and cook—on our four-wheel-drive vehicles had always been my aim, but I needed the capacity for those extra couple of 'fares' to pay the bill. With the Bedford M I could also have a large kitchen located in the back righthand corner, and much more locker space as well. To top it all off, it ran on diesel.

I could carry almost 700 kilometres' worth of fuel, and that would eliminate paying outrageous prices in some remote locations. Besides, petrol engines give no end of trouble in the electrics when there's water about. I couldn't wait to get home and start designing the body—it was perfect.

Enough of the season had gone by to reassure me that I was on the right track with vehicles that increased seating capacity. Our current operations were proving that. I ordered one Bedford M chassis for delivery in October, a second for December and three more to be delivered in 1976, then I gave Harley Evenden the drawings for the new body design and told him to get his head around that lot.

That year, 1975, I took my second real aeroplane ride overseas. I had flown all over Australia and to Bali since I had been in business, but to fly to the United States was going to be a new experience for me. This came about when two executives from the Australian Tourist Commission (ATC) phoned for an appointment to discuss a mooted 'road show' to the US, with key Australian industry figures to promote Australia to American travel agents and wholesalers. I was quite flattered, I can tell you; a 'key figure'. Goodness me!

In my mind it was the big opportunity—all those wealthy Americans with money falling out of their pockets dying to find somebody like me to give it to. I was glad we had our award-winning brochure to take; it certainly helps to sell a product if you have high-quality point-of-sale material, and we had the best.

We left Sydney on 5 September 1975 on a Qantas Boeing 707, and I was seated well down the back of 'the truck' with John Knox in a seat that seemed awfully small for such a mammoth journey that was almost beyond my imagination. Knoxy had joined AAT, a coach company established by Trans Australia Airlines at that time. It was an exciting moment. For years people had been saying to me, 'Wow, the Americans would love all that outback stuff.' They assumed I had a large number of punters from the US on our tours. The fact was there were bugger all, and I wanted to find some.

AMERICA—HERE WE COME

Our route was via Tahiti with a direct flight from there to Vancouver, we then flew on to Los Angeles and I have absolutely no recollection of that flight. It was totally erased from my memory by absolute exhaustion. Thank God we had two nights to rest up in Los Angeles.

Many of you may not believe this, but I didn't drink a great deal when I first started in the business—a few beers at the pub on a Saturday evening if there was nothing on or at a restaurant or somebody's home where we were guests. Through the week I wouldn't bother—it was a weekend thing. But when we started operating Bill King's Northern Safaris there were no weekends as such. In addition, when travelling on tour I would have a couple of tinnies when camp was set up, because it was thirsty work and everybody else did, and as we had table wine with the evening meal that I was paying for, I would certainly enjoy a couple of glasses with my food. So I gradually became a steady drinker.

Still, the US sales trip was a shock to the system. Every evening after work there was a 'bun fight', which means you pop down as much free grog as you can and pick through the wide and varied selection of canapés of dubious quality, as this may save you having to buy dinner. These days they call it 'networking'.

Our first function was on Tuesday 9 September at the Murrieta Hot Springs Resort in southern California. Managed by the Dunes Hotel and Country Club mob from Las Vegas in those days, it was a lavish establishment built in the early 1900s as a playground for the rich and famous residents of Los Angeles. The resort offered a wide range of sporting facilities, mud baths, swimming pools, spas and gymnasiums, as well as elaborate conference facilities. As we boarded the bus for the trip to the resort, it felt a bit weird being ushered along when I'm usually the one doing the mustering. This time I was a punter.

The ATC had organised big functions, not only for the American travel agents and wholesalers but for their wives as well, I assume as a sweetener to ensure a good attendance. There were Americans participating from all over the western states, from Montana down to New Mexico. A guy named Bob Godfrey organised the show. He was an Australian who had been working in the industry in Canada and had experience in conference management. Bob had a desk set up for each Australian delegate to deliver a presentation on their product and timetabled fifteen minutes with each American, of whom there were about 50. He would ring his bell to get the whole thing started and after twelve minutes ring a warning bell and after another three minutes ring it again for the Americans to move on to the next supplier. Maybe that's where they got the idea for speed-dating.

I gave my presentation and they were so eager when I talked about exploring the remote regions of inland Australia in our custom-built four-wheel-drive Desert Cruisers, experiencing nature's gifts in the peace of the bush, enjoying the camaraderie of an evening campfire. They just loved the sound of all that and so the questions began.

'Are your vehicles air-conditioned?'

'No, people spend as much time out of the vehicle as in it, and going in and out of an air-conditioned space can make people sick.'

'Do you have camps set up along your route?'

'No. It's not possible because of the nature of the terrain in the regions in which we travel; routes may vary from tour to tour, depending on weather conditions.'

'Do you have bathroom facilities in your vehicles?'

'No. Even though our four-wheel-drive Desert Cruisers are built to afford coach-style comfort, there's not the space.'

'Oh. Then what do you do for a bathroom?'

'Shovel and a roll of toilet paper.' I told them the truth, but it was becoming clear that I was getting nowhere. They just couldn't grasp the concept of what we were doing.

'I'm not sure your tours are suitable for our market,' they'd say. 'We're at the deluxe end. But if you put your tours together with hotels and use air-conditioned bathroom-equipped coaches, let us be the first to know. We just looove the sound of it.'

I discovered the so-called 'deluxe' market was the one that all of the wholesalers and agents went after; it was the blue-rinse brigade, all those 'widder' ladies travelling on their deceased husband's life insurance policy and the 'gold watch' retirees.

The common holiday was Australia and New Zealand packaged with an island stopover, usually Fiji, Tahiti or Hawaii—all in two or three weeks. The Australian part was the 'golden triangle' of Sydney, Canberra and Melbourne, with Ansett Pioneer. Jack Long, a mate of Reg Ansett's from way back, was the international sales manager and he had been working in the US for years. They were already packaged in any worthwhile brochure.

Sydney was the main gateway in those days. In fact many overseas people thought it was Australia's capital until we explained Canberra to them. There were very few international visitors arriving in Sydney who turned north to Queensland, and those who did visited the Great Barrier Reef and that was it. The Northern Territory was certainly not on the 'must do' list. (This was just before the explosion of interest in the Reef, Ayers Rock and Kakadu.) The lack of knowledge became apparent to me when I had an agent, who was organising travel arrangements for clients visiting Melbourne and Sydney, ask if I could arrange a day tour of Ayers Rock and the Olgas in between the two cities!

On Thursday 11 September the coach took us back to the Los Angeles airport for the flight to Chicago, where we were picked up and driven to our next venue, the Scotsland Resort in Oconomowoc, Wisconsin. The seminars? Same as last time—everybody loooved Bill's tours but nobody wanted to buy them.

•

The following morning I took off with Knoxy for a look about because we weren't due at the next sales venue in Quebec for a week, so we jumped on a Greyhound express bound for Nashville on Route 65, the Louisville Line. It was an educational tour on how they managed bus transport in the big world, and my word it was some operation. We asked for the two seats behind the driver so we could have a look at the goings-on. We were like a couple of overexcited school kids.

General Motors had established a bus and coach division exclusively to build the intercity express for Greyhound. The 'GM Buffalo Bus', the Greyhound in-house name for the MC1 powered by a mighty Detroit Diesel 8V71 engine delivering 370 horsepower, was an awesome machine. We changed drivers at the bus station in Indianapolis, and, because we were running a little late, we heard the depot supervisor instruct the driver to 'pick it up' a bit. And did he put the slipper into it! Pedal to the metal, we were hunting down that freeway at 70 miles per hour. The driver was constantly on the radio seeking out 'Smokey' (highway patrol) and, as the speed dropped considerably in places and then moved back up to 70, we gathered the intelligence network with the truckies was alive and well.

We went to the Grand Old Opry and the Hall of Fame the following morning before boarding our Continental Trailways Express to Atlanta. They are the two institutions for which Nashville is renowned; the Grand Old Opry has featured the stars of country and western music in weekly concerts since 1925 and the Hall of Fame museum preserves the history of American music.

The trip to Atlanta was the second of our great moments in bus travel as Trailways, Greyhound's competitor, used Silver Eagle coaches on their network and the Silver Eagle insignia as their trademark. The buses were initially imported from Europe, but Trailways eventually set up a manufacturing plant in Texas to build their own equipment. Both the Buffalo Bus and Silver Eagle used the same power plant, the 8V71 Detroit, but that is where the similarity ended. There were radical differences in the suspension. In fact I didn't like the Silver Eagle at all—you could get seasick, the ride was so soft.

For Knoxy and me, both 'bussies' from way back, those bus rides were a highlight of the US trip. Since I was that little kid sitting on my old man's knee pretending to drive a bus, it was something I'd always dreamt of doing.

AMERICA—HERE WE COME

•

We flew from Atlanta to Quebec to meet up with our mob for the next round of meetings and hospitality at the Quebec Hilton. For me, trying to sell outback Australia to French-speaking Canadians, was like trying to sell thongs to Eskimos—they all holiday in France. From there it was an unmemorable trip to Morristown in New Jersey for the same result before attending the final workshop with delegates from the northern states of the US and more Canadians.

The final meetings were at the Banff Springs Hotel and there are probably few hotels in the world that can offer the same majesty, seclusion and scenery. It was a beautiful autumn day when we arrived and I was fortunate to have a room at the rear of the hotel with a view along this vast, fir-lined valley that swept upwards to distant snow-covered mountains. All of that was scant compensation, though, for my first and thoroughly depressing foray into international marketing.

The Americans really did love the things I talked about, but they needed a bed, a bath, a dunny to sit on and transport in an air-conditioned plastic bubble—they completely missed the point of what we did.

So while my trip to the United States contained some enjoyable experiences, business-wise it was a bloody disaster. I felt guilty that I had spent so much money on an expensive 'holiday' that I did not need. There was not one agent or wholesaler I met during the entire escapade that wished to include any of our tours in their programs. I will say, though, that I did have a naive attitude to all of this—I didn't have enough flexibility in my commission rates, or the negotiating skills to offer incentives and rates linked to performance and the like. I would next time, though. And, again, I did learn some valuable lessons.

CHAPTER 14

ABOUT 'BURKE'S BONES'

BACK HOME AND IT was the second week in October and I had a deadline to reprint our tour program for 1976. We had decided to maintain the tours we revamped in 1975, giving them two years to consolidate. However, there was one new itinerary I needed to add. I couldn't believe the difference in revenue due to those three vehicles: Big Ben, Little Ben and that bitch Olga. They had turned our operation into a business in 1975. Every trip had run pretty much full during the period that I was away, and we still had some profitable loads in October, a couple in November, and Christmas departures were looking good. But this wasn't quite enough. November to March was still the millstone. We were always cashed up by November and on the bones of our backside by March.

Still, there was a glow at the end of the tunnel. We took delivery of our first Bedford chassis from Cheney's, and Harley got underway with the bodywork. I must confess to being like a kid with a new toy, and no doubt gave Harley the willies, in and out like a yo-yo, saying modify this and modify that, watching my baby Katherine (as I christened her) grow.

Meanwhile there was another job I had to do for the Australian Tourist Commission (ATC). Arthur Todero was the ATC's manager

ABOUT 'BURKE'S BONES'

in Frankfurt and he was a passionate believer in the future of European business. He believed that given an appropriate promotional budget and marketing resources, it would become Australia's prime high-yield market. The ATC, of course, was pouring its promotional budget into the United States and Japan.

Arthur had put together a group of six Italian journalists, high-profile people from major networks and newspapers. They were on a pretty tight itinerary to many parts of Australia and the highlight was to be a Burke and Wills expedition. They were to experience the real outback, not the tourist resorts that can sometimes be replicas of the places from which they have travelled, but off the beaten track, wilderness. Given their time constraints they were not doing a return journey and would fly out of Birdsville.

As well as Arthur, with them was Bruce Renton. He was a public relations consultant whom the ATC had retained as Australia's representative in Italy. Bruce, I was to discover, was a very interesting sort of bloke. Of Scottish descent, he lived on a small island in the Mediterranean.

The journalists were easily recognisable as Europeans. By that I mean they had flared trousers with pointed shoes protruding from beneath the cuffs, body-hugging shirts with large collars unbuttoned to the waist, lots of jewellery and perfume. I could visualise them in the cafés on the sidewalks of Rome, sipping cappuccinos and lattes.

By the time we departed in October the three previous years of regular rain had stimulated an explosion of growth that I had never seen before—even many of the long-term residents of the regions we passed through hadn't experienced anything like it. North of Broken Hill, the Corner Country, as it is known, had been transformed into savannah—Mitchell grass a metre high as far as the eye could see, with vast areas of spring colour, beige, brown and green, the landscape constantly changing tone in the fluky breeze.

The favourable seasons had also triggered an explosion in wildlife. Flocks of Major Mitchell cockatoos were spectacular, their pink undersides contrasting with their pure white plumage; red-tailed black cockatoos, equally breaktaking; enormous flocks of galahs; and on one occasion, when we camped near water, the corellas arrived at sunset in their thousands. There were literally flotillas of pelicans on Cooper Creek, as well as the common herons, egrets and ibis. We even spotted a couple of white-breasted sea eagles—a long way from home, they had either followed the floodplains down from Queensland or had flown up the Cooper from Lake Eyre in South Australia. Old man emus were everywhere, herding their chicks along, showing them where to feed while their promiscuous mothers were off looking for another mate to make eggs with.

Kangaroos were gathering in huge mobs in the Corner Country. Some of the big reds were bloody enormous, 2 metres high, and built like Arnold Schwarzenegger. They were locked in by the dog fence on the Queensland, South Australian and New South Wales borders. They had bred in huge numbers in western New South Wales and taken refuge from culling in the ever-increasing dimensions of the Sturt National Park. As the authorities took up more grazing leases in the west of the state, they were annexing the roos into the park. Mobs of a hundred or even more bounding across the plains were really a sight to see.

One day we came across a spectacle in the rocky hill country north of Tibooburra that was truly amazing. I could see it from a distance like a fiery glow in the late afternoon sun. It was Sturt's desert pea, miles of it, glowing blood red. The hills were absolutely covered in it. My mob were all speaking excitedly in Italian and waving their arms about. I should add that not one of them spoke English, but I knew what they wanted and was already looking for an appropriate place to stop. They were the biggest pea flowers I had ever seen—'lanterns' nearly as big as beer cans.

Our route then took us north through Warri Gate and the dog fence. The fence, the world's longest, is fabricated with wire netting about 2 metres high and stretches for 5614 kilometres from the Great Dividing Range in Queensland to the Great Australian Bight. It was built during the 1880s to control both rabbits and wild dogs but today is maintained to keep Queensland's dingoes away from the sheep country in northern New South Wales.

ABOUT 'BURKE'S BONES'

After passing through the gate into Queensland we continued north across Santos and Orientos stations through patches of really deep sand, it was really slow going. We were way out in the middle of nowhere, ploughing round this sand dune, and suddenly in the middle of the track was a bloke in a Bongo van, those piddling little things with tiny wheels and an engine of about 750 cc. What the devil was he doing way out here in that thing?

Turned out he was from Mildura and he bought this Bongo to deliver flowers for his florist's shop. What possessed him to try and drive this thing to Cooper Creek is beyond me, and I couldn't get any sense out of him at all. Maybe he thought he would get his name in the paper, I don't know, but what I do know is that it all got too hard and he tried to turn around and got stuck. He had been there for some time and had no food or water left and was absolutely desperate when we arrived.

I fixed him up with a couple of cans of grub and some water and said I would tow him out. That's when I noticed his tyres. 'You've got to have baggy tyres in sand, mate. Yours are like rocks.'

'I thought they had to be hard,' he said.

'No, soft, but you have to make them hard again when you hit the hard surface.'

So I let his tyres down halfway and told him to hop in. 'You can drive it out now.' And he did, with a push start. There was about 50 metres of sand to the hard stuff where I expected him to stop and put a bit of wind in his tyres and say, 'Bye-bye, thank you,' but, no, he was off like a scalded cat, gone in a cloud of dust and tempting a puncture, still on his soft tyres. The silly bugger probably didn't even have a tyre pump.

•

The Cooper was at its magnificent best when we arrived. The only permanent waterway between the Murray River and the Gulf of Carpentaria, it is a very special place, yet situated in some of the most inhospitable country in the land. We crossed the creek and

I took the group down to the Dig Tree, where we camped for the night.

The following day we were heading towards Burke's grave when I saw this huge snake just sunning himself in the middle of the track and I reckoned it was another western taipan. I stopped and he reared up in a striking pose and just stayed there, transfixed by the vehicle. Bloody hell, he was a beauty, and angry, too. He reminded me of the one that attacked my Land Rover some years before; they really are bad-tempered buggers.

We camped not far downstream from Burke's grave that night and my punters took an unusually keen interest in the campfire, burning heaps of wood, producing a huge pile of coals. They were all muttering away among themselves. A couple became quite voluble and were standing there gesticulating into the darkness beyond the firelight. It was getting towards the time to turn in when I saw one of them take the shovel so assumed he was off to you-know-what. But instead he took a shovel full of coals and placed them near his tent, then another, and another, until he had created a semicircle around the tent's entrance. On completion he handed the shovel to the next punter who began performing the same ritual.

'What on earth are they doing?' I said to Arthur.

He grinned and said, 'Somebody heard from somewhere that you put a circle of coals around your tent to keep the snakes away.'

I had a chuckle to myself.

We were in no hurry the next morning, we were only going down to Innamincka, so some sat about and some went walkabout while I tidied up and packed the camp away. During dinner the previous night I had related the next phase of the Burke and Wills story to the group, with Arthur and Bruce doing the translating. Because we were camped near Burke's grave, it was a very poignant moment when I spoke about another expedition returning to Cooper Creek to gather his remains and take them back to Melbourne for an appropriate burial, only to find that dingoes had robbed the gravesite and some of the remains were missing.

ABOUT 'BURKE'S BONES'

Anyway, a couple of hours had passed since they wandered off, and I had not long finished packing up the gear when into the camp puffed Bruce with a bundle of bones in his hand. 'I have found Burke's bones in a dingo's lair.'

'What!' I said. I got quite a surprise, I can tell you, but I was sceptical. It's hard to imagine bones sitting there for well over a hundred years. 'I dunno, Bruce,' I said. 'The dingoes have probably chewed on a lot of bones between then and now.'

But they were all excited and chattered away in Italian and came to the conclusion that a couple of the bones could be human. So I got Bruce to show me where he'd found them. How he came across the lair was a mystery—it was at the bottom of a small crevasse and not visible. 'Whatever took you down there?' I asked Bruce.

'I didn't have a shovel,' he replied.

We called in to Bluey Allen's camp on the way to Innamincka. Bluey was a character. He lived in a cluster of demountables with his hippie girlfriends and tribes of kids way out in the middle of nowhere on the bank of the Cooper. One of his huts was even set up as a movie theatre. His camp was surrounded by graders, bulldozers and all sorts of equipment and he had graded his own airstrip along the waterway for his aeroplane, a single engine thing.

'Who's for a ride?' he said, and one of the blokes wanted to go.

Well, did Bluey give him a work over, throwing the plane all over the place while the engine misfired so often it was continuous. Burp-burp-bip-burp—I was glad I wasn't in it.

We heard it in the distance coming towards us, low, and then it appeared coming down the Cooper which was pretty wide at Bluey's place, and just as well, because he was flat chat, flying down between the trees that lined the bank. But the aircraft wasn't horizontal—it was vertical, with the lower wing tip almost touching the water as it passed us.

'The engine's misfiring a lot,' I said to Bluey after he landed.

'It's out of Avgas. It does that when I run it on petrol,' he explained.

The guy who went up with him was green for the rest of the day.

When we arrived in Innamincka there were storm clouds threatening, and a couple of vehicles from one of the stations further north pulled in as we did and they were covered in mud. 'Big rains heading this way from up north,' they said.

'Birdsville?' I asked.

'No way. Not until it dries out, anyway,' was the reply.

Arthur made a quick decision and chartered two light aircraft from Adelaide to fly the group out of Innamincka. Mid morning the following day the planes arrived and after much hugging and kissing they all took off into the wide grey yonder.

It was a bit of a sad moment, really. The Italian journos were a great group, and I had really enjoyed Arthur and Bruce's company—in fact we became lasting friends. It was Bruce who introduced me to Scotch whisky. From the time the trip started, when ever I had no driving to do, Bruce would say, 'Time for the one, Bill,' meaning a nip out of the bottle's screw cap. I might add, 'the one' was a ritual that Bruce himself indulged in all day, every day.

•

Fast forward a year or so and I picked up an *Australian Women's Weekly* and began to thumb through it, and there was a photo of Bruce Renton. He was standing there with a red rocky hill behind him, some bones in each hand and his British Airways bag at his feet (the bag he carried his supply of Scotch in). I couldn't believe it. The heading said 'The Curse of Burke's Bones'.

It appears that Lois Miles, an Aussie journalist, was attending a cocktail party in Rome and was introduced to Bruce Renton. The story goes that when Bruce discovered Ms Miles was Australian, he immediately relayed to her that he was very worried by Burke's bones. Understandably Ms Miles was intrigued by how a dour Scotsman living in Italy, could even know about Robert O'Hara Burke, let alone have some of his bones. Bruce explained how he went on safari with Bill King and camped near Burke's grave then found the bones in a dingo's lair.

ABOUT 'BURKE'S BONES'

The curse of the bones apparently began soon after Bruce arrived back from the bush. He was involved in a motorcycle accident in Sydney. Then, on a stopover in Hong Kong, he was knocked down by a car, and in India his plane caught fire and he was forced to evacuate by emergency chute. Ms Miles also met one of the other Italians who was on the trip and he insisted that the only way to remove the curse was to return the bones to Australia. And he enjoyed his experiences here so much he would be happy to take the bones back himself. Whether he ever did so or not I have no idea, but it's a good story.

CHAPTER 15

FROM LASSETER'S CAVE TO THE NORTHERN FRONTIER

IN THE EARLY DAYS, you may recall, our survey expeditions seeking new routes and experiences were financed by advertising for punters in the *Sun* newspaper. Now that we had a list of past passengers we could do a mail-out to see if anybody was interested in a survey trip, and what do you know—we got a waiting list.

I wanted to explore the country west of Ayers Rock, the Petermann Ranges and then further west through Docker River Aboriginal settlement to Giles Meteorological Station in the Gibson Desert.

It was on that journey I first visited Lasseter's Cave. I wanted to include it in the new itinerary we were running down the Gunbarrel Highway. I was fascinated by the story of the fabled reef of gold, more particularly because of my grandfather—he and Harold Lasseter prospected in Coolgardie at the same time. I found the location of Lasseter's demise near the Docker River settlement on the Western Australia and Northern Territory border.

Ion Idriess, the acclaimed author, had quoted the last page of Lasseter's diary in his famous book, *Lasseter's Last Ride*, and I had a copy with me. Lasseter wrote:

> I think it's the worst possible death. With one's experience in this country I should never had gone alone—but I relied on Paul to follow me—what good a reef, worth millions—I would give it all for a loaf of bread—and to think only a week away is lots of tucker—the blacks are not troubling me now, they know I am dying and will wait.

Pretty moving stuff, especially when you're reading that and standing in the low light of the setting sun with the sound of silence ringing in your ears, on the exact spot where Bob Buck of Tempe Downs found Lasseter's body.

We turned south after leaving Giles, crossing dune country to the Wingelinna Hills at Surveyor General's Corner, at the junction of the Western Australia, Northern Territory and South Australian borders. We had not long crossed into South Australia and were following a pair of wheel tracks when I started thinking I had better stop shortly and clean the radiator screen of spinifex seeds. The front bumper nipped them off like a harvester, and if you didn't clean off the radiator you would certainly cook the engine.

The year before that problem had cost a man his life. Apparently this Canadian bloke rented a four-while drive in Alice Springs and took off exploring, not telling anybody where he was going. He was on the Sandy Blight Junction Track heading south towards Giles and that's as far as he reached. His radiator had filled up with spinifex seeds and he had blown up the engine. He was a forlorn cadaver when they found his remains months later, sitting in the driver's seat with his hands still on the steering wheel; he'd left a note with the emotional feelings of a dying man on the seat beside him. These things can happen very easily if people don't follow the rules.

I was cleaning the radiator in our vehicle when I noticed a tiny wisp of smoke wavering in the breeze in the distance. 'What the bloody hell is that?' I wondered as we got going and headed towards it. Then I saw the galvanised blades of a shiny new windmill revolving above a dune. I had no idea that anybody ever came this

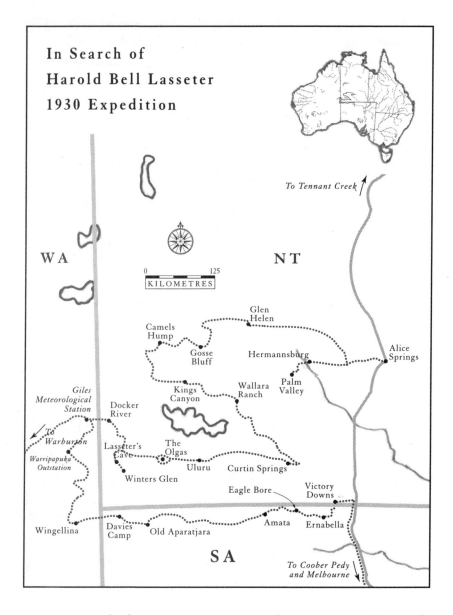

way on a regular basis. My attention was drawn to several haystacks appearing in the distance. What the devil were haystacks doing way out here? It was all very unusual.

Then, as we got closer, I could see people, and the haystacks were actually wurlies, the Western Desert Aboriginal windbreak or shelter. The people were all watching us coming down the track and I couldn't believe what I was seeing. They were nomadic people, most of them naked, and their wurlies were quite big, made from sticks arranged in a pyramid and clumps of spinifex grass jammed together to form a canopy.

We stopped and got out and they just stood there looking at us, with the little kids hiding shyly behind legs and peeping out through gaps to see what was going on. I had a big bag of oranges in the back of the truck and pulled them out to break the ice with the little people. I stood there showing the spectator group, now numbering about twenty, how to peel the fruit and separate the sections. Well, you should have heard the noise—little kids squealing, the high-pitched voices of the women intermingled with the guttural sound of the men as they all chatted and gesticulated at one another and the fruit. There was not one word of English spoken in that whole camp, but it was obvious they had never seen an orange before and they certainly weren't going to leave any. The bag of fruit was soon history. It was an amazing experience.

We headed east towards the Amata Aboriginal settlement and I pulled in to the admin block to see if I could get some fuel. As I always say, when travelling in the outback you never pass a petrol pump, money exchange or a dunny without stopping. This bloke spotted us coming in from the west and had flown out of his nest when I stopped and proceeded to give me fifty thousand words for being on Aboriginal land without a permit. He also threatened us with prosecution for interfering with the mob out at Davies Camp bore. There was only one track and he knew we must have come from there.

By the time he had all that off his chest I had extracted my permit issued by the Central Land Council to travel through that country. We had been on Aboriginal lands for the past week and I had obtained all the necessary paperwork before departure. Anyway, this ratbag cranked up his tirade again, going on about the Central Land Council having no right issuing permits for South Australia.

'Are you going to sell me any petrol or not?' I interrupted him, at which time he just stalked off—bad attitude.

I was about to load my troops back in the truck and move on when one of the young locals asked, 'You want some petrol, mate?' I nodded and he said, 'No worries.' We had a chat about the people out at Davies Camp. He didn't know a great deal other than that they had come in from the Western Desert a few weeks before and they were not from his mob. Now that was interesting: the people in the north of South Australia were Pitjantjara, as were the people who lived in the Western Desert just over the border, so if they weren't from his mob, who were they? He also told us that apart from the health people who checked them out and the blokes who installed the windmill we would be the only whitefellas they had ever seen.

I was back in Alice Springs soon after and contacted a bloke I knew at the Central Land Council to find out the full story on the people out at Davies Camp, and also the objection to our permit. On the permit issue he said that the Northern Territory, South Australian and Western Australian authorities all have reciprocity with permit, and if anyone needed a no-go zone on Indigenous land there was a procedure to be followed, which the mob at Amata had not done. He also added that the bloke who'd given me the rounds was well known as a dickhead.

The story on the tribe at Davies Camp was that they were Western Desert people from an unknown clan who had come in voluntarily because they had been reduced to one family. They were perhaps the last of the nomads in that region.

•

The second survey we did at that time was to explore the Tanami Desert, the Kimberley and Top End. We attracted a larger number on that journey, setting off with nine in our group.

One of the objectives on the mission was to find the rock carvings featured in a book published in 1968 called *Chariots of*

FROM LASSETER'S CAVE TO THE NORTHERN FRONTIER

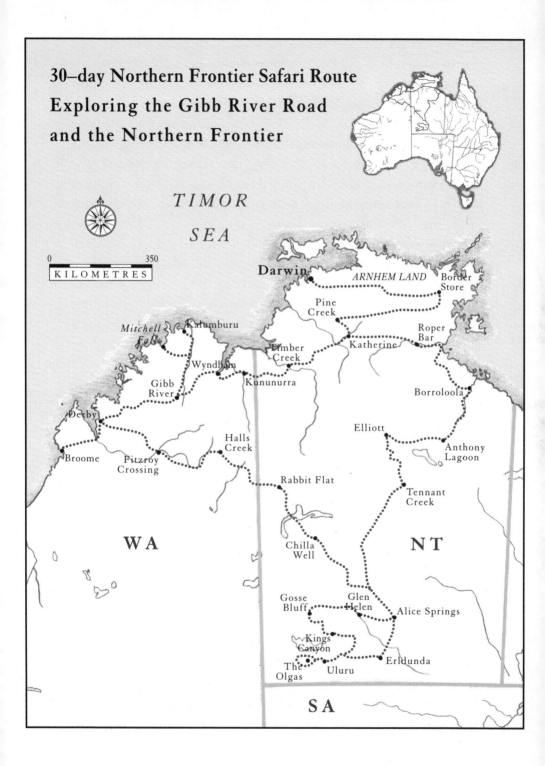

the Gods, by Erich von Däniken. He was a Swiss bloke who believed that extraterrestrial visitors had an influence on early humans and produced all sorts of evidence from all over the world to support his theory, one example being in the Tanami Desert. The book contained a photograph of a rock carving of figures that appeared to have space helmets on their heads. I knew the carvings in the photograph were in Balgo Country, near Lake Gregory on the eastern fringe of the Great Sandy Desert, and Bruce Farrands at Rabbit Flat knows all there is to know in that region and he pointed me in the right direction.

Those carvings were in a bugger of a place to get to back then, along an almost indefinable track in places, and when we got there it was no easy walk up this rocky gully to the carvings. They are primeval works, much smaller than I expected, but they are clearly figures with circles around their heads that most certainly resemble space helmets, even though they were carved thousands of years ago. It all depends on whether you are a believer or not.

I have my own theory, though. I have seen early photographs of Aborigines from the north in full ceremonial dress, crowned with headgear adorned with white bird feathers to form a circular radiance around the head. A rock carving of this figure would produce precisely the same result.

Our next stop was the Wolfe Creek Meteorite Crater, located not far off the Tanami track about 100 kilometres south of Halls Creek. It's believed that around 1.5 million years ago a missile from outer space, weighing around 50 000 kilos, crashed into the Earth and created the crater, said to be the second biggest in the world, and that must have been one big bang. It is perfectly symmetrical, and standing on the rim looking across to the other side 850 metres away and down to the floor 60 metres below, it's hard to imagine how man, using modern earthmoving techniques, could do any better.

We camped at Caroline Pool, near the ruins at the site of Old Halls Creek. The town sprang up after the gold strike by John Slattery and Charles Hall in 1885. The field was a short-lived proposition, however, and by 1889 most of the 3000-odd people who had flocked to the area had drifted away.

Geikie Gorge was our next point of interest. The boat ride through the Devonian period limestone outcrops, which are 350 million years old, is an awe-inspiring experience. Situated more than 250 kilometres from the mouth of the Fitzroy River, the gorge is not only home to some very mature crocodiles, but sharks, stingrays, sawfish and all manner of aquatic animals that live and breed in and along the waterway. The Fitzroy, which starts in the Kimberley and flows through northern Western Australia, is a bloody big river. It has a catchment area of some 90 000 square kilometres; in flood it discharges some 30 000 cubic metres of water per second through Geikie Gorge before dumping about 5 billion cubic metres of water annually into King Sound. You could add the outflow of other rivers in Australia together and they would struggle to achieve that. Flowing more than 15 kilometres wide in some places, the Fitzroy is a sight to see in full flood.

We travelled to Tunnel Creek and Windjana Gorge en route to Broome, where we visited the Japanese and Chinese cemeteries and the pearl sheds. Broome is a fascinating town with its own style of architecture: iconic Australian galvanised-iron buildings with added timber latticework and touches of red and green paint, and the occasional pagoda-style roof—traditional Australian with an Asian influence. I've never seen architecture like it anywhere else; it is uniquely Broome.

Our next challenge, and one of the prime missions on our journey, was to traverse the then defunct Gibb River Road through the Kimberley to Wyndham. This was not difficult as far as Gibb River Station, as they were trucking out cattle, but then it got really rough. Karunjie Station, situated about halfway between Gibb River Station and the Pentecost River crossing at the northern end, had been abandoned, so with no stock moving in or out the track hadn't seen a vehicle for years. In many places it had formed a floodway. Its bottom had been washed out to a metre or so below the roots of the scrub hanging out of the bank. The floodway had also exposed rocks as sharp as knife blades, and if this is sounding all too hard, it was. The so-called Gibb River Road was in some places just a deep, dry watercourse—with a voracious appetite for tyres—so we gave up.

Although there was no stock about in that country, the wild donkeys and brumbies had obviously been harassing each other, because there were huge herds of mules. I have read that mules make excellent beasts of burden and it is a pity they cannot be put to some useful task, but time has passed them by, I suppose. It would not be long before the professional hunters armed with automatic weapons in their helicopters would slaughter them in their thousands.

We travelled back to the Derby turnoff and headed to Wyndham, and what a wild and woolly town it was in the mid 70s. The abattoir was up and running and they were shipping out containers of meat, so the place was packed with meat workers and wharfies. They were also shipping out live cattle, so there were always truckies, drovers and ringers about, as well as a large Indigenous population. The pub at night was a hotbed of activity.

I went to see a bloke at the Department of Roads office and explained that we wanted to start a tour operation between Wyndham and Derby through the mountains. However, we needed a track between the Pentecost River crossing and Gibb River—that's more than 200 kilometres, so it was no small ask. We had a long yarn about the tours: what we did, where we went and who travelled with us. He was a good bloke and said he would see what he could do.

Well, he did it, sort of, but by no stretch of the imagination could you call it a road or track, really. He just ran a dozer there and back and the first heavy rainfall washed all the soil away. You had to negotiate protruding rocks and stumps and travel at little more than a crawl, but it was navigable. We were the first vehicles to traverse and open up that section of the Gibb River Road. Today it is on the must-do list for serious four-wheel-drive enthusiasts.

The Victoria Highway that links Darwin and Broome was not an all-weather journey in those days either, and the road could be shut for days in the wet season. We did encounter a couple of very deep and formidable river crossings on our drive back to Katherine. Kakadu had yet to be opened as a national park, so it was strictly dry-season travel east of Darwin as well. We did the boat trip in Katherine Gorge and customary walk to the third water hole before heading north to Darwin. There were no campsites available anywhere near Darwin because of the post-cyclone rebuilding program, so we stayed at Manton Dam, the city's water supply in those days, which is located about 80 kilometres south of the capital.

The place was alive with bandicoots at night. I was sleeping in a swag and was woken with a start by something hopping over me. In the starlight I could see these little creatures all over the place. There were dozens of them, and curious little devils they were, too. They must have thought I was a newly arrived log or something, as they hopped on and around me all night. It was a case of get used to it and get some sleep or don't get used to it and stay awake. The punters heard them, too, hopping about and bouncing off their tents.

The trip east of Darwin crossed the wetlands and Marrakai Plains between the Adelaide and Mary rivers. It had also became a haven for wildlife and teemed with water buffalo. Later, there was a concerted effort by the Northern Territory Parks and Wildlife Service to rid the Territory of buffalo. It was estimated there were about 350 000 at that time and many of them were infected with brucellosis, a disease that is contagious to both domestic livestock and humans. They did have success with the cull, but the buffalo are so far into the Arnhem Land wilderness now, they will be there forever. The buffalo, like the Bentang cattle, were brought to the Cobourg Peninsula from Bali by early settlers in 1849. The wild Bentang cattle now number about 3000, the largest non-domestic population in the world.

Our journey took us to the end of the line at the Border Store, purveyors of supplies to passersby and indigenous locals at the East Alligator River crossing. It was quite a pleasant spot at the time, but a couple of years later it was most unpleasant. One of the phenomena associated with the flooding of Lake Eyre is the proliferation of bird life. The availability of fish increases exponentially, satisfying the food chain, and so the pelican population had exploded in just a few years. But as the waters began to recede so did the food stocks. Then you would see flocks of pelicans on lakes, dams and waterholes Australia-wide, as tens of thousands flew here, there and everywhere in search of food. By the middle of the following year as the food diminished, you'd be observing thousands of dead pelicans on the same lakes, dams and waterholes.

The tidal turn of the East Alligator River occurs at the Border Store crossing. At low tide the heap of pelican carcasses would recede with the tide downstream and at high tide float right back up to the crossing again. Bloody hell, did they stink! The problem was that crocodile hunters in areas within proximity to civilisation had culled the animals to a point where there were none left at all. Crocs are the natural cleaners of the waterways—to them all that dead stuff is very tasty indeed. But they were gone, so unfortunately the rotting pelicans were not.

We were now passing through a region that in years to come would form the centrepiece of Kakadu National Park. The following day we visited the Indigenous rock art at Obiri Rock, or Ubirr as it is called today, and Nourlangie, before continuing on to camp at Yellow Water Billabong near Tom and Judy Opitz's place at Cooinda. The next day we made for UDP Falls—Uranium Development Project Falls was a dreadful name for such a special place. Rising near the headwaters of the South Alligator River, Waterfall Creek is a series of small falls that lead to the escarpment where the crystal clear water tumbles down 70 metres or so into the pool below. Surrounded by pandanus, palms, paperbarks and eucalypts, it is truly an idyllic setting that now has the Aboriginal name of Gunlom. Nearby is a place called Christmas Creek, which houses an extensive collection of rock art that is now deemed a sacred site not available to the public.

The survey expedition through the Kimberley and Top End was a success and we decided to add it to our itineraries. We introduced our 31-day 'Northern Frontier Safari': Alice Springs to Broome along the Tanami track, Broome to Darwin through the Kimberley and along the Gibb River Road. The tour then turned south through Arnhem Land to Roper Bar and Borroloola before heading back to Alice Springs. The tour could be purchased whole, or in sections in and out of Alice Springs, Broome and Darwin.

That was a pretty adventurous experiment in those days, I can tell you. It was tough country, the biggest problem being the section between Roper Bar and Borroloola. Black soil country! Any water about and it's like driving through glue. But I knew I was on a winner.

CHAPTER 16

IT'S HARD TO GET GOOD HELP

AND SO IT CAME time to analyse where we were at. We had pioneered a segment in the travel industry and developed an Australia-wide reputation, and business-wise we now knew what we were doing, sort of. Product-wise we had tried all manner of options and we now knew what worked and what didn't, sort of. We don't live in a perfect world.

We still suffered from the seasonality plague which we would dearly love to address, and I did have some ideas, but first we needed to get the tours we had committed to operating smoothly. That would tell us if the fly/road and fly/in, fly/out itineraries we loaded into our program would continue to improve.

We had a good cash flow, but there was still not much sticking as it went past. However, there was plenty going back into the business. Of concern, though, was Australia's economy. It was not very stable in those days as inflation was alive and well, and interest rates were on the rise. I used often to reflect on the fact that we still had no serious opposition. The 'mushrooms' kept popping up here and there, but they faded as quickly as those in the fields. The odd ones that hung on were operating in regions where we hadn't developed a presence, like Cape York and Perth. We were available

IT'S HARD TO GET GOOD HELP

as a model, but to take us further in the markets we now dominated would require a lot of time and money, so we felt comfortable putting all our revenue back into the business.

Staff was still a major cause of concern. Manfred Leis lasted one year. He met a lady on the tour and left to marry her. That woman would have no idea how much she cost us. Peter Harrison was a sook. He gave us all this bullshit about the tours he used to take into the North African wilderness. He had references, too, but I don't think they had bush like we had bush. I think they went from village to village where you could get help. Left to his own devices he was as useless as a glass eye at a keyhole. John Knox had taken his position with AAT. Dusty 'retired' to his camp at Borroloola to write books and Rosey got busy building Abode houses in Eltham.

So we had Brian, myself, number-one son Russell, or 'Boss' as he was known, and Ian 'Sticko' Weatherly as tour leaders and Peter Hartigan, Peter Rynia, Mick Grey and Bob Wagstaff, either in training, or about ready to lead their own tours. With more trucks on the road the time had come, however, when crews could disappear for weeks before I caught up with them. Regrettably, it had become more impersonal. What I had to get my head around was a training manual. We needed to have a formal script so that tours were operated our way. It needed to be documented, and I had to be able to 'point to the rules', so to speak.

The first step was to see if an applicant could drive. I do not mean work the steering wheel, knobs and levers; I mean handle a machine. In our work the driving had to be smooth, real smooth, as to me there's nothing worse than your head being thrown about when a vehicle accelerates, brakes or corners. Our job was to make the passenger feel relaxed and secure, and if an applicant did not have the natural feel for driving in the appropriate manner, he was no good to us. Poor driving also has an adverse effect on fuel consumption and brakes, and when a vehicle is clocking up big kilometres, that is costly. So that was it, no second go. I had no interest in teaching people how to drive. The applicant either had the feel or he didn't.

The first document in the manual was a general knowledge questionnaire on inland Australia that anybody looking for employment was handed, along with an application form requesting name, address, previous employment and the like. They were to complete the documents and call back for an appointment on completion.

Did it drive applicants away? It sure did, but if they weren't interested in further education they were no good to us either. Education was the most important part of our business: creative leisure, have a holiday and learn a little at the same time. It was interesting that those who did the work to answer the questionnaire sooner or later got a job with us; our method eliminated much of the interviewing procedure.

We then created a running sheet for each tour that contained a commentary for each day with pertinent information on points of interest, good sites for bush camps with mileages, names of contacts in national parks, camping parks, stores and the like. It also listed businesses where repairs, services, spare parts might be obtained, and so on. They were detailed to such an extent that an experienced tour leader working a particular itinerary could, in an emergency, switch to another without the need of a familiarisation tour. There was also a cook's manual with menus for ten days, recipes and information on ingredients and brands, together with shopping locations.

The one regret I had when employing tour leaders was that I couldn't employ females. We had some great girls working as cooks who would have made fantastic tour leaders but for physical limitations. Manhandling spare wheels down from the back of trucks, changing flat tyres, replacing leaves in broken springs requires a lot of brawn. And there was no road-side service out there.

•

When I first began driving a coach it was a bus, a coach captain was a bus driver, and tourism was an embryonic industry. There was no concise regional history that could be imparted to clients. There was not one scrap of information available on tour guiding or people management. And certainly there was no school on basic psychology. I soon learned that I had better give that subject some very close attention because people management was 75 per cent of the job. It didn't take me long to understand that we were unique in the world of business: we lived with the purchaser of our product for 24 hours a day until they had consumed that purchase. Not an easy task and certainly not a job for everybody.

There is a saying that all people are different. Well, they are, but after a while I found there were only three types that travelled with us; they just arrived in different appearances. I called them the Vague, the Venturesome and the Vocal.

The Vague are those who, when on holiday, just let their mind slide into neutral. They ask the same questions every day, become generally helpless and follow you around like a pet. They are nice people really, but can get under your skin at times. I recall one who was with me on a highland tour in Papua New Guinea. Years later I took groups there for the big Highland Sing Sing. When we arrived back at the hotel in Port Moresby on the return journey, I asked the folk to bring their air tickets down to breakfast so I could organise a group check-in. They followed instructions faithfully and while I was sitting quietly at the table having my breakfast, one Vague, dear soul, put her ticket on top of my buttered toast.

Another Vague encounter remains etched in my mind—it occurred when we were camped at Granite Downs near the top of the old Oodnadatta Track on the way to Alice Springs. I should add here that the most important thing that needs to be addressed when people are living in such a close environment is hygiene. It's not easy to put into practice, but you try. Because if one gets a bug, you all get a bug.

Toilet training was always discussed first night out. Obviously, there are no ablution blocks in many places so the simple camp system was girls out to the left and boys out to the right. Camp selection took this into consideration and reasonable shelter was a requirement. The first thing that should be set up in a camp is a dish of water and soap, and then you inform people not to wash hands in the dish, just scoop some water out and I'd keep topping it up.

The 'shovel dunny' is another training requirement. When we first began the tours with Land Rovers, I had a spade strapped to the front mudguard. Later when we designed and built our Desert Cruisers with a compartment for all manner of equipment, I had two long-handled shovels so we could move it along in peak periods. Burying ablutions was an absolute must because there is nothing worse than sitting around the campfire and having a piece of secondhand toilet paper fluttering through the camp on the prevailing breeze. Thus the necessity for lectures on the management of one's own personal waste disposal system.

Anyway, on this particular journey I was up early as usual because I like to get my head around the day in peace and quiet. At this camp girls to the left was south and boys to the right was therefore north. So I headed east, away from any early morning traffic, straight into the rising sun where there was a bit of shelter so I could be alone with my thoughts and anybody looking in that direction would be blinded by the sun.

There I was squatting behind a little bush when I saw this woman, a Vague, striding out from camp, lit up like a biblical vision and walking straight at me.

'Excuse me, I'm here,' I yelled in warning.

'Oh, Bill,' she said, lengthening her stride. 'There are a couple of things I wanted to ask you.'

Jesus Christ! 'Excuse me,' I said. 'I'm busy.'

'Oh, sorry,' she said. Then she spun 180 degrees, gazed in every direction and walked north towards the boys' bushes. It's bloody embarrassing, the last thing anybody needs at six o'clock in the morning.

The Venturesome ones are the majority. They spend their money on a holiday that they have researched thoroughly, they are determined to enjoy themselves, and they are collectors of experiences. They were the key to the success of our creative leisure concept. They were all too eager to keep the show rolling along to feed their passion and they were an absolute delight to travel with. There is a high number of mature females in this group, skinny little things with wire legs, walk forever, climb anything. Many of them had been to every corner of the globe.

Venturesomes came from all walks of life, too: the daughter of a British prime minister, internationally acclaimed academics, journalists and writers whose names were household in both Australia and their country of origin, ministers in the government of the day, a famous surgeon, the most senior police officer, shop assistants, students, retirees, construction workers and wharf labourers—the list goes on. They were people not drawn together by demographics but by inner need.

Finally, we have the Vocal: it is in this mob that you get the most variation, from those who know all things, to the ones who just love the sound of their own voice. They exceed the ratio of balanced communication, i.e. 50 per cent listen and 50 per cent speak, with an unhealthy bias towards the latter.

Then there are the insidious bastards, Vocals who are always in somebody's ear, not satisfied until they are dissatisfied and constantly working to make everybody else dissatisfied and undermine the success of the tour. The itinerary is wrong, we should have more time here, less time there, the food's unhealthy, camping parks substandard, on and on they go—they are a real pain in the arse. I really struggled with some right up until the last day and kept saying to myself, 'This will be over soon, this will be over soon.' And one day it is.

So it's no picnic in the park taking a group of people into a harsh and unfamiliar environment—it can be bloody stressful. I have come home from trips absolutely drained then had to service the equipment, reprovision and attend to the too-hard basket, before leaving again in five days. What makes it worthwhile is a good group of punters, who just want to get on with it and have a great time.

·

Writing about the business has reminded me that over the years I have had several people, both men and women, thank me for giving them the opportunity to not only take part in the building of the business but for the influence their time working with us had in developing them into the people they are today. It was character-building stuff, and if any of them read this yarn they will know who I am writing about.

It also reminded me about a couple of the employees who passed through the system fairly quickly, before we formalised our training manual. There weren't many of them, actually, which is probably why they stuck in my mind.

Roy and Vera came as a team and completed two tours. On the first one he returned with a tooth off a gear. I put that down to bad luck, but I was to discover Roy had absolutely no 'feel' for a vehicle at all. He could never sense something might be amiss, never hear it, never see it and never smell it, nothing, and you can't put brains where there aren't any. Their second tour was a Burke and Wills in a Bedford and I got a call from Tibooburra saying he needed a new engine. Roy had developed a radiator leak between Broken Hill and Tibooburra, kept driving and cooked the motor, and then he even had to go to the town workshop to ask what was wrong. So I told Roy to get it into the workshop and give the bloke a hand to pull the motor out and I would deliver a new one. For the life of me I do not know how he got under my guard, because a mandatory requirement for the job was to be a 'Mr Fixit'.

The following morning I took off in the old Holden Kingswood, the only vehicle we had available at the time, to Don Kyatt's to pick up a motor with gaskets, filters and necessary bits before heading to Tibooburra. It was about seven o'clock at night when I got to Broken Hill and I was buggered, so I pulled into the West Darling pub in the main drag and booked a room, dropped my stuff and headed to the bar for a long cold beer, or two, and a steak sandwich.

I got to Tibooburra the next day, unloaded the gear in the workshop, discussed the project with the local mechanic, then pulled Roy and Vera aside for a serious chat. I was in no mood for debate. I pointed out that the sixteen days that they would be away on this tour would provide employment for them and, hopefully, enjoyment for the sixteen people on board, but was a financial disaster for me. However, what was done was done. My interest now was the brand new engine in his truck. 'Look after it like a newly born baby,' I told Roy.

When they eventually arrived back and I debriefed them, I noticed Roy kept holding his hand up to his face every time he spoke. Weird, I thought. He also looked like he had cold sores. I went through the unpleasant procedure of having to let them go, the downside of employing teams; losing one loses them both. Roy had given me no alternative, though. Apart from the gearbox and engine disaster, he only produced five comment sheets from sixteen passengers, which meant he had destroyed the bad ones, and the ones he passed in weren't too good. So he had stuffed up big time, and later I was to find out why.

Something came up about Vera when I was talking to one of our other girls and she said, 'Oh, didn't you hear the story?' She thought it was the funniest story she'd ever heard and proceeded to fill me in.

Apparently there was a female on the trip who took a fancy to Roy, and he, being flattered by the attention, did nothing to arrest the way things were going—more the opposite. As days went by Roy grew more desperate and decided to let his ferret out for a run, organising an early morning rendezvous with the female passenger. Sneaking together out the back of the camp somewhere they immediately went into an embrace, at which time the young lady asked Roy what his relationship was with Vera. 'None—there is no relationship,' he replied.

At precisely that moment they were both illuminated and blinded by the beam of a torch which moved quickly towards them. On arrival the light paused, then accelerated around them in a great arc before coming to a sudden stop, when the torch hit Roy in the mouth, splitting his upper and lower lips and knocking his two front teeth clean out of his head. 'So now there *is* no relationship,'

Vera said, and stalked off. Well, that immediately dampened Roy's ardour and he scampered back to the truck to nurse his wounds, while the little nymphet, I gather, fled in great haste.

Can you imagine the tension on the rest of that tour? It was enough to make me cringe.

CHAPTER 17

ALL ABOUT BUSINESS, BEDS AND BARRAMUNDI

The travel industry in the 70s was going through a pretty tough period, with rapidly increasing inflation, interest rates and wages. These were three very critical issues with our business. For example, we released our brochures in January of each year to give lead-in time to the tourism calendar of April to March, and therefore we priced our tours in November, prior to going to print, and we had to carry that price for fifteen months. We had no option other than to put a 17 per cent hike on each year and pray it was enough, and hope to goodness people would still buy it.

Imagine the difficulty we got into with the holidays we packaged with Ansett. We included the airfare to offer an easy-buy package and shot ourselves in the foot because they changed their airfares four times in 1977. The airlines were in the same boat as everybody else. Similarly, when I commenced the project of building our first two Bedfords, I did my sums on the basis of 16 per cent interest and thought that was outrageous. By the time they were ready for the road, the interest was more than 20 per cent. How do you run a business in that climate—on a bit of a wing and a prayer?

Government spending seemed to be at ever-increasing levels, although one exception was the travel industry. There were those among Whitlam's advisors and bureaucracy who saw it as a junket and would dearly have loved the Australian Tourist Commission (ATC) to be done away with altogether. I often wonder if the ATC 1975 promotion to North America, the one in which I participated, was seen by management as their swan song, because the miserable budget they were given to work with was about right to pay their rent. Fortunately Cabinet prevailed and we still retained Frank Stewart as Minister for Tourism and Recreation, so we did have a voice, for a short time.

When the Fraser government was sworn in on 22 December 1975 we were naive in thinking there would be a quick fix. Nothing could be further from the truth. He put the brakes on everything, even dispensing with portfolios; we didn't even have a minister for tourism. Bloody hell, and here we were reading newspaper advertisements next to ours on the travel pages of the dailies offering cheaper holidays to nearby overseas destinations, while we priced ourselves out of business and fattened the moneylenders. But then, I suppose, the government had no money left anyway. There is no money tree.

What the government did do, though, was form a select committee from both sides of the House of Representatives to study 'The Significance and Potential of Tourism'. I felt so strongly about all this that I drafted a submission and forwarded it to the committee. It was quite a lengthy presentation, and the key areas addressed were the following:

> Tourism offers an essential service, providing the facility for people to enjoy their leisure time constructively and creatively. It is educational. The leisure and hospitality industry employs a significant percentage of Australia's workforce and generates 1.5 billion annually. Surely it is important enough to warrant the appointment of a minister.
>
> Government assistance is needed for staff training; also tax breaks on the production and distribution of promotional material and on vehicles, spare parts and fuel excise in line with our near competitors. (New Zealand being one.)

> The Australian Tourist Commission should be given a wider role in tourism promotion and development with both domestic and international markets in their charter. It is an incongruity in that it stands apart from the development of the product that is its responsibility to promote, a product that is domestically uncoordinated and bereft of any statistical analysis. The ATC should be the link between government and industry.

I was called before the committee as a witness on 9 February 1977. There were four members present. Mr Robinson was acting chairman and Mr Cohen, Mr Jull and Mr Sainsbury were the members.

I was chuffed when the committee findings were published and Mr Cohen, the Labor MP for Robertson, offered the following which I copied from the official Hansard Report:

> I would like to congratulate Mr King on the quality of his submission and say that my own personal feeling is that people who are doing what I consider quite a courageous thing for the Australian tourist industry, people like Mr King, should be encouraged. I hope we come up with some solutions to the problem.

Now all of that made me feel very positive. Maybe, just maybe, we were making progress, although the acting chairman then gave us food for thought by stating that there was a serious conservation lobby to contend with. These 'greenies' believed there should be no tourist facilities at all in major national parks. Of course, being an elitist group, they did not bar 'themselves', whomever 'they' were, from access. I discussed this issue after the meeting with Barry Cohen. The committee members were well aware that these green groups were more prohibitionist than conservationist.

So that was the climate we were working in and we needed to plan our business strategy for the next two years: what tours, for which market, and what equipment we needed to do the job. We also decided that the time had come to shift the whole operation to Alice Springs and lease a suitable workshop, leaving sales and reservations in Melbourne.

So we had several new tours to add to our offerings in 1977–78, and it was not without difficulty that we floated our first initiative of 'Bill King's Red Centre Tours' with lodge accommodation. It was time to capture some Americans, we hoped.

We needed rooms with dunnies at Kings Canyon, Ross River, Ayers Rock and of course Alice Springs, so off I went to see the proprietors. I got beds at the Telford property in Alice Springs, Ren and Joy Kelly's Red Sands at the Rock, Di Byrnes's Mount Sonder Safari Lodge at Glen Helen (dunnies down the hall)—all 'no worries'—then I struck a snag. Gil Green at Ross River and Jim Cotterill at Wallara Ranch on the track near Kings Canyon told me to go and see Keith Castle at the Central Australia Tourist Association (CATA) as he had management of their rooms.

I thought, 'That's bloody ridiculous.' I had been in and out of both properties for years and while they would be full when a CATA tour went through, other nights they might not even sell a bed. So I went to Wallara Ranch again and saw Jim.

I told him that CATA weren't giving him 100 per cent occupancy, and I wouldn't rectify that problem either, but I would print a new tour in our brochure featuring his property and I'd guarantee to put 30 tours through next year. I explained it was a new initiative for us and I was upfront with him. 'I make no promises other than to dedicate a vehicle and all our marketing skill to the project,' I said, 'and we'll pay you a cheque for our accommodation as we walk out your door.'

'Leave it with me,' he said.

Was that a proposition too good to refuse? Obviously it was, because Jim gave us the beds.

I purposely waited until Jim came on board because I reckoned Gil Green at Ross River would be a little harder to move, but I need not have worried. Word had got around. 'Tell me what you need, Bill,' Gil said.

And so we had our new 'Red Centre Safaris' program with lodge accommodation, and even though we were a minnow in the scheme of things, we now had tours that appealed to all segments of the market.

•

The next initiative was to establish a barramundi fishing camp on the lower end of the Gulf of Carpentaria. A bloke in Alice Springs had approached me to bring our people to this hunting and fishing camp he was going to set up at the old Port Roper site, near the mouth of the Roper River. 'A little piece of tropical paradise,' he told me, 'rich in wildlife and game.' Well, that may have been true, but the Roper River was, and still is, a crocodile-infested waterway, so Val and I went with him for a look, Val and I in one Toyota ute and this bloke and his girlfriend in the other.

It certainly wasn't the most welcoming place I had ever been to. There were big stretches of wet black soil country to negotiate, and somebody had warned us that we might have to run the gauntlet with a rogue bull buffalo who hated motor vehicles. He had attacked a Land Rover once and all but tipped it over, with one of his horns jammed through a side panel. It was only when the horn snapped off that the Landy came back to rest. We did see the nasty old bastard—known as 'One Horn' for the obvious reason—and he was bloody huge, pawing the dust, throwing his head about and moving forwards threateningly, but he never came after us.

At disused Port Roper the floods had washed away the piles of the old jetty that was hanging out of the bank at a crazy angle. There was a big steel-framed shed that had lost half the iron sheets off its roof and sides in some cyclone, and the sheets that had blown off were lying all over the place, twisted and torn. It was just on dark when we got there, so I just rolled our swag out on the concrete floor of the shed under what was left of the roof and after a bit of grub we turned in.

I woke up in the early hours to answer the call of nature and saw in the moonlight some unexpected wildlife. There were snakes everywhere—moonbaking. They were just relaxing, lying on the warm part of the concrete that had been in the sun. Thankfully they weren't at our end of the shed so I quietly snuck out for my pee and wriggled back into the swag, making sure not to disturb Val and the snakes, otherwise we would have been spending the rest of the night sitting up in the front of a Toyota. Humans weren't prey for little reptiles and I reasoned that if I minded my business the snakes would mind theirs. I must say, though, I didn't get much sleep, keeping one eye open in the direction of our 'room-mates'.

The snakes had slithered off as the concrete grew cold, so I got up early and walked over to the river. It was a sight to behold in the morning sunlight. There is 80 kilometres of water between the mouth of the river and the high-tide mark at Roper Bar, and when it turns, as was happening that morning, it really comes down with some force, a head-on collision, with the waves coming in from the gulf creating a foaming mass of currents and counter-currents. What's more, there was a feeding frenzy in progress, a couple of dorsal fins wheeling and diving in and out of the swirling water, hunting the food coming down with the tide. I would not have fished there for all the coffee in Colombia.

It was about that moment I saw it. I was standing on a small beach in the middle of a slither mark. It was nearly a metre wide with claw marks as big as dinner plates. Bloody hell, he must have been a monster. Then I noticed the claw marks in the wet sand just under the water were visible with little clouds of silt still floating around them. The crocodile must have either heard me coming or by pure coincidence decided to go for breakfast just a minute or two before I arrived.

I never looked back, I can tell you. I scampered up the bank on all fours. I have never moved so fast. With the hair on the back of my neck still bristling, I threw our stuff in the back of the ute and Val into the front seat, then fled that Godforsaken place, vowing never to return. 'I'm off!' I yelled at the fool who'd brought us to this 'tropical paradise' and the site of his mooted fishing camp among snakes, sharks and crocodiles. The idiot was still in his swag, and I discovered later he had never been there before either. He had sucked himself in with his own bullshit.

•

Val and I went and saw Ray Fryer at Urapunga Station, and we came to an arrangement to camp on the Wilton River, which bordered his station lease. The Wilton is a tributary of the Roper and we set up a campsite a couple of kilometres up from the junction. We bought two boats with Mercury outboards and a heap of fishing gear that we could keep in a shed on the station. Our ten-day Roper River barramundi fishing safari out of Katherine, packaged with Ansett, was ready to go.

It was a great area for fishing. We could fish the Roper down as far as Kangaroo Island, the Hodgson River, and of course the Wilton. We each had our favourite fishing spots and boasted to one another about river knowledge and the like—this, of course, was governed by where you caught your last decent fish. I tried the tributaries and didn't like them much. That Hodgson was bloody spooky. It was serious crocodile territory, with really still water, and you could literally feel the eyes looking at you and smell the rotting flesh. I couldn't relax in that waterway.

I preferred the Roper near the mouth of the Wilton. That's where Val caught her big one. It was about four in the afternoon and we were idling along the north bank when Val hooked a snag, or what we thought was a snag, because the line anchored and the boat spun around. 'Ease it off a bit and I'll try and unhook it,' I said, grabbing hold of the line. No sooner had I got hold of it when it moved around to the other side of the boat. 'Shit, you've hooked something.' Her rod nearly bent in two. Whatever it was, it was big. I hoped it wasn't a croc. It had gone to the bottom, and we were idling in a circle around it. Then it took off, with Val hanging on for grim death.

It eventually stopped and she started to reel it in and so began a struggle that went on for about an hour. When Val finally won the battle I looked over the side and there was the biggest 'barra' I'd ever seen. I dived for the gaff but it wasn't there—always a problem with many people using the gear—so I hung over the side of the boat and grabbed it in the gill, hoping to Christ that no croc was eyeing it off for supper and took my arm with it. I heaved it on board and it was a sight I'll never forget—all 19.5 kilos of fish and all 49.5 kilos of Val, both lying exhausted in the bottom of the boat.

And what was it like to eat? Absolutely delicious. One of the station hands had his own secret recipe for barra, and it fed the mob at the station for dinner and there was still enough for a breakfast. Is there a better eating fish than fresh barramundi? I doubt it.

Unlike me, Ian 'Sticko' Weatherly liked the Hodgson because he caught some good fish there. On one particular trip he had a young honeymooning couple on board who were really keen on fishing. They quietly moved up the Hodgson—putt-putt-putt—Sticko took the boat under the lee of a huge fallen tree sticking out from a clump of pandanus on the bank. 'A likely spot for a bite,' he muttered to himself, when all of a sudden—splash! A croc must have been basking on the log, camouflaged by pandanus. It heard the boat coming too late and had to crank its heart rate up to get some movement, and by that time the boat had arrived. The crocodile shat itself, rolled off the log just as the boat passed underneath, and landed on board, half in, half out. This thing was nearly as big as the boat and it was only by some miracle that it didn't land on anybody, but it flipped the boat up in the air, whipped its tail around, and by the sheer weight of its tail took Sticko down with it.

Did I say the crocodile shat itself? Spare a thought for Sticko. Imagine being submerged on the bottom of the river with a huge freaked-out crocodile. Luckily Sticko was able to disentangle himself and swam the few metres to the bank, where he was relieved to see the honeymooners standing there hanging on to one another, their faces ashen to match his own. But here's the mystery. Sticko swears the couple was bone dry. 'How did you get ashore?' he asked.

'Don't know,' they replied.

Sticko said it was weird, they really didn't remember how they got onto the bank and his theory was that they either did a Jesus—their feet moving at such great speed that when they hit the water they ran across the top—or when the boat flipped it did so with enough force to throw them to the bank. Either way, they were dry.

The crocs must have really liked Sticko because he had another close encounter after that. He was heading towards Darwin and passed a small mixed farm on the river near Katherine. There was a sign out the front reading 'Pigs for Sale'. It sounded like a good idea for a barbecue, Sticko thought. So he stopped, saw the bloke and picked out a pig in the pen to have it all dressed out and ready to cook on his return.

At the camp Sticko rigged up a spit out of a couple of fence droppers and wire, but the pig took much longer to cook than he estimated, and by the time it was ready the punters were eyeing one another off as food. In the meantime the cooking smells had been wafting off down the river for hours, and when they were sitting around eating their meal in the silence that occurs when the guests are desperately hungry, Sticko heard crocodiles barking down by the river. He grabbed his torch and there they were: four sets of red eyes. The sneaky buggers had followed the scent up the river and were all lined up on the bank, waiting for their dinner. Sticko threw some firewood at them and they took off, but the punters slept in the Desert Cruiser and on its roof that night.

For the rest of us crocs weren't a problem at the campsite, although the little Aboriginal kids from nearby Ngukurr, who swam in the Wilton at 'Flat Rock', as they called it, never took any risks. Flat Rock was a huge sliver that protruded well out over the river a short distance upstream from our camp. They told us that a big rock dropped on top of the sliver echoed like thunder underneath, so they always dropped a couple to frighten the crocs away before diving in. Their ancestors had probably been doing that for thousands of years.

Most people think that crocs, snakes, spiders and other creepy-crawlies would be most likely to strike fear in the hearts of the city-dweller, but they're not—in fact, it's the green frogs. These amphibians breed in septic tanks in the tropics and the canny little devils have the instinct to travel through the system and arrive in toilet bowls. Imagine the yells from the female ablution block the first time somebody lifts a lid and there's a big green frog floating in the bowl! Then again, imagine the scream that reverberates throughout the camping park when one or more of the amphibians have concealed themselves under the rim of the bowl and start leaping about when an unfamiliar posterior replaces the toilet lid. Now I can tell you from experience it feels like being touched on the bum with a cold and clammy hand. It's bloody awful and, for the unsuspecting punter, crocodiles, snakes and creepy-crawlies pale into insignificance.

CHAPTER 18

HITTING THE BIG TIME

So we had our new program up and ready to go. We did another great brochure with Rennie and Beau and again had it packaged with Ansett. There was a blend of old favourites and new initiatives, and I was convinced we were gradually moving towards marketing the ultimate in outback holiday experiences. We had a mix of fly/fly and fly/road tours, twelve in and out of Broome, 135 in and out of Alice Springs, 65 in and out of Darwin, 52 other tours that were all road from Melbourne, and we had our fishing camp packaged with Ansett in and out of Katherine—250 departures with a wide range of choices.

It was not without some nervous feelings, I might add. Sticking our head in the noose to fund the new machinery made us very apprehensive indeed as the economy was not improving, and although passenger numbers were increasing our load factor was decreasing as we kept introducing more seats to service our new tours. But we were as ready as we would ever be. We took the punt that sooner or later the economy would make the turn and we would have the seats available to capitalise.

We still had Big Ben, Little Ben and Olga as backup vehicles and our four new M series Bedfords lined up to operate the main program. I had also ordered a Bedford VAM chassis with the 466 cubic inch engine to build a 28-seat Desert Cruiser to support Gertrude. So we were in for a shilling, in for a pound. We also had two Greyhound coaches on charter to fulfill our coach-touring program in peak periods.

The first advertisement we ran featuring our fishing camp at Urapunga on the Roper River prompted a call from the producer of the ABC's *Holiday* show. He wanted to send a crew to join one of our 'Barramundi Fishing Safaris' and gave frontman Jeffrey Watson the job, along with a cameraman, director and soundman. Sticko took them in one of the new Bedfords and I went along as 'mine host', and I must say the few days on the Roper did make great TV.

We had an unplanned night of campfire entertainment when a bloke wandered in and said, 'Share your campfire?' It was Buddy Williams, the legend himself. Buddy was regarded as the father of country and western music in Australia. He was the first Australian country singer to ignore the American origins and do original Aussie stuff. He was passing through Roper Bar to do a concert at Ngukurr settlement the following night. He and his party had camped nearby.

'Always wanted to go on a Bill King safari,' he said, as he and his mates pulled up their stools.

People would have paid a lot of money to be entertained the way we were that night as the stories and stubbies flowed around the campfire.

•

By now the unique style of holidays we offered was attracting constant media attention. We had something happening all the time. More than that, we had a regular stream of photojournalists approaching us for contra deals. We even got choosy, having been caught by one or two who did nothing. We asked to see examples of their work, something they were accustomed to anyway, we discovered. Not a week went by without Stan Marks, the publicity officer at the Australian Tourist Commission (ATC), calling me to see if I could help with some writer or forwarding me material their worldwide clipping service had come across.

Bruce Renton, the PR consultant and journalist with Arthur Todero's group of Italian media people, turned out to be a prolific worker. He wrote a story titled 'Il Mondo di Bill King' and it was featured in all manner of newspapers and magazines throughout Italy.

Almost as prolific as Bruce Renton was Götz Weihmanns, a German journalist from Stuttgart. Arthur Todero had contacted me in 1975 about taking him on a charter job in the Land Rover. Götz was a delight: he was twenty or so years older than me and a well-educated and active gentleman. One of his main clients was *Mit die Auto Zeitschrift*, the equivalent of our *Royal Auto* magazine, and later Götz began sending me copies of his work. For six issues in a row they featured lead stories on the Australian outback. I couldn't believe it, like, was this ever going to stop?

We were still the only operator in the Kimberley, as nobody else had the equipment to take on the Gibb River Road. Frank Palmos, a journalist with a new travel magazine, *Australian Trek*, invited me to write the lead article on the Kimberley for their forthcoming issue. Why wouldn't I?

The story that really made things happen, though, was in the Melbourne *Herald*. I received a phone call out of the blue from journalist Kenneth Joachim, who wanted to come out to Eltham for a chat. He duly arrived, we sat down and he started to interview me: 'You must have a lot of funny stories to relate. Tell me some of those.'

Well, it was at that moment I discovered something about myself—I was no stand-up comic. Sure, I could relate some funny stories, but not on cue. In conversation things lead to this and that and 'I remember when's'. But his question threw me, and I sort of shrugged my shoulders and said, 'Oh, they'll come to mind shortly,' then sat there waiting for the next question.

The longer we sat there looking at one another, the more uncomfortable it got and the less I had to say. It was really painful. Eventually he slammed the blank notepad and pencil onto the desk and said, 'Why do they send me out to do jobs like this when you're giving me nothing to write about?' Well, if I was intimidated before, how do you think I felt after that spray? I wanted to crawl under a truck.

Thank God for Sticko who knocked on the door and needed to talk to me about something. It was only 'shop talk', as he had just returned from the Centre, but I'd never been happier to see him.

I apologised profusely for the interruption to the journalist. 'Not at all,' said Kenneth, and he began asking questions. 'What did he mean about this?' and 'What was that about?'

Things began to thaw. He was an inquisitive journalist and knew as much about our business as we did. He ended up spending hours with us, talking to Sticko and Sandy Chapple, his cook at the time, and me.

The story was published in *The Herald* weekend supplement on 12 February 1977. It was a full-page feature, titled 'The Joy of Being King of the Outback', and had photos of Sticko, Sandy and me. Despite our uncomfortable start, he did listen to what we said and he did 'feel' it, and his words reflected those feelings: 'There's a land and people and birds and beasts and natural phenomena out there that combine savage beauty and serenity unmatched anywhere else in the world. It will ravish your eyes and your senses.'

•

The story also coincided with the release of our 1977 program and we could not believe the impetus that it gave us. At the time *The Herald* was the only evening newspaper in Melbourne and had a huge readership. We had produced a classy brochure, and more importantly the Northern Territory was beginning to grow as a priority destination with Australian holiday-makers. Bill King's Northern Safaris was now regarded as the way to do it.

Things began to move in Europe, too. A Dutch wholesaler came to visit me and wanted to see our programs when they were ready. Helmut Voss, the principal of German wholesaler Inter Air Voss, called from the ATC office in Melbourne and came out to Eltham to talk about working with us the following year. We were starting to get European bookings, people just coming out of the woodwork, and I had a real gut feeling that when we did become packaged with wholesalers the business would come.

So, all was going to plan. Our bookings were reaching the targets we hoped for, and while we weren't operating with full decks, we were paying our way. And on the horizon was a windfall—August was always our best month because of school holidays, and we were fast reaching the 'sold out' sign.

By then I was not taking out many tours. With eight of our own vehicles now operating and two more on the way, plus two on charter from Greyhound, I was flat out making things happen, which was good—I could sit back a little and look at things objectively because I wasn't obliged to make decisions on the run. I was backwards and forwards to Alice Springs almost weekly at the start of the year, making sure the remote-control process was working with documentation and the like. We were still using the pay-as-you-go system. It became a little difficult at times with our biggest account, Ansett, paying us monthly, but I resisted the temptation to use credit.

Moving the whole operation to the Alice was keeping me busy as well. I found a factory development that was about to begin so we massaged the plan a little, arranged to have a pit installed in the floor and ordered a building virtually to our design. Bob Kennedy, the real estate agent, was a good bloke and when I said I was also looking for a shopfront sales office, he suggested, 'Why not here?', so we came to the arrangement to share his premises at the end of the Todd Street Mall. That was more than 30 years ago, and AAT Kings still operates from that same office.

With our affairs in Alice Springs in order I looked for a retail office in Melbourne and settled on premises in Ivanhoe. Val still had itchy feet, so she decided to share the shop with Bill King's Northern Safaris and establish a general retail travel agency as a Jetset franchise.

Although the summer trough was gradually levelling, we still had capacity for more work between October and March so I hired a vehicle and did some extensive exploration on the Tasmanian west coast, then with Sticko did a survey of the Australian Alps. That gave us two new itineraries: we began a 'Summer in the Mountains' program to operate out of Melbourne and shipped Bob Wagstaff and his Desert Cruiser across to Tasmania to operate a Tasmanian west coast tour.

So there we were in 1977, feeling good, with our itineraries established, our sales outlets open, our equipment up to scratch, and our marketing plan coordinated. All we had to do was make it all work.

CHAPTER 19

INTO SURVIVAL MODE

ON FRIDAY 19 AUGUST 1977 Ansett pilots called a snap strike, over what I have no idea. No planes were going to fly on Saturday or Sunday and we had all these people booked to fly out on that weekend. We had one Desert Cruiser in Darwin, four in Alice Springs and two in Melbourne; we had a Greyhound chartered coach in Darwin, another in Alice Springs and Gertrude in Melbourne—all waiting for passengers.

I was sick with worry. I was on the phone until midnight on Friday with Ansett's reservation manager, rescheduling all of our people for Monday. We could still pick up enough time and run a tour. I spent all day Saturday making arrangements with agents and the people who contacted us, informing them that they were departing on Monday instead. All but a few accepted the delay. Well, Monday never came. The pilots didn't fly until later in the week. We were stuffed.

I spent days going through our commitments and forward bookings. We had thousands of dollars to be refunded to clients. The new Bedford VAM was ready for delivery. We needed to get our brochure underway for the following year. We had the instalments on vehicles, our wages, we were heading into the quiet season—it went on and bloody on, and thank God I had not run our daily operations on credit. We were broke.

We needed $35 000—that's about $250 000 in today's money—and we needed it now. So I gathered up all my paperwork, forward bookings and history of business for the same period the year before and projections for 1978, and went to see my bank manager.

We had equity in our property on Main Road in Eltham, so I floated the request for a second mortgage. It would take some weeks before the bank could give us an answer, and we were sliding deeper into the shit—remember me saying that it was only the depth that varied? Well, we were reaching the bottom of the pit. I do not remember anguish like that before or since, and I'll never forget the day the bank manager called and said he had recommended the transaction be approved. It was like a tonne weight being lifted off my shoulders.

An ever-present worry was still vehicle reliability, apart from the M series Bedfords. Nothing, it seemed, would ever save us from vehicle breakdowns. They were as inevitable as the sun rising in the east, and it was just a question of how nasty they turned out to be.

Russell had a beauty out near Kings Canyon. He broke the rear axle housing in half on Big Ben, dropping the differential banjo into the dirt, with the tyres jamming in the wheel arches and dragging the whole shooting match to a halt. For those unfamiliar with the workings of a motor vehicle, to say that was a serious breakdown would be a gross understatement. He was about 20 kilometres from Wallara Ranch, the nearest telephone, and there was bugger-all traffic on that road, so he set off for a nice walk.

We got a differential banjo from W&P Machinery, pulled the back seat out of the Kingswood, cut a hole through the panel from the boot into the car with the oxy so we could fit the thing in, and Brian set off on his non-stop mission to deliver the differential to Kings Canyon in a Holden Kingswood. While we're on the subject, the Kingswood was a bloody good car. It would go anywhere. If it rained, however, you were in trouble, so you just stayed home.

Peter Rynia then had a corker when a connecting rod went through the side of the engine block. For the uninitiated again, if there are six cylinders inside an engine driving it along and a part of one breaks and flies out through the side of the motor, leaving a gaping hole, you're in deep shit. More so when you're halfway down the Tanami Track.

Our Peter was not one to be deterred. He dismantled the engine and discovered that all the damage was confined to one cylinder, a bit of luck, so he took out the remaining bits of piston and connecting rod, the rockers off the head gear to blank off the valves, and lo and behold he had a five-cylinder Bedford instead of a six.

The next problem was the gaping hole in the side of the engine block. He couldn't start the motor because it would have thrown the oil out of the hole. For whatever reason, he had a sheet of fibreglass and some resin in the truck, so he bandaged the dreadful wound, sealed it with resin, waited overnight for it to cure and limped back to Alice Springs, only two days late.

Mick Grey was another who got in strife on the Tanami, breaking the front cross members, the ones that hold the engine in place, which left the motor dangling off the gearbox and resting on the ground. Mick used a bit of ingenuity, some chain and the winch cable to create a cradle for the engine to rest upon so he could get the truck back to Alice.

Bob Wagstaff was not to be left out of those stories. He was well up the Oodnadatta Track, beyond William Creek, when I received the call from someone or other that one of our trucks had broken the ball off the front live axle housing. This awful occurrence left a front wheel lying on the road, and who the bloody hell had ever heard of that before? The message was to just get a ball and a front brake line to William Creek and he could fix it. There was weather about and there was no way I could risk driving the Kingswood, so I started ringing the air charter guys at Moorabbin Airport for a quote and we soon took off on our mercy dash.

We were flying above Leigh Creek, dodging around these monster black clouds that if you came anywhere near would blow you in every direction. Suddenly the pilot started yapping on his radio to DCA (Department of Civil Aviation). 'Your missus wants you to give her a call urgently.'

'Bloody hell! What now?' So down we went in a spiral, with my stomach in revolt and my eardrums threatening to burst. He landed at Leigh Creek and taxied up to the shed that served as an airport terminal with a public phone on the side.

I phoned Val and the problem was Gertrude. She'd broken down near Kingoonya and needed a water pump. So I called Detroit Diesel in Adelaide and arranged for one to be at the Adelaide airport at a place designated by the pilot, and we continued our mercy mission.

Bob was waiting for us at William Creek. One of the blokes from Anna Creek Station had kindly given him a lift. So it was one down and one to go. From there we flew straight to Adelaide to pick up the water pump and deliver it to Kingoonya to get the show on the road again.

•

Kingoonya, or not far from there, was the scene of my worst breakdown ever. Gertrude was only about a year old in 1968, and John Knox and I were bringing a school group down the South Road after a trip to Ayers Rock. It had been raining lightly on and off for the whole tour, but when we left Coober Pedy it dropped by the bucket load. We only needed to make it to Pimba, where we would hit the blacktop, then, as we started to churn through mud, we thought that if we could just get to Kingoonya we could hire the local hall and have some shelter until the rain stopped.

But that wasn't to happen. The Allison automatic transmission gave up the ghost just after we struggled through a monster bog hole. And remember that the South Road in those days was not the South Road of today. It was a dirt track, and we were stuck about 80 kilometres north of Kingoonya.

Good fortune was on our side, though. We had broken down on a rise but were surrounded by water. Knoxy got a lift back with a passer-by to see if we could get hold of a vehicle at Mount Eba Station to ferry our group to Kingoonya. He did better than that. The owner and one of his blokes came back in a couple of Toyota four-wheel drives and offered to ferry our mob firstly back to Mount Eba and then to Woomera. The rocket range covered the whole of the station lease and had tracks all over it that were obviously known to them.

Now that was some operation, getting 40 kids and two teachers to Woomera in a pair of Toyotas. Those Mount Eba blokes did an incredible job. Knoxy had also arranged for a coach to set off for Woomera to pick up the group, it was all blacktop to there. So they were taken care of but now we were on our own.

We started the serious business of fixing the transmission, and it soon became obvious it was stuffed. But we were lucky again. A car load of drink-sodden Yugoslavs from Coober Pedy came by, the last vehicle we would see for some time, and Knoxy got a lift to Kingoonya to organise Detroit Diesel in Adelaide to send up a transmission and an engineer. Beer was also on his shopping list. We had plenty of grub and beer but it was Southwark, hardly my favourite beverage. Meanwhile I began the task of removing the transmission and by the end of the day had gone as far as I could without help.

So the wait began, one day, two days, then three days—but no traffic and no Knoxy. By the fourth day my mind was playing all sorts of tricks. He's pissed off and left me, maybe the Yugoslavs kidnapped him, maybe he's crook. Then I reasoned that there was no traffic, the roads must be shut and he was dependent on a lift, so that's why he hadn't come back, I hoped.

There was a dead mulga nearby, its single trunk as straight as a gun barrel, which was unusual, so I began throwing the endless supply of rocks at it, then as the pile grew I began building a cairn. I remembered that's what Sturt did to keep his men occupied way back in 1844 when he was stuck at Depot Glen, although he was stuck because of the heat and I was stuck because it was still raining.

The monument grew and grew and another day went by and by this time I was getting a bit stuffed. I was sitting by the campfire drinking a stubbie and I saw this ant grab a crumb that had dropped off a biscuit I'd eaten. He was one of those spindly ones about a centimetre long that you see everywhere in the bush. They build vast nests and when rain is coming they all stand around facing inward with their bums and back legs up in the air waving about, having a little corroboree.

This little ant pushed, pulled, dragged, shoved and fought with others who wished to relieve him of his prize in his determined effort to replenish his larder, all of this even before he had passed from my line of vision. I was intrigued, so I grabbed another stubbie and wandered along in an extremely slow pursuit. He came to a puddle and ran here, ran there, keeping an eye on his prize, then he circumnavigated the water, and I could see he was taking the same straight line to his destination. I had no idea how far I had gone until I looked up, and our camp must have been at least 150 metres away. I didn't know ants would travel that far for food. I had followed him for hours and he still hadn't reached his destination; he was still pushing, pulling, dragging and fighting off bandits when I got sick of it.

Day six, and I was really starting to worry. It was as if I was the last person left on earth. I split a bit of mulga for the fire, and it was full of little black ants. There was also a natural compartment in the middle and in it was a skink about 20 centimetres long that had grown to the shape of the compartment. Unable to escape his chamber, he had apparently spent his whole life feeding on the little black ants that tried to walk past every day. He was transparent, too. I could see his organs working inside him. There was no movement, his body was just limp, as if he was dead, but he was pumping away on the inside. It was amazing. I put him on a rock in the warm sun that had begun to appear now and again and he slowly began to darken. Then I went to move him, I didn't want him to get sunstroke, but before I touched him he was off. There was no thank you, kiss my bum, nothing—he was gone.

It was day eight, really early in the morning and I heard a vehicle coming from the south. It was so quiet I could hear it for ages before I saw this speck in the distance that grew larger and larger. You have no idea of the apprehension that consumed me while I waited for that little speck in the distance to become a reality. Eventually the speck became an old Austin tray truck, and, thanks to the good Lord, Knoxy was on board.

Knoxy had got the lift two days before with no idea that Amin, the guy who picked him up, was a Muslim. At sunset the little bloke in the truck went off to pray to the east, and the following day was also his day of prayer, so five times he went off into the scrub to pray to the east while Knoxy sat by the truck and twiddled his thumbs. Little did Knoxy realise that they were only a few kilometres down the road from where I was. He could have walked back, but with all that was going on when he left he couldn't remember exactly where we were.

Amin stayed while I cooked them some breakfast and traffic began to appear. The road was open. Amin told us he had a business carting supplies from Adelaide to Coober Pedy. He would enquire around town to see what would sell well then scoot down to Adelaide to buy it. This particular trip he had capsicums, chillies and cement. He reckoned he would make 'good dollar' in that lot.

Knoxy and I had plenty of time to fill in, waiting for the engineer from Detroit, so we began picking up the two-man rocks to put around the one-man rocks that I had started the cairn with. We finished the job, and I must say that the monument looked very impressive indeed, well over 2 metres high and similar through the base, so much so that in later years it became a legend of the South Road.

You have no idea of the stories that came back to us about that cairn. There was a murder there when a stage coach hold-up went wrong. It was one of John McDouall Stuart's base camps on his 1861 expedition across Australia. It was a depot for the camel trains that used to ply their trade between the Adelaide market and the stations up north. Our blokes, of course, knew the real story, but when they told people the truth about Knoxy and me being stuck there for nine days, building the monument out of sheer boredom, nobody believed them anyway. The other stories were much more interesting.

The new South Road is nowhere near the original so I went searching for the cairn a few years back. I found it, too, but it was no longer a monument. Before the opening of the new road people from bus tours were climbing all over it to have their photos taken and had reduced it to a heap of rubble, still with the mulga tree sticking out of it, but at a crazy angle.

CHAPTER 20

THE GERMAN EXPEDITION

THE TIME HAD COME to put my head around 1978. This was the year it was all to come together, the culmination of all of our plans. It was our tenth year in business and I well knew where we had been, I knew where we were at, and I knew exactly where we were going.

The good feeling paid off, too. The Fraser government released the findings of its Select Committee on Tourism and increased the Australian Tourist Commission's (ATC) budget more than eight times, and gave Phillip Lynch the job of overseeing tourism under his portfolio of Minister for Industry and Commerce. So my trip to Canberra had been worthwhile.

Staff-wise we had never been better off. After try, try and try again we had finally put together crews who took pride in their work. They sorted out problems themselves. If we put somebody on who wasn't up to the mark, the crew would take it upon themselves to say, 'Hey, mate, we don't do it that way. Do it right.' So the cream eventually came to the top. Quality fosters quality. I felt also that I had finally developed a bit of business acumen, too; I wasn't born with it but I certainly learned a lot over ten years, the key being to surround yourself with the right people. They weren't perfect, mind you, and from time to time made wrong decisions, but anybody who says they haven't made mistakes is either a liar or too old to remember. It's part of the learning curve.

•

I had a huge program of tours to put together for 1978. We printed seven brochures and two flyers. One flyer was for tours to Papua New Guinea that I was to escort, the first of which was to attend the annual Highland Sing Sing. The second flyer was for two expeditions to Cape York to seek endangered parrots: five of the world's rarest birds. I had decided to experiment on both of those concepts with our past passenger list and top up with advertisements in the Melbourne *Sun*, if need be. We would test the water and see how they worked before releasing a full program of departures. We took a zoologist with us on the 'Seek the Rare Parrot' expeditions, and Sticko and Robyn Rynia, who had taken over as Sticko's cook, did the job.

We were seeking firstly the eclectus parrot, a large bird, up 40 centimetres in length. It is one of the most colourful of Australian birds and confines itself to the tropical rainforest canopy. Wary by nature, it is found on the east side of Cape York, near Princess Charlotte Bay.

Sharing the same habitat is the rarely seen red-cheeked parrot, a much smaller bird with a noisy 'voice' and bright green plumage that blends with the rainforest canopy.

The golden-shouldered parrot grows to some 30 centimetres in length and is one of our rarest and most strikingly beautiful birds. Even though it inhabits a substantial area of savannah woodland from the western tip of Cape York, across the Gulf of Carpentaria into Arnhem Land, it is not often seen.

The palm cockatoo is a large and conspicuous bird that is widespread in Papua New Guinea. However, in Australia it is confined to the rainforest on the northern tip of Cape York. A big bird of some 60 centimetres in length, it has black or dark grey plumage and is probably the most raucous of all Australian birds.

The little fig parrot is one of the smallest and least known of our colourful parrots. It inhabits small pockets of rainforest from Cooktown to South of Cairns and a small colony exists on the New South Wales and Queensland border.

We were successful in identifying all of the birds on both of our expeditions, and that led to a story in *National Geographic*.

•

One day I received a call from Arthur Todero, the manager of the Australian Tourist Commission in Frankfurt. He must have received some dollars from the new ATC budget and wanted to put this road show together and travel across Germany doing agency seminars, with me as guest speaker. 'Fair go, Arthur,' I said to him. 'Firstly, I've never done any public speaking in my life, and secondly, I don't speak one word of German.'

'Doesn't matter,' he said. 'Everybody in travel here speaks English.'

'Yeah, but not my English.' I recalled taking Götz Weihmanns through the outback and there was a big difference between his English and mine—mine being very Australian.

But Arthur refused to take no for an answer. And it was a pretty good deal. I only had to get myself there and pay my own expenses and they'd take care of the rest.

Arthur had got in Qantas's ear, and Heinz Wellbrock, the sales manager for Germany was in, so I assume that gave him a lead on Richard Tunbridge, Ansett's manager in the UK and Europe, who came on board. That left John Fleming, sales manager for Trans Australia Airlines (TAA) in Europe, with no option. With Manfred Dreke, PR consultant for the ATC in Germany, that was the team.

We were doing shows in eight cities—Frankfurt, München, Stuttgart, Hanover, Düsseldorf, Cologne, Berlin and Hamburg—and Arthur had invited travel agents and wholesalers to the hotels for an 'Australian dinner': I use the term loosely as, understandably, some of the hotels struggled with the theme. We had no idea what to expect and were shocked when more than 250 agents accepted for the first show in Frankfurt. Imagine the bill!

Arthur ran the shows, introduced himself, talked a little about the ATC and its role in Germany and then introduced Richard Tunbridge, who talked about Ansett services. John Fleming was up next. He had a German mother and English father, grew up in England and spoke 'kiddie' German. He was well aware that it created mirth when he spoke to Germans; however, he had never done it in a presentation before and it had them rolling in the aisles. This broke the ice for Heinz Wellbrock, who showed all of the TV advertisements that Qantas did in the 70s joined together: they were fantastic, and featured a real koala as a passenger on Qantas flights in all sorts of humorous situations.

Then it was my turn. My first foray in to after-dinner speaking in a foreign country was quite a daunting experience. Arthur did the introductions, referring to me as a modern-day explorer, a pioneer in the travel industry, king of the outback and on and on. 'Jesus Christ, Arthur. Shut up and let me get on with this,' was all I could think. Arthur had insisted that I wear my Akubra hat, my sleeveless sheepskin vest and my uniform shirt with the wedge-tailed eagle shoulder patches, but when I got to the rostrum he said, 'Here, take this,' and shoved a boomerang in my hand. Well, I have never felt like such a bloody galah in all my born days!

My mind was in turmoil, but somehow I managed to talk about the unusual experiences that can only be encountered when you leave the main roads, about living close to the earth, following bush tracks and century-old camel-train paths, absorbing the gifts of nature in the peace of the bush. Australia was a place where you could do these things, just pull off the road in a dry creek bed, set up a camp, gather some wood, light a campfire and sit around having a yarn and a few beers in complete safety. It was the unique quality of life that we enjoyed in the lucky country. I filled in my 30 minutes and I was relieved to get the first job done. The audience applauded but I don't know if they were just being polite, because I felt a pretty forlorn figure, like a freak in a circus.

And that was the format of the road show. Arthur really had the gift of the gab and the attendance at each show was amazing. It was successful beyond all our expectations.

For me as a tourist it was an eye-opening experience, from the vineyards in Stuttgart first planted by Benedictine monks more than 1000 years ago, to München, where in 1972 eleven Israeli athletes were slaughtered by the Black September mob, a dreadful happening in such a beautiful place, and Hamburg, a centre of international trade and one of the most important ports in Europe. 'Can't come to Hamburg without a visit to the Reeperbahn,' said Heinz Wellbrock. In those days the Reeperbahn was something else: it had strip clubs, brothels, sex shops, sex theatres and sex museums. What amused me most, though, were the coach loads of senior citizens. As we know, in Australia our senior citizens take their bus tours to the clubs along the Murray River to play the pokies. At the no-holds-barred sex theatres in the Reeperbahn, they watch the 'pokies'.

Our final show was in Berlin, at the Hilton Hotel. West Berlin in the 1970s was a fascinating place, with this bloody great wall that was never out of the news. People told me about living with their bags packed, ready to go, in a cash-only society, there were no credit card facilities outside of a few big hotels and large stores.

It seemed the Berliners of the 1970s were either young or old. The young were a 'way out' lot, to say the least, wearing their rebellious attire and attitude with pride. On the other hand the older folk would not pass out the front door without being 'properly' dressed, even when going for coffee and cake. Men in dark suits, with collar and tie, topcoat, hat and scarf; and the ladies in tailored suits or dresses with appropriate hose, modest-heeled leather walking shoes, with a smart topcoat, hat and scarf. They maintained the formal dignity of an era long gone.

The older residents had lived through the siege of Berlin, and many of them still bore the scars of that conflict. I had never seen so many limbless and wheelchair bound people before in my whole life. You couldn't sit at a sidewalk café without being conscious of the number of physically handicapped people, many in my age group, continually passing by. They were some of the 2 million or so who tried to hide in basements and cellars, while the Russians all but obliterated the city above them.

In Berlin I had an in-depth conversation with Manfred Dreke, the ATC public relations consultant, and he enlightened me about the travel industry in Germany and the size of the market, which was the biggest in Europe, and the reasons for it being so.

It was all about the aftermath of WWII. Everybody in Germany at that time was either born and grew up in the Cold War, or lived through and survived WWII. That history was still part of the German psyche. The Americans had nuclear weapons in silos all over Germany pointed at the Russians; the Russians had nuclear weapons all over Russia pointed at American targets on German soil.

The Germans couldn't wait for their holidays so they could get out of the place, hoping that if the big bang was ever going to happen it would be while they were somewhere else. Post-war Germany had become quite affluent. There were around 50 million people, they had worked hard, the Deutschmark was a strong currency at that time and they were buying more than 8 million package holidays a year. Research had also proved that they would travel 'long haul', an industry expression for long-distance flights, which meant that Australia's isolation was not an inhibiting factor.

Manfred asked me about our operation and I told him of our beginnings, following in the footsteps of the great overland explorers: Burke and Wills, Giles and Sturt. I described our first itinerary that went from Melbourne to the Gulf of Carpentaria to relive the tragedy and drama that surrounded the Dig Tree, the death of Burke and Wills and the survival of John King.

He was intrigued, so much so that when I looked at the Berlin newspaper that was under the door of my hotel room the following morning, there was a small photo of me on the front page. Even though it was in German, I could read Bill King and Burke and Wills in the headline and John King and Bill King in the caption beneath it. 'Read that for me,' I said to Manfred at breakfast, and he did so with a huge grin. It was about the Burke and Wills story and how John King survived by living with the Aborigines and now modern-day explorer, Bill King, a descendant of John King, was in Berlin to lecture travel-industry personnel on the Australian wilderness.

'I never told you I was related to John King,' I said. 'That's bullshit.'

'I know,' Manfred replied, 'but it's a very good story and I would not have got front page without it.' PR consultants!

•

I learned a great deal on that journey, including how to better qualify Australian colonial history to international visitors. At that time the term 'more than a hundred years old' was a common phrase used by our tour leaders as a measure of being history. That would mean nothing to a European of my age—that's when their father was born. I was of the opinion that we shouldn't measure our history by age at all, rather, we should emphasise the fact that we are a young nation that contains fine examples of colonial architecture and a very special natural environment around which our cities have evolved. They offer what we know as 'The Australian way of life', a quality of life unlike any other in the developed world.

That German promotion was really a feather in Arthur Todero's cap. Stan Marks, the ATC publicity officer, forwarded a handwritten memo to me on ATC stationery, which I found in my stuff when I began this story:

> AGM—SM 4-9-79
> For Bill King—at last trade support is having
> impact with our tours without our ATC involvement—
> I consider Bill's promotion here in 78 directly
> responsible for this starting.
> Regards, Todero
> Please pass regards to Bill from all here.

I was quite chuffed when Stan sent that memo to me. To make a contribution in developing an overseas market made my efforts feel worthwhile.

Business-wise the promotion had been fantastic. Opportunities had presented themselves at every venue, and several wholesalers had approached me for rates and itineraries to reproduce in their programs, saying 'We're so glad you're here.' Many of them had built their business on African adventures and safaris, and that had all turned pear-shaped with the likes of Idi Amin, who was at the height of his mischief-making by then, and bad things had happened to Germans in Africa. We were on the threshold of becoming a very successful inbound enterprise.

Germany was so busy—in fact the whole of the developed world was busy, and had been for a long time. I remembered reading a quote from Thomas Beddoes's play, *Death's Jest-Book*: 'Nature's polluted, there's a man in every secret corner of her, doing damned wicked deeds. Thou art, old world, a hoary atheistic murdering star.' Well, that was published in the middle of the nineteenth century. Goodness knows what he would write about today.

When our German market became established, they sometimes outnumbered the Australians on our tours. The Germans were nature-lovers and Venturesomes, and I could sense they shared my feelings when travelling through the outback. 'Wunderbar,' they would say, just gazing out the window at endless open space. Back then we could drive for a day and not see another vehicle. Drive the autobahns of Germany in 200-kilometre per hour traffic and as you pass by one little village you will see the church steeple in the next.

People would ask me, 'What are the Germans buying, Bill?'

My tongue-in-cheek reply was always, 'Nothing. I sold them nothing because they love travelling through nothing.'

CHAPTER 21

IN SEARCH OF SKYLAB AND PEOPLE GONE MISSING

At the conclusion to the German road show, Arthur had some business to do in the UK, which was fortunate indeed for me, as I had intended to visit the UK also. We were getting a lot of Brits on tours, appearing out of the woodwork, coming down to Australia to visit Auntie Myrtle, if you like, then getting sick of one another after a couple of weeks and deciding to have a bit of a look about. I was seeking a suitable sales agent or a wholesaler to package our tours at the source.

When I arrived in London I went to the Australian Tourist Commission (ATC) office to see the UK manager Bill Walker. He was sitting with his back to a window, and through the shaft of sunlight streaming in I could see silken threads, cobwebs, then I noticed a couple of them reaching down to his shoulder. I don't think Bill moved much. I told him of my mission and his reply was, 'It's a waste of time. The English market is all VFR.' VFR is the trade term for visit friends and relatives. 'The English aren't adventurous. They all go to Spain and sit in the sun.'

I then went to see the powers that be at Qantas and received the same answer: 'All VFR. The English aren't adventurous. They all go to Spain and sit in the sun.' I caught up with Richard Tunbridge at Ansett. He had no faith in the English holiday market and neither did John Fleming at Trans Australia Airlines (TAA). 'The British, adventurous?' Flemo scoffed. 'No way. They go to Spain and sit in the sun.'

I was perplexed. The British not adventurous? You could have fooled me! When I went to school the map of the world in my atlas was nearly all pink, and that was all British Empire. There had to be some Brits that didn't want to sit in the sun and I was determined to find them.

I had read somewhere about the British Airways Arts and Adventure Club, and thought 'That's us'. So I went knocking on their door and after much searching through an office complex as big a shopping mall, I found a bloke to talk to. I told him about our tours, our philosophy and the markets we sought. 'Great stuff,' he said, making me feel warm and fuzzy inside, but then he told me that since the African problems they had shelved the club and weren't doing anything with it. The arts and adventure club was virtually defunct. 'Have one of our ties,' he said and, you guessed it, it was a VFR tie, their family reunion club.

I was very depressed, to say the least, but walking along Piccadilly I glanced into an arcade and saw a sign, Boomerang Travel. 'That looks interesting,' I thought, and deviated in through their door.

A friendly fellow said, 'May I help you?'

I introduced myself and, not wanting to take up too much of his time, said we ran safaris in Australia along the same lines as they do in Africa: this was a quick and easy way to explain. Then I asked, 'What have you got on your shelves on Australia?' Well, there was nothing, not one brochure, not one piece of information on holiday destinations, no information on anything—all you could buy was an air ticket. I couldn't believe it.

I showed the bloke in Boomerang Travel a set of our brochures. 'Wow!' he said. 'Can I get a supply of this stuff?' I happily handed over a few to go on with. Then he added, 'Why don't you go and see the guys at Kensington Travel in Earls Court Road? They advertise a bit on Australia.' Well, thanks to the bloke at Boomerang Travel I got a lead that set us up with a sales agent in the UK.

Peter Siklos looked after our business at Kensington Travel. He was a Hungarian who sneaked out of the country in the 1956 uprising and got himself to the UK. He came down to Australia and hopped on a couple of our tours to familiarise himself with our product. Peter was a delightful bloke who was really passionate about our tours and from the first day he worked incredibly hard in that marketplace to promote our business.

o

A lot can happen in a year, and the Australian Tourist Commission began to allocate more resources to the United Kingdom and Europe. Ken Corbett got the job of putting together the first road show in the UK, in the same format as the ATC North American extravaganza in 1975, but condensed to a couple of weeks, which was much more sensible. Qantas got more serious, too, opening up a Jetabout office in Chiswick to put buyable holiday products into the UK travel agency distribution systems to support the destination information that the ATC began to publish.

It was the ATC's plan to develop a chain of 'special agents', and educate them on Australia by feeding them a constant stream of information and brochure material, plus ongoing support from the ATC office in London and the incentive of familiarisation tours to Australia. I participated in that exercise. We had already set up a sales office in London, with Peter Siklos at Kensington Travel, so it was most certainly a timely initiative for us. There were to be five workshops, the first to be held in London the day after our arrival at one of the airport hotels at Heathrow.

I remember that quite clearly because Brian Milnes, a good mate of mine, who was marketing manager of Ansett Pioneer at that time, announced to all and sundry who gathered in the bar after we had settled in, 'Champagne for everybody,' reaching for his wallet.

Having been to the UK the year before and discovering the Australian dollar was valued like 'Monopoly money', I said to him, 'Bloody hell, Brian. You'll need more than your wallet to pay for that.'

'Bullshit,' he said. 'They make the stuff in France, just over the Channel.'

To this day Brian and I still share that story. He went white when he saw the bill, but it was too late then. I don't think I ever said thank you to Brian.

We finished the UK promotion and the ATC were underway in setting up their special agent initiative. Britain did develop into an important inbound source for us, second only to Germany. Our international marketing had been through a long and expensive process, five years and three overseas missions, but it was now coming to fruition and justifying the considerable investment. The only market where I couldn't really get a foot in the door was the US, the people who, back in my naivety, I thought would have money falling out of their pockets for me. But that was about to change.

•

Some of you will remember back to 1979 when the media started telling us that NASA, the National Aeronautics and Space Administration, had announced that the 78-tonne Skylab research station, the largest apparatus man had ever maintained in space, had been abandoned and was about to be brought back to earth. 'Bloody hell, that's exciting stuff,' I thought, and I was certainly not alone. The Skylab story was big-time worldwide and huge in the US, and naturally when NASA first released that information everybody assumed that because it was American property it would arrive on American soil.

It became very commercial. Telescopes and monogrammed hard hats went on the market, insurance against being landed on was advertised, as were odds from bookmakers on a multitude of happenings, and basement Skylab parties became the thing to attend. The *San Francisco Examiner* even offered a $10 000 reward for the first piece of debris delivered to them within 72 hours of the crash.

However, it was soon revealed that NASA had not the slightest idea of where the thing was going to land. There was talk of China, then India, which sent the population into such a panic that some diplomats from Washington had to rush over and placate the prime minister at the time, Morarji Desai, who then issued those famous words of advice to the population along the lines of, 'It's no good thinking about dying until you're dead.'

NASA chiefs gathered in their HQ in Washington to collect the information on where it would land. They reckoned the time for decision would be when the space laboratory reached 120 miles above Earth, 48 hours before entry. Then it became known that the key decision would be made when it was 90 miles above Earth, when it still had enough fuel to fire it up and steer it somewhere. By this time, of course, people in the US were becoming apprehensive. NASA issued a statement saying that they accepted all responsibility and the government put together a huge team of experts, including police, fire services and medical teams.

Recriminations were now rife. 'The thing was built on the cheap: if it had been done properly it could have been brought back to earth safely.' Or 'The 2.5 billion dollar budget was not enough—a little more and it could have been saved.' The flak was coming thick and fast. Everybody was saying that if a bit of stuff hits some poor bugger, there would be hell to pay. The lawsuits would be endless. And then NASA released those famous last words: 'Don't worry, it's okay. It's all okay. It's going to land near Australia, about 1000 miles west of Perth in the Indian Ocean.'

Well, it's now history that on Wednesday 11 July Skylab started to break up over Papua New Guinea then left a 4000-kilometre 'spray' of debris right across Australia on a line through western Queensland to the Great Southern Ocean, with the bulk of it falling between The Olgas and Kalgoorlie. It missed the Indian Ocean by a very long way indeed. Sorry, somebody said.

If Skylab was big news in the US before it landed, imagine what it was like in Australia when the junk selected us to land on. It was media frenzy, and newspaper journalists and TV crews were all over the place trying to find out exactly what occurred. And when young Stan Thornton, a kid from Esperance, found the first little scrap, a Perth radio station sponsored him to go and get his $10 000 from the *San Francisco Examiner*. Then three blokes from the settlement of Rawlinna on the Transcontinental railway line found a big bit, about 2 metres long, which they loaded on a trailer and dragged off to Kalgoorlie for everybody to have a gander at.

I had a big map of Australia on the wall behind my desk so I took a good look at it, then checked our vehicle availability and thought, 'Why not?' We had two vehicles coming off their regular tours later in the year, so we could do it. I rang Terry Watts, our advertising agent, and said, 'Hey, get yourself over here. I've got a couple of ads I want you to place in the Melbourne *Herald* and the Adelaide *Advertiser* this Saturday.'

Well, I had hardly walked through the office door on the Monday morning when the phone rang. It was a bloke from Australian Associated Press (AAP) and he wanted to find out more. 'Do you know where "it" is?' he said.

Obviously none of us had any idea where 'it' was at that stage. 'I know exactly where it is. It's in the Great Sandy Desert,' I said. He seemed to be satisfied with that. He asked me several questions, thanked me profusely and promised to put in his release that it was the wildflower season. 'I may as well have another string to the bow,' I thought.

The phone never stopped all day. I had several phone calls from other journalists and radio stations and continued to do so for days, including a call from the ATC wanting information on the Skylab trip. They had received requests from all over the world for details. The AAP bloke's story created a remarkable amount of interest. In the United States it received no end of exposure with highly

Val's 'barra', all 19.5 kilos of fish, and all 49.5 kilos of her telling me 'Hurry up or I'll drop the bloody thing.'

SKYLAB SEARCH

A 4 wheel drive expedition will be leaving Alice Springs on Sept. 29 and Nov. 3, down the track called the Gunbarrel Highway, concluding in Adelaide. The itinerary is a flexible "search and see" mission taking in the Olgas, Lasseter's Cave, Warburton Aboriginal Mission, Kalgoorlie and Experance. Following as near as possible Skylab's "spray path". Metal detector carried on board.

15 days. $580 ex Alice Springs, plus we will arrange your special economy air fare.

Bill King's NORTHERN SAFARIS

For information contact:-
Northern Territory Govt. Tourist Bureau
157 North Terrace, Adelaide. Ph. 212 1133

We search for Skylab, and find the front door key to the American market.

Seite 6   **AUSTRALIEN**

Tournee durch acht Grosstädte
Australien-Werbung in der BRD
Fremdenverkehrszentrale und Qantas rührten Reklametrommel — Reisen verlost

Sydney (korr.). — Der fünfte Kontinent ruckt als Urlaubsland in den Blickpunkt. Noch vor einigen Jahren galt Australien als erstrebenswertes aber vorläufig kaum erreichbares Ferienziel. Günstige Flugverbindungen und ein umfangreiches, auf europäische Urlauber zugeschnittenes Angebot, machen eine Australienreise heute längst nicht mehr aussergewöhnlich. Das steigende Urlaubsinteresse, 1977 waren es 15 000 Besucher aus Deutschland, hat die mit Reise und Urlaub befassten australischen Organisatoren wie die Fluggesellschaft Qantas, TAA, Ansett sowie die Australische Fremdenverkehrszentrale veranlasst, erstmals in gemeinsamen, grösseren Veranstaltungen für das Reiseland Australien zu werben.

Durch acht Städte der Bundesrepublik Deutschland und Berlin führte kürzlich eine Informationsreise für die Reiseindustrie. Reisebüro-Expedienten und Mitarbeiter von Reiseveranstaltern konnten sich ausgiebig über das Urlaubsland Australien und das Transportangebot der Qantas unterrichten.
BREITE PALETTE

Arthur Toredo stellt dem deutschen Reisepublikum einen echten australischen Abenteurer vor, Bill King, der Urlauber ins australische Outback führt.

Arthur Todero and yours truly, hanging on to that boomerang, launch the German campaign in Frankfurt in 1978. The event was recorded in the German press.

OUTBACK AUSTRALIA

Overland expeditions with Bill King's Northern Safaris

Explore the Australian outback on a 4 wheel drive expedition. Itineraries vary from 3 to 30 days. Living deserts, pre-Cambrian mountain ranges, fascinating wildlife and 40,000 years of Aboriginal culture. You too can now experience the unique ecology of "The Timeless Land".

Bill King's Northern Safaris
224 Upper Heidelberg Road,
Ivanhoe, Victoria 3079, Australia.
Telephone (03) 497 3800.   Telex 33408.

Katherine, the first of our Mark 11 Desert Cruisers that we constructed on an M series 4 by 4 Bedford chassis. It was the image that became synonymous with our brand and was the vehicle that turned a dream into a reality.

One of the four brand new Dennings that we obtained, with our brand, when we merged our resources with AAT.

The Inbound Tour Operators Association members who did much of the groundwork in developing the American market with the Great Australian, the victim of a daring 'koala napping'.

L–R: Qantas Sales Manager from Germany, Heinz Wellbrock, Yirrkala tribesmen Murphy Dhulparippa and Michael Bungapidu, myself, and Ralph Nicholls, resplendent in his Northern Safaris uniform at ITB.

Steve Gregg and myself looking very pleased indeed, with the Australian Tourism Award in the category of Tourism Marketing for our Yulara Resort project.

Glynt, our heritage-listed retreat on the Mornington Peninsula.

The Bill King 'tent' in the foreground at Longitude 131, the exclusive and luxurious wilderness lodge that overlooks the spectacular sunrise at Uluru.

The boab tree carved by Phillip Parker King in 1820 at Careening Bay on the Kimberley coast.

The camel train at the Bangemall pub. They were still working the supply route to the Bangemall goldfields in the 1920s.

Photo taken by my father of Aboriginal tribesmen and women from the Yardie clan fishing Yardie Creek with traditional three-pronged spears and nets of woven vines.

'Jacko', the senior tribal elder of the Yardie clan, riding a turtle in the Indian Ocean.

regarded publications such as: *New York Times*, 'Skylab Searches!'; *The Chicago Tribune*, 'Go look for Skylab: Now there is a way you can'; *Newsweek Magazine*, 'Skylab Debris: Finders Keepers'.

Stan Marks, the ATC publicity officer, sent us some 28 clippings from American newspapers and magazine. We also received a huge amount of publicity in the UK: James Gilheaney in *The London Evening News* wrote, 'Now the Skylab Safari Lifts Off' while Georgina Walsh in the London *Evening Standard* wrote, 'Holiday Hunt for Skylab!—Space Age Adventures with Bill King'. Both included quotes from Peter Siklos.

On it went—the Netherlands, Germany, France—I had no idea that those two piddling little ads we ran could generate that much publicity. Our first tour was fully booked in the first week with Australians, then I received a telex from the Society for the Study of Space Fragments, or some such name, wishing to charter a vehicle for their group.

This was followed by a fax from the Audubon Society in the US. Somebody in their organisation had read a Skylab story in a publication that elaborated on who we were and what we did, mentioning programs like 'Seek the Rare Parrot Safari'. They were keen to seek rare birds, and we were happy to oblige.

Then I got another telex, this time from the Cornell University Herpetology Society, requesting information on an expedition to the outback for research, and yet another from the Sierra Club.

Bloody hell, nothing from the US for years and suddenly I found the key to the front door.

•

I no sooner got my breath back from that lot when I had a group of German wholesalers to take on an expedition for the Australian Tourist Commission. They were important people from major organisations and the ATC requested that I personally take the tour. I needed ten days away like a dose of Bali belly with what was going on, but that's the nature of the job.

We had eight in the group, and did the standard nine-day Red Centre expedition which visits all the gorges and chasms west of the Alice, Kings Canyon, Ayers Rock and The Olgas. All went according to plan until one of the lasses came up to me when we were walking through the Valley of the Winds and asked me to take her to the dentist. A crown on one of her front teeth had come off and all there was to see was a little peg poking out of her top gum and the crown in the palm of her hand.

'Well, my sweet,' I told her, 'there's only one dentist way out here and you're looking at him.' That frightened the bejesus out of her, but she got the picture. I had some Loktite in the truck that I knew was really good stuff, used for securing nuts and bolts under stress, so that evening I got her settled on a stool and laid all my 'tools' out on a table. I took her crown and did a test run to make sure I knew how it was supposed to fit then I packed around the tooth with cotton buds to keep it dry, so far so good. Next I put a little Loktite on the peg, followed by a little in the crown. I fitted it back on with my thumb, pressing the tooth firmly upwards until the adhesive went off. I held it for about five minutes to be sure we had given it every chance to work—until we got back to Alice Springs, anyway.

This was the least of my worries, though. The following day we did the walk up Mount Olga Gorge and I began to get really nasty chest pains. I had to sit on a rock while the group hiked up to the end of the gorge. I joined them on the return journey. By then the pains had subsided. 'Thank God for that,' I thought, and wondered later if I should do something about it.

Work-wise there was more and more going on. For months I was flying to Alice Springs on Sundays and back to Melbourne on Wednesdays, this only being interrupted when it was necessary for me to pursue some sales or marketing initiative. The Australian Tourist Commission continued to come up with new ideas. Destination Australia Marketplace was to be held on the Gold Coast and it was their intention to bring some 50 international wholesalers, travel agents and travel journalists to experience the destination first-hand and to meet with Australian suppliers.

By then the government was getting really serious about the export dollars generated by the travel industry and they kept up the ATC funding. In fact the states and territories' funding had been increased, making a total of some $30 million dollars, as I recall, allowing them to pursue all manner of new initiatives. And why wouldn't they? Once established there is no more cost-effective export than tourism. There's no freight involved, the consumer buys a dream off a page or two of printed material, the sale is confirmed in the same manner. What's more, the money paid for the product is doubled with the amount spent after arrival. In fact statistics show that consumer spending by visitors from some markets far outweighs the original purchase price of the holiday.

It had been a long hard road, though, and more than once over the years certain politicians and bureaucrats have questioned the value of investing in tourism and fought hard against it. And I do remember at one stage a trade publication taking a politician to task who thought the international traveller coming to this country was an import. Spare me.

I was feeling more and more tired—stuffed, really. We had been working on our project for twelve years without a break other than a couple of industry conventions that Val and I registered at, if you could call that a break. We had not had a holiday for fifteen years and we were in a business that operated 365 days a year and 24 hours a day. I had a notepad and pen on the bedside table.

•

To be awakened late at night or in the early hours of the morning was not uncommon. The vehicles all had CB radios and they were really a marvellous method of communication. However, they do work better at night. I remember getting a phone call in the early hours of one morning from a girl in Adelaide who had picked up a distress call from Sticko, who was stuck on the Tanami in bad weather. He had a broken rear tail shaft and was pulling the truck along in front-wheel drive and needed the part to be waiting in Halls Creek or Kununurra. She had him on the radio and me on the phone and acted as go-between. Those CB fanatics just love all that stuff.

Val got the worst call we ever had. I was away and she had to deal with it. It was Sticko and Robyn again—weird how Sticko and Robyn are involved so much, and I didn't realise they were until I began to record all of this. Anyway, they were at UDP Falls, marked on today's maps as Gunlom Falls, at the lower end of the Kakadu National Park. The water comes down off the Arnhem Land high country, and through its journey tumbles over a series of small falls before reaching the edge of the escarpment, where a waterfall plunges more than 70 metres to the pool below. There are those who argue that it is the most picturesque place in the whole of the Northern Territory, and not just the waterfall—the large plunge pool at its base is surrounded by giant paperbarks and pandanus.

A climb to the top of the escarpment was part of every tour for the young and energetic, and one girl with a group of her new friends took on the challenge. From what we know she began taking photos standing on a rocky outcrop where the water tumbles over. Then she appeared to slowly lose balance and fall off the edge. The theory was that she was looking downwards through her camera viewer and lost vertical perspective, and this caused her to lean forwards and be unaware that she was losing balance until it was too late.

Robyn was at the edge of the pool when she hit the water with a loud smack and immediately dived in and swam across to assist. Even though the rescue response was immediate, the impact on the water would have been like hitting concrete from that height and the girl passed away soon after Robyn brought her ashore. Naturally, there was much to be done. Police and ambulance from Katherine attended, and it was early hours of the morning when Val received the call from Sticko. It was her responsibility to inform the next of kin, in this case, the parents.

IN SEARCH OF SKYLAB AND PEOPLE GONE MISSING

I took the bad call on another occasion, again late at night, when Bruce Johnson, one of our tour leaders rang. The story was they were camped at Katherine and one of the passengers, a German travelling alone, had not returned to camp and was last seen in the early afternoon. By the time Bruce called me, police were involved and a search was to be conducted at first light on the following day. But despite searching all day there was no sign of the missing tourist and the hour of decision was fast approaching. For how long do you hold the tour? If the man has wandered off and got lost, it might take days to find him.

The remains of the missing person were found the next afternoon, miles down the Katherine River. He had been eaten by a crocodile. Now, the likelihood of being killed by a croc was thought to be pretty remote, as the river was inhabited by the freshwater Johnson River species. Katherine was always believed to be too far up river for big salties, so the consensus at the time was that he probably died on the riverbank and the smaller freshwater reptiles decided not to let him go to waste.

Today, there is no doubt in my mind that he was killed and eaten by a big salty. Some years ago it was discovered that there were saltwater crocodiles in the Katherine River near the town and the rangers began setting traps for protection. Fourteen saltwater crocs were trapped near Katherine in 2010, including a 4.5-metre monster that was snared in August.

I also had a passenger go astray on Cooper Creek—fortunately it wasn't tragic but it was a real headache. We had set up camp on a waterhole not far from the Dig Tree and a few of the punters said they were going for walks, so I gave them the usual advice: 'Take note if you're going to walk upstream or downstream so you know which way is home—and stay near the water.' Well, you guessed it, one bloke didn't return, and nobody remembered whether he went upstream or downstream. Bloody hell, he kept me awake all night worrying. Had he gone for a swim, or fallen in, got into trouble and drowned?

So early the following morning I had a meeting with four of the younger and fitter passengers to discuss the problem and the consensus was that two go downstream and two go upstream for four hours before returning. At their four-hour limit the pair that went downstream were sitting on a log, munching a sandwich, when they heard a motor vehicle in the distance coming towards them. It was Mike Steele, of Red Rover Tours from Adelaide. He had been camped overnight on the Cooper well downstream and had just packed up, ready to move on, when this bloke fell into his camp, absolutely spent and badly dehydrated. He had walked for more than twelve hours and had not once taken a sip of water from the Cooper, because he didn't like the muddy look. And why didn't he listen to words of advice? He said he did, but when it came time to return to camp he had forgotten if he went upstream or downstream.

CHAPTER 22

THE END OF AN ERA

We were operating ten vehicles by the end of the 70s, plus two Greyhound coaches on regular charter and another two as backup in peak periods. The problem that vexed me most was that the Greyhound vehicles and crews weren't really under my control and importantly we weren't presenting vehicles painted up in Bill King's Northern Safaris livery. And while I was uncomfortable with that arrangement, I couldn't bring myself to face the alternative of buying four new Dennings when we needed more four-wheel-drive equipment.

To add to that problem, more than 40 per cent of our business was now coming from the inbound market and we were averaging loads of 80 per cent plus—we were filling those empty seats. We began to say, 'Sorry, fully booked,' on many itineraries. Now that's bad enough when you're dealing in the domestic market, but when an overseas operator invests a lot of money on a brochure featuring your tours and you're turning them away, they're going to get very upset. We needed to borrow more than a million dollars and even to think about that at the time was stressful.

I was about to embark on a trade mission back to Germany to participate in ITB, or International Tourism Bourse (which translates as 'International Tourism Exchange'), the largest tourism exhibition in the world. The Australian Tourist Commission (ATC) had researched the industry for several months to see if it was feasible to have representation and on receiving a positive response, had, for the first time, registered for an Australia exhibition hall.

When I say ITB is big, I mean it is huge. Berlin has acres galore set up as a commercial park with a series of 24 exhibition halls, each full of stalls and displays from every country on the globe. Even the so-called Eastern Bloc and Middle Eastern countries that were in conflict with the West, some of them with one another, still had their displays at ITB. Buyers from all over the world attended. It was a cost-efficient one-stop shop to see what countries could package and sell in their marketplace.

To start walking on any given morning, for a brief look, would take a full day. The Germans, of course, were the most prominent of all of the buying groups and I was fortunate to have been working in that market for the two years prior to the ITB mission. We were already packaged with several major wholesalers.

Publicity-wise we were never out of the news, with major Australian and international publications featuring stories of adventures with Bill King's Northern Safaris. *The Daily Yumiuri*, a Japanese–English publication, featured a full-page story headed 'Safari into the Vast Outback'. The Australia Family Reunion Club magazine in the UK, *Get Together*, and London's *Sunday Times* ran stories. The German magazine, *Status*, devoted four pages with colour photos; and *Town and Country* in the United States did a two-page story with colour photos, titled 'Adventuresome Australia'.

The BBC *Holiday* show in the UK did a whole program on Australia, and Meredith McGlynn from the ATC London office wrote in her report: 'We received more commercial identification than we ever believed possible on national BBC TV. Bill King's vehicle shots led the program in and were also featured on a ten-minute segment on Alice Springs.'

Bill King's Northern Safaris was now recognised worldwide as Australia's foremost adventure tour operator.

THE END OF AN ERA

•

It was late in 1979 and I was at an industry lunch at the Melbourne Hilton sitting next to John Knox, my old buddy from way back. He was by then the tours manager at Australian Accommodation and Tours (AAT), the coach company set up by Trans Australia Airlines (TAA) and Mayne Nickless to compete with Ansett Pioneer. So we nattered on about this and that, getting the safaris up and running, and how the pressure of operating an international business was taking its toll. I was running on a cocktail of adrenalin and alcohol and that was not a healthy lifestyle. I explained how hiring equipment from Greyhound was not a satisfactory way to progress our business, but the answer to that problem was too difficult to contemplate.

I said the bottom line was that we really needed to borrow a lot of money to buy four new Dennings, and that was just to replace the equipment we were chartering from Greyhound. We also had two new Desert Cruisers on the drawing board and the following year would in all likelihood require two more. Our business was fast outgrowing our seating capacity, and building a rapidly growing business out of revenue was putting a great strain on whatever quality of life Val and I thought we had.

Now for whatever reasons the AAT–TAA–Mayne initiative had never really worked. I didn't know whether it made money or not, but it had never given anybody any competition and was identified in the industry as 'Arse About Tours'. It had gone backwards from the day it began.

As we sat there yarning Knoxy said, 'You know, it would make sense if we talked. You've got the bums and we've got the seats. We have four new Dennings, a million-dollar-plus investment, sitting out at the Oakleigh depot, which are underutilised, and they'd look pretty good in your livery. Do you have any interest in selling out?'

Well, that was out of the blue. I had never thought about selling and to even think about it was a bloody nuisance because I hardly had room in my head for what I already had to think about, so I just parked it away in the back of my mind and got on with the job.

Around the middle of 1980 we had a couple of Greyhound tours return that I was not happy with at all. They were okay in the sense that there were no passenger complaints, but their 'coach captains' were operating the tour with a 'song book' mentality. It was not the service or style of tour we set out to provide. The fact was those tours were not only out of my control, they were out of the control of our top tour leaders whom I relied on heavily to ensure things out in the field were done right. We just had to get our own equipment.

I rang Knoxy and said, 'Do you want another chat about the buy-out discussion?' That led to a series of talks with the directors at TAA–Mayne Industries, directors at the airline and some of their sales people, who I knew were quite excited about taking over our air traffic into Alice Springs that at the time was with Ansett.

Our air traffic was significant. In peak times we had the best part of a Boeing 727 load of people in and out of Alice Springs every weekend, and that was apart from those through the week, and Darwin was steadily building, too. I felt a bit of a rat because Ansett were not aware of what was going on, so I rang Dick Bennett, who was general manager of Ansett Pioneer, and told him there was an offer in the wind. I asked if Ansett Pioneer would have an interest.

'No interest to us, Bill,' was his reply.

'That's a pity.' And it was, because I enjoyed our relationship with Ansett Airlines.

Never having sold a business before, I had no idea in the wide world what I was in for. I had accountants in every nook and cranny. We haggled over the price and my role in the new company, and my salary had to be satisfactory.

What would we do about premises? Capricorn Travel, our retail operation, was not part of the sale, so we would need new premises, and some staff had duties in both operations. Bloody hell, who stays with the retail office and who comes with me on this new adventure? What a nightmare.

Worse still, I was in limbo. I couldn't make one decision because I didn't know whether they were going to buy us out or not.

THE END OF AN ERA

I couldn't print brochures for the following year because there would be two programs to be merged and address and phone numbers could change. I couldn't order vehicles because it might not be my decision—on and on. I just had to remain in a stalled position. I was lucky to get any sleep at all.

Another thing that continued to rear its ugly head was Arse About Tours, and I well knew our competitors would be pointing the finger and hoping that AAT would drag us down rather than us elevating our parent to be a genuine player in the market. But I knew, by then, that if you believe in something hard enough and you work at it long enough, you will win in the end.

And then it finally happened. Len Simmons, AAT's general manager, acknowledged the sale in a press statement to *Inside Tourism*, the industry publication who released the following article on 8 December 1980:

> Bill King in AAT 'Reverse Takeover'
>
> AAT has acquired the camping and safari operator, Bill King's Northern Safaris.
>
> But the name of the latter company will be retained as a division of AAT and King will head it as general manager.
>
> It will market both existing Bill King products and the AAT camping and safari range of holidays.
>
> AAT general manager, Len Simmons, described the move Wednesday as a 'reverse takeover'.
>
> He said: 'Bill gets a bigger operation, plus our administrative and financial backing. We feel we are getting the best of both worlds. Bill's got the expertise we want, and which will give us the opportunity to take our major camping/safari competitors head on.'

So that was it. In view of a pending sale I had taken a punt, securing an option on the lease of the first floor of the building in which our retail office was located, so we only had to move upstairs. I had also made the long overdue decision to employ an operations manager, an appointment I needed to make whether I sold the business or not.

I advertised in the Melbourne *Age* and got several applicants. One stood out. Tony Blunsom was a young English bloke who had just migrated to Australia and had formerly been employed by Treasure Tours in the UK. They had gone belly-up, and that was one of the reasons he moved to greener pastures. Tony was the perfect back-stop, because that is what he aspired to be. He was a godsend—by then I felt like my gas tank was on empty.

There was one other thing that I did when the sale was first mooted. Ever conscious of the Arse About Tours label the company was stuck with, I registered the business name Australian Adventure Tours, so we could change the name and operate as Bill King's Australian Adventure Tours, giving a new meaning to the AAT brand.

•

Val and I had reason to celebrate—we had done well out of the deal, plus, it was the most profitable year we had enjoyed since we began the company. We still had our retail agency, we were happy with the sale price, I had an excellent remuneration package and the responsibility to manage what was virtually my own business. Yet I felt strangely flat, like when your offspring come of age and flee the nest.

But I had work to do. I didn't know where to start, really. We had new brochures to produce and we were a month behind schedule. This had always been my responsibility, but in the new regime I was to do that in consultation with the tour planning man at AAT.

Our four-wheel-drive expeditions and our Red Centre tours were fine, that was our domain, and we did what had to be done to get our itineraries, dates and prices ready for artwork. Our coach tours were the problem, and the reason we did the deal to get hold of AAT's four new Dennings.

When I went to see the AAT bloke I discovered he had all these odd tours planned off a map and hadn't taken into consideration at all the tours that we had been operating successfully for the past twelve years. He said, 'That sixteen-day tour you have is the same as Australian Pacific and Centralian.' (Centralian, I should explain, had risen like a phoenix from the ashes and they were again a serious player in the market.) 'You have to have something different.'

'Why?' I said. I then explained that we had our preferred agency deals with our own distribution channels, so the fact that we had the same tour was irrelevant. What was relevant was that with its three options it was our most profitable itinerary. The first section fed the 'Ayers Rock Air Safari' and the second section fed the twelve-day 'West of Alice Safari', two of our bestsellers. The seats on those sections generated 25 per cent more revenue than the sixteen-day riders. And, importantly, TAA wanted the air traffic.

But the bloke wouldn't budge, and it was quite evident that he hadn't given our brochure more than a cursory glance. He was a dimwitted drone and I was stuck with him. I was really pissed off. I can't stand fools now and I was worse then, so I went to see Len Simmons. He was very conciliatory. 'In a big organisation you have to have various departments that are responsible for various functions, and the lines of communication should be through the heads of those departments and the outcomes should be in line with the policies . . .'

'Len,' I said, interrupting, 'why did you pay a lot of money to buy me and my business when you have blokes already employed who think they know more about my business than I do?' I got up, walked out of his office and went back to Ivanhoe, seething.

The next problem I encountered was crews. I discovered I did not speak with crews—there was a supervisor at the Oakleigh depot with whom I communicated, and he relayed instructions to crews. I was worse off than I was with the Greyhound crews—at least I briefed them directly.

Len Simmons phoned me on some matters after a while and said, 'Oh and go ahead and do the coach camping tour brochure.' This was a huge relief, but by then it was Christmas 1980, so I spent all of Christmas Day, Boxing Day and the following week writing and preparing a brochure for artwork.

I thought I was going to eliminate some stress when I sold the business, but the pressure involved in working within that company's guidelines was bloody intense. Everyday things that were just part of the day-to-day operation of the business had to be explained and justified. Within a month of the sale I discovered why the company had degenerated into Arse About Tours. The whole organisation was stifling in a bureaucratic fart.

CHAPTER 23

AN AUDIENCE WITH THE GRIM REAPER

AFTER A LONG DRAWN-OUT process and a great deal of difficulty, we finally released our programs and it was time to head off on my third visit to Germany and the second International Tourism Bourse (ITB) in Berlin. I must say with all the recent pressure it was a relief to get away, but I was really feeling buggered.

I arrived in Berlin on 28 February and checked into the Sylter Hof Hotel on the Kurfurstenstrasse, a really nice small European establishment handy to the showgrounds. I spent the following day putting my booth together at the Australia stand, which incidentally was a replica of the Birdsville Pub. It looked terrific. I had a light snack that night and was feeling absolutely at the end of my tether so I went straight to bed, only to be awakened in the early hours of the morning with severe chest pains. 'Shit. What's all this about?'

I had experienced a couple of episodes over the previous eighteen months, but they were different. This was more persistent. My mind was telling me I needed exercise—why it did that I'll never know—so I got dressed and went for a walk and the pain became more intense. Then I knew I was in real trouble and I phoned my brother Ron, who was in the same hotel. I told him I had a problem and needed to get medical help and asked him to look after my stuff until I returned. He called hotel reception, they called an ambulance and a fire truck turned up with a compartment in the back that served as an ambulance.

When I checked into casualty a bloke helped me onto a gurney and pulled my shirt off and hooked me up for an ECG. Then he started talking in German in an agitated voice to somebody while I was thinking, 'Jesus. Give me something for this pain.' By this time I knew there was a big problem but I was also busting for a pee, which was not helping my discomfort, so I pointed and said, 'Toileten.'

'Nein, nein, heart attack,' he said.

'But I really need a pee.'

The next thing he was yelling at people and we were headed at great speed along this corridor. All I could see looking forwards was my two feet sticking up in the air and fast-approaching doors, which he hit with the front of the gurney; they burst open, and there were more corridors. The pain was so intense it felt like a Desert Cruiser parked on my chest. I could see blokes in white coats rushing everywhere and hear agitated German voices, and then it all stopped.

I had heard silence before: camped way out in the bush, relocating a vehicle alone when heading home after a one-way trip, rolling out the swag for a kip, early hours of the morning, nobody for hundreds of kilometres, no breeze, nothing. The ringing in the ears can become intense, louder and louder as they strain to hear a sound other than your heartbeat, yet your hearing is elevated to such a pitch you could hear a leaf drop in the sand; it is the sound of silence.

This sensation was different; there was nothing, just profound and absolute silence. With it came a vision of white, whiter than white, like light that grew and grew with an intensity I find difficult to describe. That was all there was, a white and silent place.

I awoke with a feeling of wellbeing. The pain was gone, and thank goodness for that—it was the most excruciating sensation I had ever been subjected to. I was on a ground floor with a large window overlooking a courtyard. It was snowing lightly and there was a deciduous tree, a beech I think, and the snow was gathering on the top of branches, pure white against their underneath that looked so black in contrast. Every now and again the weight of snow would become too much for a branch or twig and it would sag, dropping its load on the ground before springing back up for more. It was the prettiest sight I had ever seen.

I was alone in an intensive care ward—that was obvious, because I was hooked up to all manner of tubes and gadgets and had an oxygen mask on. I thought back to when it was all going on and wondered what happened to my pee.

My brother Ron and Doyley—Bob Doyle from the Northern Territory Tourist Commission—came in to say g'day. No visitors other than relatives were allowed in intensive care. I couldn't talk with the oxygen mask on, so I gave them the one finger salute and they knew I was okay.

It only took Val two and a half days to get to the hospital—not bad, really. John Knox fixed it with Qantas's help. It was not easy to do at that time, either, because there was an aviation fuel crisis. Iran and Iraq had gone to war and the Qantas flight she was on arrived in Frankfurt via San Francisco on a route over the North Pole.

Nobody spoke English in my ward. I found that strange, because the majority of Germans I came into contact with in the travel industry did. It must be the nature of the profession. A doctor who did speak English came to see me after a couple of days and we had a chat about what had gone wrong and the story was I had a 'diaphragmal cardiac infarction'. A blood clot landed in one of the three main arteries in the ticker, blocked it and killed off that section. The heart compensated for that problem and was functioning again. The treatment they used when I was admitted to casualty was to insert a tube into an artery under my arm, running directly into the heart, and flood it with Marcumar, a derivative of Coumarin, a chemical compound/poison found in some plants. Its anticoagulant properties dissolved the blood clot.

'The use of the drug in question can be dangerous in certain circumstances. We need your permission to use it,' the doctor said.

'Do whatever you need to do,' I told him, wondering about his question because they had already given me loads of the stuff. I figured Germany was no different from anywhere else: you cover your arse.

'You a smoker?' he asked, and I confessed. 'You've had your last cigarette, then.'

'You're overweight,' he said, and I would have been foolish not to agree. 'You need to lose some.'

'Do you have any stress in your life?'

'Stress is my life,' I said.

'You need to get rid of stress. Any questions?' he added.

'When can I go home?'

'You will be with us for some time yet,' he replied. 'We need to monitor you. You are very sick. You just got to the hospital in time—we lost you for a bit.'

I'm glad you found me again, I thought.

•

I was in intensive care for eight days before they moved me to a peripheral station and then into a two-bed ward that I discovered was near the Berlin Wall. It was a nice room and my bed was near the window, so I could look up at clouds and sky. I had a rude awakening, though, when in the early hours of one morning all hell broke loose; it was like the beginning of World War III. One of the nurses told me later that some parts of the wall, like the one adjoining the hospital, were guarded by automatic weaponry and even if a flock of pigeons flew through the sensor it would activate the system.

I was discharged from hospital on 28 March, 26 days after that ride in the fire truck in the early hours of the morning. I felt quite feeble. I had felt safe and secure in the hospital. Now, however, I had an almost overwhelming feeling of apprehension and anxiety, almost panic.

My physician had said to avoid long flights and take breaks where possible, so we flew from Berlin to Frankfurt with Pan Am, followed by Washington and San Francisco with United Airlines for a break. After that we took a Qantas flight to Honolulu for another break and then home. It was a beautiful feeling when Qantas finally put me down on Australian soil, I can tell you.

•

Back home I saw my physician and told him my medical report from the hospital was in German. He checked me over, said all was okay and sent me off to see a cardiologist who also gave me the all-clear, but told me I needed to lose some weight. 'Get rid of that muck,' he said, slapping me on the belly with the back of his hand.

'When can I go back to work?'

'Next week,' he said.

However, the feeling of anxiety had not disappeared and as the next week came closer it became more acute. I hopped in the Renault I had at the time and headed down to the office in Ivanhoe, and on the way I could feel myself getting the shakes. Then I started sweating profusely, I was having difficulty breathing, and the anxiety was building to the point where I thought I might have to stop the car. When the dreaded moment arrived and I was outside the office, there was no way I could get out of that car and walk in. It was a feeling that bordered on panic and it only began to subside after I made the decision to turn around and go home.

That drive home was a nightmare, I was shaking so much. 'Bloody hell. What's happened to me?' was all I could think. Val rang Len Simmons to tell him I was unwell and would have to see the physician, and I knew what he would be thinking—'When is this guy coming back to work?'—and that gave me another anxiety attack.

I made an appointment with my doctor to talk about rehabilitation. They had mentioned it when I was in the Berlin hospital. 'Just do plenty of walking,' he said, but I explained I needed more than that, and somebody had told me about the Cardiac Rehabilitation Unit at the Caulfield Hospital.

'You don't need any of that. Just do plenty of walking,' he said.

'I need a referral,' I said, refusing to be deterred.

Caulfield Hospital, in Kooyong Road, is a long way from Eltham, and Val was stuck with driving me on her way to work at Capricorn. Then she had to do a repeat when I was ready to come home. There were three girls sitting at a desk when I walked in on the first day and people all over the place. I gave them the doctor's referral and they gave me a form to complete then told me to wait. The place was a bit of a madhouse and one of the three finally got around to me and asked about my episode. I told her what I knew and mentioned that I had a report from the hospital in Berlin, but it was in German. 'Give it to me,' she said, and added, 'I know somebody who will translate that for us.'

She took my blood pressure and pulse and said, 'Go and walk twice around the sports oval and come back and see me.' Walk twice around the sports oval? I was aghast. 'This bitch is trying to kill me! I've had a bloody heart attack.' But I did as I was ordered and when I came back she took my pulse and blood pressure again then sent me off to the exercise class. So there I was with about a dozen people, mainly oldies, stepping up and down off boxes, bending over, spinning backwards and forwards from the waist. Bloody hell I was exhausted, and it was only my first day. 'I've had a heart attack,' I kept telling myself. 'What am I doing here?'

I got the translation of my medical report back the following week and it had a significant passage:

> He needs the following treatment; anticoagulation therapy and physical training according to a stage plan. This will have to be continued in Australia up to complete rehabilitation. As Mr King from the medical point of view is definitely not able to handle affairs and as he certainly needs mental assistance, we consider it necessary that his wife accompany him back on his flight to Australia.

Well, I was bloody stupid. Why did I not get a translation of that report when I came home? Because I assumed its contents would be just common knowledge that my physicians would be aware of anyway. I had learned over the years that I should assume nothing; obviously I was still a slow learner. They had diagnosed me as a screw-up at the hospital in Berlin. Why my doctors in Australia did nothing about my anxiety attack I will never know.

The Rehabilitation Unit made an appointment for me to attend a session with the psychiatrist. Dressed in his light trousers and black jacket, with a black and white spotted bowtie, he was hard to miss. He was a really odd bloke and I wondered if years of working with the troubled had rubbed off on him. We went through the art of learning to relax, which included me lying on the floor, focusing on each part of my body and finally the mind, until I was in a state of total relaxation. It takes a bit of concentration but it works and helps in stress management.

Then he talked about stress. The doctor in Berlin had told me to 'Get rid of the stress.' 'Can't get rid of stress,' the psychiatrist said. 'A certain amount of stress is good for you. We're never going to get rid of it, so what we must do is learn how to manage it.'

Stress is one of the most basic and important human instincts, going way back to primitive man. The instinct is needed to trigger the adrenalin rush when our ancestors were faced with the decision of flight or fight. The problem with modern humans, though, is that the stress and adrenalin rush is not occasional—it could go on all day every day and overpower their lives.

'Don't get stressed about being stressed,' I told myself.

I had several sessions with the psychiatrist, who made sense of my disability and made me understand that what had happened to me was a confidence thing. No big deal—I had just lost the belief in my ability to confront an issue, to analyse the situation and bring it to a logical conclusion. These days I think they call it depression.

The day came again when I had to walk back into that office, and it was not without anxiety that I drove to Ivanhoe. Could I get through that door? I must confess I did have the shakes and I was out of breath walking up the stairs, but I made it. It genuinely felt good to be back and I could tell that the crew was really pleased to have things back to normal. I'm sure the people at HQ were, too, because a couple of months had passed since I had made a contribution.

There was a gym at the bottom of the main street in Ivanhoe in those days so I joined up, and the young bloke and his wife who ran the show worked out an exercise routine designed to suit my problems. Often the pressures of the office would be building by the afternoon and I could feel the approach of an anxiety attack. I'd go and spend an hour or so in the gym doing my routine, then get pummelled in the spa by the heavily chlorinated water, before walking the kilometre back up the hill to the office, feeling pretty good. It is amazing how exercise can relieve stress.

•

There was, however, still much work to be done. I had met all of the AAT staff by then and was really impressed with Steve Gregg, the sales manager in Brisbane. He was a genuine self-starter who understood where we were coming from, and I pushed hard to get him relocated to Los Angeles to work out of the Trans Australian Airways (TAA) office, selling our itineraries to US wholesalers to include in their brochures. This was approved.

We needed a similar appointment to do likewise in both the UK and Europe. I had always been impressed with the work of Val Flackl, who was assistant manager of the Northern Territory Tourist Commission office in Sydney. I also knew she was of German extraction and spoke the language fluently. She would be the ideal person to manage our European office from the TAA base in London. I raised the subject with her and we spoke about our needs and her ambitions. She was really excited about the prospect, so I took her application to Len Simmons and made the recommendation that she be employed by the company. That was also approved.

We then came to an agreement with Qantas that we believed would significantly increase volume from the UK. Our entire program would be released in Britain in a Qantas Jetabout holiday brochure and sales would be coordinated with Qantas Chiswick head office.

Len Simmons sent a press release to *Travel Week* informing the trade that in the coming year Bill King's Australian Adventure Tours would operate all the company's touring programs except for Tasmania. We had both camping and accommodated holidays packaged with rail, the Ghan and Indian Pacific, as well as air with TAA. We had a full range of tour options in Western Australia, the Northern Territory and Queensland.

Within one year we had Bill King's Australian Adventure Tours positioned in the marketplace to give Australian Pacific and Centralian serious opposition, and they knew it. We had certainly given the industry a major shake-up. And Arse About Tours? They were a thing of the past.

•

I received a phone call one morning that really surprised me: 'Bill, it's Paul Everingham here.' I well knew who Paul Everingham was, Chief Minister of the Northern Territory, but I had never met him before. Why the devil was he calling me?

After a bit of chat he explained he wanted to talk to me about the Northern Territory Tourist Commission. He needed somebody to back up Eric Poole, the chairman, somebody in the marketplace who had a finger on the pulse. He only wanted a commission of three, 'so things will get done', and he already had David Astley, who ran the local TV station in Darwin on board. 'Would you take the job as the third commissioner?' he asked.

It was about the time when all governments were coming to grips with the real value of the tourist dollar, the Northern Territory in particular. Cattle weren't going to be a real growth industry and neither were minerals in the short term, so tourism offered the feathers to fly with. The economic and social importance of tourism was being realised in Canberra as well. And even though

Australia's share of the international market was pitifully small, it employed nearly 350 000 people, more than 5 per cent of the country's workforce, and provided almost 5 per ent of the country's gross domestic product (GDP). Government figures indicated that tourism generated more than $12.7 billion for our economy. I felt quite honoured to be invited to join the commission and readily accepted.

Then there was a change of government. Virtually on the eve of an election Bob Hawke was given the job as leader of the Labor Party, then lo and behold he rolled Malcolm Fraser and we had a new mob in power. What would happen to us? The last Labor government, Whitlam's crew, was no advocate for our industry. Would Hawke's lot be any better? Malcolm Fraser and co. had not rectified the mess that Whitlam left. Maybe, just maybe, the new government could do the job. My interests, naturally, were tourism and environment. John Brown and Barry Cohen got the ministerial responsibility for those portfolios and they were both making the right noises, so we would have to wait and see.

CHAPTER 24

THE GLOBAL MARKET— ON OUR TERMS

I HAD JOINED THE Inbound Tour Operators of Australia (ITOA) organisation in 1979, as Bill King's Northern Safaris, but not been to a meeting for months, and after getting things on track in the company I decided to involve myself in industry affairs again. I must say Len Simmons took a broad view of that involvement, understanding that my high profile presence in industry affairs did elevate the company's standing and I was close to the policy-makers and could have a say.

An inbound operator could be likened to a broker who accepts responsibility for destination management, a one-stop shop based in Australia that takes care of all manner of travel arrangements for overseas tour wholesalers, incentive houses, conventions, study tours and ordinary holiday-makers. When I first joined the Sydney-based organisation, there were 30-plus members at that time, about half inbound operators and the remainder known as 'allied' members, the suppliers who were mostly accommodation houses, coach tour operators, cruises, attractions and so on.

It had always been my belief that a much greater allied membership was essential if the organisation aspired to be the voice of the Australian industry rather than the voice from Sydney. There was, though, a lingering reluctance from some inbound members who harboured a fear that somehow the tail would start to wag the dog.

However, if we wanted to position our organisation as the voice of the industry and reach our goals, we also needed funding. Obviously, membership fees were our bread and butter, although an annual industry symposium that included the ITOA award for a deserving individual had become a good source of revenue and a premier industry event. It was the brainchild of Billy Wright of ID Tours.

For some time I had had the seed of an idea running around in the back of my mind for an ITOA trade mission to the United States. Having been on many Australian Tourist Commission (ATC) trade missions, often as not with ITOA members, I could say there were several of us who were an authority on 'trade shows'. I had also come to hold the view that there was a lot of money to be made out of such a venture, even if we charged a lower registration fee than the ATC did for their events.

The ATC had as many staff in attendance as there were delegates on their missions, and that of course had to be funded. In our scenario the delegates would run the shows. I reasoned that the cost saving would be significant if we could somehow get a deal on air tickets.

Now, as we all know, in life there are unforeseen moments that occur every so often that in later years you reflect upon as being almost divine intervention. Well, it so happened that I was in Sydney at a travel function and was introduced to Paul Glaser. He was an Australian residing in the US and we began to chat about this and that and I discovered he held a very senior position with Continental Airlines. They had recently begun to service the Australia–US route, and being a US domestic carrier they had also introduced some innovative 'on carriage' fare deals, meaning that on the purchase of your international flight, you had access to rock-bottom airfares in the US with Continental.

Paul was based at the airline's corporate headquarters in Houston at the time and was the director of international sales and development—when I heard all this, green lights started to flash.

I immediately floated my thoughts of staging an ITOA road show in the US. I asked Paul if he would be interested in providing 25 air tickets and support from his sales staff if we ran a Continental Airlines–Inbound Tour Operators of Australia promotion in key cities that the airline serviced.

'No worries. When?' he said without batting an eyelid.

There it was—out of the blue we had our road show.

I went to an ITOA meeting and put forward my concept of a road show to the US. 'All very well,' the other members said, 'but the air travel would be too costly.'

'What if I said we had free air tickets with Continental?' Well, that floored 'em.

There were 26 of us ready to go. We formed a working committee to organise registration, venues and accommodation—there was plenty of behind the scenes work to be done. I took on the job of working with Continental's regional sales managers in the twelve cities we would visit, organising venues and the invitations to travel agents. Telex machines were running hot in those days.

That mission was an outstanding success, not only in its educational aspects for the American agents, but we also proved to ourselves that we could run an international trade mission and return a handsome profit at the same time.

With all of that I still felt there were limitations in the variety of product we displayed in the workshops, and I continued with my campaign to broaden the membership base. Apparently this was to some effect, because Trevor Haworth, founder of Captain Cook Cruises on Sydney Harbour, who was due to retire as chairman, said, 'If you feel so passionate about it, why don't you take the chair and do it yourself—put up or shut up?' So I did; put up, that is.

•

I became chairman of the Inbound Tour Operators of Australia in 1983 and immediately set about consulting with the board to select a committee, formulate a plan to increase membership and elevate our organisation to the peak body in the Australian travel industry. I was soon to discover that wasn't going to be easy, given the constraints the organisation worked under, for we were a division of the Australian Federation of Travel Agents (AFTA). They provided our association with a secretary, and Margaret Walton's job was to take minutes at meetings and report back to the AFTA board. I was soon to learn that the mood of the parent body was: 'Hold on. Where do you think you're going? We run this show.'

It was at the November 1983 meeting of members that I informed them of the following, which is an extract from the minutes:

> More and more of these people are turning to ITOA for guidance and membership and our AFTA criteria is seen by potential members to be a barrier.
>
> The executive is unanimous in its feelings that ITOA could best serve its members and the industry as a whole by functioning as an independent body given that the roles of AFTA and ITOA both in philosophy and objectives are so totally divorced.

The book, *ITOA—25 Years*, published in 1996, contained the following quote:

> The statement was a watershed, to be recognized in the years to come as one of the major determinants of ITOA's success. By casting off the shackles of AFTA, ITOA was able to broaden its membership base, increase its revenue and provide greater support to a dynamic and growing industry.

Now the big problem with all of this was money—our money was in the AFTA bank account. We could have started a new organisation in a day, and our members would have backed it 100 per cent, but AFTA had more than $50 000 of our hard-earned money, and that was why the bastards were playing hardball. In our naivety we hadn't even dreamt that they would set out to nick our piggy bank, but they were sitting on it and weren't about to give it up.

It was not until December 1984, almost two years from when we first floated the concept of an independent body, that we finally made our breakthrough. Yes, we could break away and form an independent organisation, but they would keep half of our money. In other words it cost us $25 000. Their justification was that they would spend their $25 000 on 'benefits for both organisations and the industry as a whole'. To my knowledge it was never seen or heard of again.

So we were free, and to quote from the book *ITOA—25 Years*:

> While ITOA was poorer financially, it was richer in many other ways. Its decision to step away from the AFTA umbrella saw membership numbers surge 55 per cent to 114 in 1985 and the organization develop a pride and focus that would make it one of Australia's most successful industry bodies.

Back in history I used to say there were 1000 prospective members out there who needed our organisation and one day that would happen—well, it has. Our little organisation has grown to be the peak body in Australian tourism. It is now known as the Australian Tourism Export Council (ATEC) and the current membership has grown well in excess of the 1000. All is going according to plan.

•

While all this was going on, we had also been putting our heads around our international marketing plans for Bill King's Australian Adventure Tours and it was time to return to my 1981 disaster zone—ITB (International Tourism Bourse) in Berlin. This time, though, we were going to raise our presence to a new level.

We had been involved with Ralph Nicholls's Bwung Gul group for a couple of years doing promotional work. Ralph was the son of Sir Douglas Nicholls, an Aboriginal leader who did much to elevate the understanding of Indigenous issues in Australia. Ralph had formed a group to visit schools and give children an insight into Aboriginal culture with song and dance, didgeridoo playing and fire lighting. I saw great potential promoting Australian tourism with his show and worked with him in introducing some minor modifications to his presentation to make it even more appealing to adults.

I began negotiations with the Australian Tourist Commission with the intention of taking Ralph and the Bwung Gul to ITB as part of Bill King's Australian Adventure Tours contingent where they would stage several corroborees.

That initiative really tickled the ATC's fancy, so much that they asked if we were prepared to go to London for a performance following the show in Germany. 'Cost you nothing,' they said, and they were prepared to put substantial resources behind publicising the event.

'Why not?' said Ralph.

And that's how there came to be a corroboree at the Waldorf Hotel in London.

It was an historic event, and Murphy Dhulparippa, Michael Bungapidu and Ralph Nicholls were wonderful ambassadors of their culture, and indeed Australia. It was a privilege for me to compere the presentation, alongside Ron Hewitt, the UK manager for ATC, and Ian Auchinachie, the Qantas representative.

While they were in London, Ralph, Murphy and Michael took the opportunity to visit the grave of Yemmerrawanyea. They were the first Indigenous people ever to do so and *The Times* published a story about their visit, entitled 'Pilgrims from a World Away'. Yemmerrawanyea and Bennelong had sailed to England with Governor Arthur Phillip in 1792 to meet King George III, who was keen to meet two of his Australian Indigenous subjects. Bennelong returned to Australia but Yemmerrawanyea stayed in England. He did not adapt to the climate at all, though, contracting a lung infection that proved fatal. He passed away in May 1794; he was only eighteen years of age.

•

THE GLOBAL MARKET—ON OUR TERMS

I was at the 1983 ITB in Berlin, just after I had been appointed chairman of ITOA, when I was approached by Sir Peter Derham and John Rowe, chairman and chief executive officer of the Australian Tourist Commission respectively, for a meeting to discuss our organisations' differences. The timing was opportune, because we at ITOA had voiced our concern at the ATC plan to use their overseas offices as sales centres. We believed that decision would have a negative effect on the existing distribution systems and inhibit the development of any new ones. Why would the British travel trade invest in promoting a destination when the destination is endeavouring to compete with them in sales? We believed the ATC should be the country's marketing arm and their role should be strictly destination promotion and their offices information centres.

I sat there and let them go on to see where all this was leading. I was in 100 per cent listening mode and discovered that they interpreted ITOA's initiative to go it alone with Continental Airlines in the previous year as a rebellious act against their 'sales office' policy. Well, actually, the sole reason we had participated with Continental in the US promotion was to make some money, not as a protest.

And then the breakthrough came. They announced that the ATC had decided to change their strategy. They would no longer pursue their policy of sales offices and would continue to act as a marketing and information service. Bloody good, I thought. Common sense had prevailed and the ATC was going to stick to its knitting and do what it did best.

But that wasn't all—they really bowled me over when they asked, 'Would your organisation have an interest in a joint Qantas–ITOA promotion in the United States, with ATC involvement later in the year?'

I was speechless; I couldn't believe what I heard. 'Er, probably. Don't see why not,' was my eventual reply.

We were going to make some more dollars, because our proviso would be that we run the functions with Qantas support—the same format as the Continental effort. Life was lovely. It's funny how things just come out of the blue; it was exactly twelve months since that chance meeting with Paul Glaser, when we put together the first ITOA road show with Continental.

•

I contacted Ralph Nicholls and he came on board again with his Bwung Gul dance team. This time he was supported by Robert Mununggurr and David Yunupingu, both members of well-known Yirrkala families in Nhulunbuy, and so we were under way with 'The 1983 Australian Corroboree', the title we gave the road show.

The 1983 Qantas–ITOA trade mission got underway with a presentation in Tampa that attracted 135 delegates. We then did Atlanta, Georgia; followed by Kansas City in Missouri; Hartford, Connecticut; Cleveland, Ohio; Toronto, Ontario; Salt Lake City, Utah; and Los Angeles, California. It was another successful event that added to our coffers.

There were 21 of us in the group plus The Great Australian, a huge koala mascot with the aforesaid printed across the front of his T-shirt—and when I say huge I mean he was almost the size of an adult human. He was so big the airline needed to make arrangements for him to travel safely. The only problem we had with him was in Los Angeles. We used to sit him up on stage near the podium in full view and I had just stepped down from welcoming the delegates and people were starting to move about when I glanced back and he'd disappeared—there one minute, gone the next.

Shit! Somebody had knocked him off. A quick glance about and it was easy to see he was not in the room. I dashed out into the hotel lobby and said to somebody, 'Have you seen the big koala?' and they looked at me like I was crazy. Out the door I went and there he was tearing through the car park, head and shoulders above the cars. I couldn't see what was propelling him along, but I set out in hot pursuit, arriving at a scene where he was sitting on the ground and this woman was rummaging in her handbag for her

THE GLOBAL MARKET—ON OUR TERMS

car keys. Seeing me she snatched him up with this mad look in her eyes and started screaming, 'He's mine, he's mine!'

By this time I had hold of him as well and was yelling, 'In a pig's eye he is. He's mine!'

Can you think of anything more demeaning, standing in a car park with people about, staring in amazement while you're having a tug of war with a giant koala and a stupid woman who has had enough alcohol to believe the bloody thing was hers? By the grace of whomever I was saved by a member of the hotel staff and could still hear the woman screaming at him as I re-entered the building with the koala and as much dignity as I could muster.

There was another disappearing act on that tour. We did a show in Honolulu on the forward journey, the first-ever Australian promotion in Hawaii. On the night we arrived Ralph knocked on my door in the early hours and said, 'The boys have gone and my bloody didgeridoo has gone with them.'

'Oh no! Bloody hell!' I put on some clothes and we hurried down to reception to ask if they'd seen David and Robert.

'No, we haven't seen them,' the desk clerk said.

We started walking the streets and checking the nearby bars and by this time, I can tell you, Ralph was nearly beside himself with worry. Just as we arrived back at the hotel, a taxi pulled up and out jumped the two missing persons with the didgeridoo. 'Where have you buggers been?' yelled Ralph.

They both stood there with silly looks on their faces then started turning out their pockets, which were absolutely stuffed full of American dollars. They had been busking in a bar somewhere with clap sticks and the didgeridoo.

Ralph turned to me and said, 'They frightened the daylights out of me. Do I look pale?' He did have a great sense of humour.

•

There was so much going on at that time, including new initiatives by the ATC. Kim Dunstan had set up an office in Singapore and floated the concept of an Asian road show. The destinations included Jakarta, Kuala Lumpur, Singapore, Kota Kinabalu, Bangkok, Hong Kong, Seoul and Taipei.

I must admit I was sceptical. If people from those counties had become affluent enough to afford an overseas holiday, there was no way it was going to be in a tent. We did, however, have our fully accommodated, coach tour itineraries functioning well by then, but whether or not they fitted the market's travel patterns was the question.

I returned from the workshops with a negative attitude and the report I did for Len Simmons reflected that: 'They are markets that will never produce significant volume in my lifetime.' I could not conceive that their economies could catch up to ours.

That promotion we did back in 1983 was pioneering stuff: more than 1 million people arrive in Australia from those markets today and there's even bigger growth from mainland China where the forecast is for more than 1 million visitors by 2013.

It just shows you how much I know—bugger all, it seems.

CHAPTER 25

WE BUILD THE 'MOGS'

It was about that time when Frank Hutchinson from Don Kyatt Spares in West Melbourne called and said, 'Hey, mate, I see the British Army Occupation Forces in Germany are having a disposal sale of surplus goods and there are two M Series Bedford chassis included in CKD form. We could bring them in as spare parts.' CKD is manufacturers' jargon for 'completely knocked down', when the whole vehicle is packaged in pieces right down to the last nut and bolt. They were subject to a much cheaper import duty than vehicles.

'If I'm thinking what you're thinking that would be a very good deal indeed,' I replied. He was. We could assemble them here and have two new chassis ready for Desert Cruiser bodies for the cost of one. 'We'll have 'em,' I said to Frank.

Well, getting them was the easy part. It was only when we unloaded the freight and got to assembly stage that we discovered the British army had built them to European specifications—they were left-hand drive. But we got hold of the stuff to convert them to right-hand drive and by that time we were the 'knowers of all things' when it came to building off-road vehicles. We would use them on our day tours to Palm Valley and without the luggage locker and kitchen in the rear end we would have a net gain of sixteen seats. The time had come to pension off Big Ben and Little Ben.

At that time I was also investigating the availability of additional equipment for the long-haul stuff, and although the Bedfords had done a good job I had seen a newspaper article about Mercedes Benz Unimogs being trialled by the Australian military forces. This captured my attention. I had contacted Mercedes some years before regarding the feasibility of importing Unimogs for our application, and it couldn't be done. Mercedes would never sell a vehicle unless they had appropriate service and spares backup, and that wasn't possible with one-off importations.

The Unimog is a unique machine that came into being because of the Second World War. Even though engineers were working on the concept back in 1942, it was not until the last shot was fired that the authorities got serious about inventing this particular vehicle. A syndicate of engineers, industry executives and farmers were assembled, and their job was to research the diversity of applications required for an all-purpose vehicle to work in the rebuilding of post-war Germany. In 1946 the first chassis was constructed for practical testing and from that came the first Universal Motorized Vehicle, or Unimog as we know it today. The 'mog' is regarded as the finest light duty, all-terrain, all-purpose vehicle in the world.

Anyway, I spoke to the Merc mob again, and any deliveries in Australia would be dependent on a positive response from the army. If they placed an order, Mercedes would tack on an order from us on the end of the army's. Well, we were ecstatic, I can tell you, when the Australian army ordered 1295 of the UL 1700 models in the first batch and we tacked on four to their order: a big investment.

I got my drafting instruments out again and designed an all-new 21-passenger Mk III Desert Cruiser with much improved storage for gear and highly advanced kitchen and food storage. We had enjoyed years of practice building the Internationals and Bedfords so we reckoned we knew what was needed to build an off-road personnel carrier second to none. We retained Centurion Transport Engineering to build them; they shared our vision.

One aspect of the construction that needed research was the flexing or torsion effect on the body when negotiating extreme off-road conditions, such as when the left front and right back suspensions are compressed to the maximum and the right front and left back suspensions are extended downwards to the extreme. The twisting motion puts enormous strain on the body mountings, can toss passengers about and cause vehicle body and mounting breaks. Although the German engineers had perfected all aspects of the chassis, we had to ensure that the body, particularly the mounting system, was equal to the task.

Through being involved with Mercedes Benz Australia we had developed a relationship with the military people taking part in their mog projects. Their engineers were most interested in our application, so we were able to do our testing on the Department of Defence proving ground at Monegeeta, in Victoria. The testing track offered the maximum in off-road variations, so we took our first experimental vehicle with body shell in place for evaluation. Our engineers came up with the theory of three mounts along the spine of the body with shock buffers on the perimeter; this would allow maximum flex on the chassis with minimum strain on body mounts. We also had to convert the chassis to forward control. Moving the driving position forward more than a metre entailed the repositioning of clutch, brake and steering systems. The modifications also had to be evaluated and approved by Mercedes.

The Unimog's performance was exceptional. Powered by a 5.7-litre, 6-cylinder turbocharged diesel engine, it cruised effortlessly at 95 kilometres per hour on the blacktop, 10 k per hour more than the Bedfords, and the 8-speed forward and 8-speed reverse gearbox eliminated the challenge of any terrain. The constant all-wheel drive and the independently activated front and rear differential locks made varying road conditions a breeze, and it had amazing ground clearance. Water hazards well in excess of a metre deep could be negotiated without special precautions, and the centre of gravity allowed traction on a side slope of more than 42 degrees.

Mercedes Benz Australia continued to take great interest in our project, and their PR consultant organised an initial delivery ceremony at Emu Bottom, an historic homestead north of Melbourne. A large media contingent had been invited, including Channel 9, and I drove them across some undulating terrain to give them a demo of the vehicle's capability. Hans von Brockhausen, the managing director of Mercedes Benz Australia at the time, was in attendance, and presented me with a giant Mercedes Benz key adorned with the three-point star to mark the occasion. It is now included in our Wall of Memorabilia at the National Road Transport Hall of Fame in Alice Springs.

We had articles published in most of Australia's dailies that week, but surpassed that publicity when we relocated the first Unimog to Alice Springs. Greg Smith was taking the vehicle north with two cooks on board, Jenny Davies and Karyn Ven, who were relocating to Alice Springs. It seemed a good opportunity, so we invited several motoring journalists to experience the product first-hand and travel via Ayers Rock. I went along for the ride—no show without Punch, and besides I felt like a break. It was at the time Chief Minister Paul Everingham indicated the Northern Territory's intention to grant the Anangu people native title to the then Ayers Rock–Mount Olga National Park. They had lodged a land claim to the region in 1978 but it was not until October 1986 that the Federal Government recognised the claim and granted title to the 1325 squre kilometres that were to become known as the Uluru–Kata Tjuta National Park—Uluru being the family name of the senior traditional owner from the Pitjantjara tribe.

In 1993 the monolith was renamed Ayers Rock/Uluru and in 2002 it was again changed to Uluru/Ayers Rock; it is the only dual-named feature in the Northern Territory. Today it is a World Heritage site, recognised initially for its outstanding universal natural values and later for its universal cultural values. Around 450 thousand people a year visit the park these days, a far cry from the time there was only the colonel, three ladies and me, camped under the lee of the north-west face.

The exposure we received from the group of journos was fantastic. Steve Brooks did a four-page story with colour photos in *Truck and Bus* magazine under the heading 'A Star in the Outback'. Ric Williams filled eight pages with his impressions and colour photos in *Bushdriver* under the heading, 'On Safari with Bill King'.

Mercedes Benz Australia took the trial very seriously indeed. It was the first passenger application of a Unimog in its 37-year history, and was big news for the company. Mercedes headquarters in Stuttgart flew a journalist to Australia to join the safari and write an article for *In Aller Welt,* a magazine published in many languages and distributed worldwide by the company as *The Magazine for Friends of the Three-Pointed Star.* But it was Doug Hicks's 1983 story in *Australian Trucking Action*, 'Unimog—Out Back with Precious Cargo', that really summed up the success of our project:

> Watching the vehicle over super rough terrain from the outside was, however, a rather unnerving experience, seeing the chassis and suspension bashing and crashing all over the place while the body appeared to be totally remote and calm—almost as though the two were not connected. Overall the Unimog and Bill King's operation were very impressive.

Passenger comfort was uppermost in our minds when we conducted the exhaustive testing on the proving ground at Monegeeta; it was nice to be reassured that our engineers had got it right.

•

The Unimogs were an important milestone in the company's growth and we had a large program of presentations organised to launch our brochures and tours. The first of these was to be staged in the ballroom of the now demolished Australia Hotel, in Collins Street, Melbourne. We approached management at Trans Australia

Airlines (TAA) and suggested they join us with a joint promotion, to which they readily agreed, and so an invitation from TAA, Bill King's Australian Adventure Tours, Dunk Island, Great Keppel Island, Wanderers' Paradise and Bedarra Island was distributed to the travel trade, as well as travel publications and news media.

At that time Aussie bush bands were in vogue, and the Bushwackers were at the top of the tree. They were attracting big numbers to their concerts and we were fortunate indeed to have them agree to do our launch.

Our invitation stated: 'Warning: Bushwackers at large in Melbourne Town'.

To use a theatrical expression, the event was a 'sell-out', an embarrassment, really. We couldn't fit them in the door. And the interest in the Unimogs, generated by the massive amount of exposure, was nothing short of amazing. In the aftermath we had people booking tours who wanted to ride in 'one of those Unimog Desert Cruisers'.

It was in February 1983 when we introduced them—the four most sophisticated off-road passenger-carrying vehicles in the world—and they were an addition to our existing fleet. We planned to operate 30 different itineraries with more than 300 departures that year, during which we carried more than 10 000 passengers. We had become one of the world's largest adventure tour operators.

CHAPTER 26

CHANGING TIMES

On 1 July 1983 the decision was made to abandon the Franklin River Dam project and the issue finally began to settle down. The Greens, of course, had led the battle to save the Franklin and the plan to dam the river by the Hydro Electric Commission was halted for all time, so it seemed to me an appropriate juncture to stimulate some study of the relationship between national parks and tour operators.

I had begun to develop views on how parks could be developed under universal guidelines of control and management. We had been in the business for more than fifteen years and there were still no uniform regulations from state to state. There were no common regulations even within some states, and many parks were managed using guidelines set down by the particular officer in control.

The Franklin announcement got me thinking again about the subject and stimulated me to put pen to paper. We had a very strong interest in the development of tourism in Tasmania, having pioneered 'off the beaten track' tours in the west coast some eight years prior, so I wrote a letter to the editors of all the leading dailies in Australia.

Then for good measure I copied in the appropriate powers that be: the Rt. Hon. Mr R.J. Hawke, Prime Minister of Australia; the Hon. Mr J. Brown, Minister of Sport Recreation and Tourism; the Hon. Mr Robin Gray, Premier of Tasmania; and Gordon Dean and John Rowe, general managers of the Tasmanian and Australian Tourist Commissions respectively.

My proposition was that, depending on the capacity of the region in question, there should be defined areas of utilisation. Firstly, a lock-out zone for scientific purposes only, where future generations would have access to a nursery, a time capsule if you wish, where plant species would be available to re-create unique natural environments. Secondly, areas reserved for foot traffic only, and thirdly there needed to be defined areas for approved tour operators to service the needs of the old, young, incapacitated and general holiday-makers, to introduce them to the unique facets of nature that the park offered. And finally, heavy impact areas should be set aside as recreation reserves for the short-term visitor.

The letter was published in all the major dailies. Bob Hawke handed his to Barry Cohen, Minister for Home Affairs and Environment at the time, for a reply. Robin Gray passed his on to Ronald Cornish, his Parliamentary Secretary, and John Brown replied himself. All of the letters concurred with the comments and drew attention to the fact that the Hawke Government had allocated $5 million dollars to the Tasmanian Government for the development of tourist facilities in the southwest. Precise projects were obviously yet to be identified, but input from John Brown's department and the Tasmanian Government would be involved, and both said my correspondence had been forwarded to the appropriate people.

The correspondence was obviously distributed far and wide and did have an ongoing effect. I received an invitation from the Tasmanian Parks and Wildlife Service to speak at their conference in Launceston on national park issues. I assume that there were people among the delegates from the Victorian Department of Conservation, Forests and Lands, as I was invited as guest speaker at their conference at the Cumberland Resort in Marysville. The subject was 'New Tourism Opportunities in Parks and Forests'. Later again I received an invitation from the same department to be guest speaker at a conference they were staging with Tourism Victoria at the Lakeside Reception Centre at the Melbourne Zoo. This time it was 'Cultural Tourism—New Markets for an Information Age'.

There was, however, a growing voice of disapproval from 'green groups' who were quite beside themselves with the authorities having conferences discussing subjects like 'tourism opportunities in parks and forests'. They likened tourism development, such as amenity improvements and accommodation facilities, to mining and other noxious industries. The greenies had always used tourism as the main weapon against what they perceived to be unsympathetic development in or near national parks, and indeed it was the weapon that ultimately led them to the successes they enjoyed in blocking development such as mining, logging and the like.

Now they were gratifying themselves in academic elitism, 'defining' who they perceived as sharing their views and restricting the utilisation of parks to the super active, or the 'commando' set, if you wish. They believed parks should be set aside for them alone. Bugger the old, the young, the family, the incapacitated and the people who work hard for a living and have limited time for leisure, who rely on the tourist industry to provide the transport, the accommodation and the means by which they can enjoy the regions they have been attracted to by TV documentaries and promotional literature. I actually had a member of the 'green movement', who was with a group objecting to an accommodation facility within a national park, say to me, 'We don't want resort-type people here'. Spare me.

Since Bob Hawke swept into power on 5 March 1983 and the Department of Sport, Recreation and Tourism was created, and John Brown got the nod as minister, it had become obvious that the tourist industry was set to reach new levels of recognition and development. Brown was undoubtedly aware that Australia's receipts from the lucrative international tourist trade were very meagre indeed, well below our European competitors. Yet to put the true worth of Australian tourism into perspective, at the time its contribution to the gross domestic product (GDP) was greater than the textile, clothing and motor industries combined.

Australia had up until that time, even with all of the road shows and industry promotions we had participated in, not even scratched the surface of the world markets. We received 944 000 international visitors in 1983 and John Brown set the target of 2 million in 1988, more than double, and all to be generated within that timeframe. He had been able to extract additional funds from Treasury, and, working with the Mojo advertising agency, was set to release some radical and exciting international advertising campaigns.

As chairman of Inbound Tour Operators of Australia (ITOA) I was invited to become a member of John Brown's Tourism Advisory Council, and gave a presentation on ITOA's role in developing overseas markets to the first meeting in Canberra on 26 July 1983. I also drew attention to the fact that while 2 million international visitors was a commendable goal, we still had much work to do in elevating the quality of the Australian product. We were still emerging from a cottage industry and while there were major development projects underway, we had regions that could only provide basic accommodation, we had regions that because of road conditions were not accessible all year round, and we had a road transport industry needing constant upgrading that was lagging behind in vehicle replacement due to high interest rates and inflation. The most pressing need, though, was education. Staff training facilities were virtually non-existent and that was probably the major issue to be addressed. Unlike other industries, hospitality and tourist services can never be automated. It takes people to look after people.

In 1984, as the Federal Minister for Tourism, John Brown introduced the National Tourism Awards to draw attention to the benefits the industry brings to Australia's economy and to highlight the associated employment opportunities. There were various categories in accommodation, tourism services, marketing campaigns, transport and the like, with nominations put forward by the state tourism bodies and the Commonwealth. The winners were then selected by a judging panel, chaired by Ms Ita Buttrose, with panel members Sir Peter Abeles, Sir James Hardy, Mr Bobby Limb OBE, and Mr Emanuel Klein. This event was to be held at the Wentworth Hotel in Sydney on 27 September, to coincide with World Tourism Day. It created the interest he'd hoped for, too, the awards night being programmed live on TV.

I received a letter from Minister Brown asking if I would accept his nomination in the Award for Excellence in the category of transport. I can remember feeling deeply honoured to have been nominated by the minister and even more so when selected by the judging panel as the inaugural recipient.

●

About this time it came to my ears that Australian Adventure Tours was up for sale. Trans Australia Airlines (TAA) had spent big money introducing the new wide-bodied airbus to their fleet. The market was slack—there were too many empty seats—so there were those in Franklin Street HQ saying, 'Hey, why are we fooling about with buses, islands, resorts and the like?' and questioning the business they were in. 'We've taken our eye off the ball. We fly aeroplanes. Let's stick to our business and get rid of all the other stuff.'

I also heard that Australian Pacific were sniffing about and I made a call to a TAA-Mayne director and said that if the company was up for sale we would be interested in buying it back. The fact was, however, it was never going to be sold to anybody other than Australian Pacific, who at that time used Ansett for their package tours. TAA desperately wanted that business, so a sale to anybody else was not on. I assumed that air travel would have been locked into the contract of sale.

After the takeover had settled down I thought it appropriate to speak with the owners of Australian Pacific, Mayer Page and Geoff McGeary, about my role in the organisation, where they saw the future, and my remuneration package. It was a matter I was to have taken up with Len Simmons, but it got lost in the system when the sale proceeded. My job specifications and duties had changed dramatically from when I first joined the company. My initial title and area of responsibility was manager of Bill King's Northern Safaris, and that was the outback tour program we operated from our address in Upper Heidelberg Road, Ivanhoe.

However, things did change, and quickly. The tour programming and brochure production were transferred back to Ivanhoe. We changed the name of our operation to Bill King's Australian Adventure Tours and within a year all the company's tours, apart from capital city day tours, were then operated under the Bill King's Australian Adventure Tours banner.

At that time we were also given the go ahead to set up an operations base in Darwin. I also accepted the responsibility of opening the company's sales offices in London with Val Flackl, Los Angeles with Steve Gregg, and began working with Penny Briscoe, the sales manager in New Zealand. By that time I carried a second business card that read 'International Sales Manager' for the group, and the sales offices in London, Los Angeles and Auckland were my responsibility.

I also continued to be the face of the organisation at international and domestic trade shows and held regular sales meetings with the domestic sales staff in both the Sydney and Brisbane offices. Our sales crews in both of those capitals were really active within the domestic travel trade and organised periodic agency promotions, where I supported them. I also continued to allow the company to use my image in their advertising, although there was no financial reimbursement clause in my contract for that.

So, obviously, my role had changed dramatically.

I called Geoff McGeary for an appointment to discuss my position in the company and my remuneration package. He said he would get back to me—he did, too, after a few days, and said there was no need for an appointment. He said I was 'about right' where I was. That was it then—about right where I was, whatever that meant.

It was soon after that when I got the message that the Ivanhoe office was to close and we were to move into an office in West Melbourne. 'We may lose some of our key staff,' I said. 'So it might be wise to offer a small incentive.' I forget the precise reply Mayer Page gave me, but it left no doubt in my mind that losing staff was part of the strategy.

Dennis Staff, the reservations manager at Australian Pacific, was appointed manager, and other administration positions were taken up by their employees. I was allocated an office but did not have a title or any responsibility and the company name was changed to AAT Kings.

Page and McGeary began regular meetings with AAT Kings sales staff, who were expected to attend with ideas and suggestions for the betterment of the company, but after the bosses heard all the offerings they would then tell everybody what was going to happen. Everything was always predetermined, so it didn't take people long to recognise the procedure. The meetings became known as 'playing charades'.

It was a management style totally alien to the people from the sales and maintenance departments at AAT and Bill King's Australian Adventure Tours. They were self-starters who had over the years introduced many worthwhile initiatives to the company. What they found hard to live with was being asked for an opinion which was never going to be considered in any case. I'm not saying that their management style was wrong. How could it be? They were very successful businessmen. What I am saying is that it was different from what the people in the company were accustomed to, and, as we all know, one of the hardest things for human beings to come to grips with is radical change.

•

There was one saving moment for me in all this and it began at the ITOA Annual General Meeting dinner at which Sir Peter Derham, as chairman of the Australian Tourist Commission (ATC), and Lady

Derham were at the head table with Val and me. Val was seated next to Peter and the conversation got around to the Mornington Peninsula, where Peter had his Red Hill Estate vineyard well underway. They chatted about this and that for a while and Val mentioned we had some land in Mount Martha parked away for a retirement project.

'No need to build a house,' said Peter. 'I have one you can buy that's perfect for you and the grandkids, friends and whoever. It's on the market—go down and have a look.'

Val later enlightened me about the conversation and we both agreed we weren't interested.

The following week I was attending an ATC-sponsored promotion in Alice Springs, where international tour wholesalers and media were invited to workshops with Australian suppliers. At the official dinner I was sitting at the head table again with Sir Peter and he said, 'Hey, Bill, did Val tell you about this place I have in Mount Martha? It would suit you down to the ground as a retirement project.' I just nodded and said yes and at that moment decided it was probably best to go down and have a look, then we could say it didn't suit.

It was Saturday morning and pissing rain when Val and I set off from Eltham to drive to Mount Martha to look at Glynt, the five acre property Peter had for sale near the village. Well, we found it okay, or thought we had. There was a heavy white timber gate closed across an imposing driveway lined with Canary Island palms, and it led through this great expanse of manicured garden surrounded by thick bush. There was no end in sight and I could see no house.

We were full of indecision and unsure about opening the gate and just driving in, so we drove up Bay Road a little and parked the car where I could hop over a post and wire fence to head off through the bush and waist-high grass. Wet as a shag in no time, I was, scrambling up this hill, only to be confronted by a 3-metre hedge, through which I finally located a gap, and there it was, like a castle out of a spooky movie, almost camouflaged by the pouring rain.

'Bloody hell, and bloody hell again, I must have it,' I was thinking. I scrambled back to the car and said to Val, 'Come and have a look at this.'

'No way,' she said. 'I'm not getting out of the car in pouring rain. Get in. We're off.'

'No, you've got to have a look,' I replied.

'Bugger off,' she said.

'I'll carry you.'

Not to be deterred, I dragged her out of the car, hoisted her on my back for a piggyback through the scrub, then I finally pushed her through the gap in the hedge.

I reckon she stood there in the downpour for a full minute, maybe two, without saying a word, and for somebody who has spent her whole life worrying about getting her hair wet that was some period of think-time. 'We have to have it!' she said. And that was how it happened.

When we bought Glynt it was not officially recognised as historic, but it is now, classified on the Registrar of the National Estate as:

> Historically important because it is representative of the grand summer houses that were established in expansive garden settings in the wake of the 1890s recession brought on by falling export prices, over-borrowing by speculators, banks going bankrupt and a general Depression.

Sounds familiar, doesn't it? It could be 2009.

It took us eleven months to complete the renovation, restoring Glynt meticulously to the period. There were twenty rooms plus five bathrooms involved, and these included the five ball-and-claw cast iron baths. I discovered a place in Richmond where the baths could be sand-blasted to bare metal, then recoated in porcelain enamel and oven-baked. All the exposed plumbing, shower heads, taps and bathroom fittings were stripped back to polished copper and brass and then coated with clear enamel and oven-baked for longevity.

The whole house had to be re-plumbed and the roof leaked like a sieve. I had an electrician climb into the roof to check the wiring and heard 'Jesus Christ!' echo around the rafters. He scrambled down and said, 'I'll have to shut the power down. The rats have eaten the insulation off the wires. There are exposed live wires all over the place. It's a wonder the whole joint hasn't burnt down.'

It was all major stuff, but our sons Martin and Russell were both in the building trade, were excellent tradesmen, and the end result was nothing short of magnificent.

•

On completion of the Glynt renovations I decided it was time to get out of the futureless environment. Even though I had a few months of my contract to go, I called Geoff McGeary and told him I was not really contributing to the development of the business, had never done so since the sale, so it was probably time to go our own ways.

Geoff eventually phoned me for a meeting in their office, to which I duly fronted up, and there they all were, the full cast of Australian Pacific's hierarchy. They asked the obvious question as to why I wanted to leave. I was non-committal and was not about to enter into any debate whatsoever, so I just said, 'I'm off.'

They wanted to have a new agreement signed, in essence to ensure that I would not involve myself in the coach tour business in opposition to them, which was fine by me. I had no intention whatsoever of becoming involved again with four-wheel drives and buses. I raised the issue of the ten weeks holiday I still had owing and Mayer got very surly and said he was not going to, quote, 'pay you to sit on your arse: you can work it off'. So there was no option, it was sign the new agreement and I was back sitting on my bum again in West Melbourne for ten weeks instead of sitting at home. It didn't really matter; there was an end in sight.

So finally it was time to flee the nest. It was a sad time for me, really, leaving the few remaining crew members with whom I had an affinity; it would have been very easy to become emotional. The most memorable moment came, though, when Dallas Newton, the accountant, gave me my final pay slip and a cheque for $91.10, representing the 72 hours I was owed, calculated at approximately $1.27 per hour, ordinary time. He arrived at my worth as being $50.61 per week. I still have that pay slip as a reminder of the time I spent with Page and McGeary.

I had not read the fine print in the new agreement requiring me to 'do time' for the money I was owed. I just assumed the salary package would be the same, but I was wrong. I can only assume that Dallas was instructed by Mayer to find the lowest legal wage rate for the final payout. How often have I said, 'Assume nothing'? I'm still a slow learner.

It was 26 September 1985, more than twenty years from when I took my first tour to Uluru, and short of a few moments of sadness when I shook hands with my old colleagues, it felt really good to be free from that place. It also gave us a good reason to celebrate, and Val and I put the $91.10 towards dinner and a bottle of good red wine at Herman Schneider's Two Faces Restaurant in South Yarra. A fitting reward for twenty years work, don't you think?

CHAPTER 27

NEW DIRECTION

VAL WAS STILL WORKING at Capricorn Travel and I sat about being a house husband for a while, although I was having great difficulty adjusting to this new life of leisure and contentment. The guilts came and went every day. I felt I should be doing something—but what? It was like I was in the dark, groping for something and not knowing what I was groping for.

It was about that time I began doing some part-time work with Steve Gregg. He had been our sales manager in the US, but had moved on when the Australian Pacific team moved in. Steve had founded Destination Australia Marketing, a tourism consultancy that I thought he would do well at. The tourist industry had flourished since the Labor government took office and tourism-related companies and developers were investing huge amounts of money in all manner of infrastructure. The banks and moneylending institutions, naturally, were asking for their feasibility studies, which in the main were provided by accounting practices.

Soon after this Steve and I had formed a partnership and were offering to not only provide a feasibility study, but a marketing plan designed for the particular segment of the market the investor wished to attract. Our business flourished with all manner of projects to review and manage. It was like the beginning of a third life.

We secured a consultancy for the New South Wales Government to explore the feasibility of future tourist development in Broken Hill. They saw a sunset on mining and were seeking ways and means to provide sustainable employment in the future.

We did the feasibility study, site evaluation and final plans for the traditional owners to develop the tourist resort at Watarrka National Park, as Kings Canyon is now called. At that time we also accepted a brief from the Aboriginal Development Corporation on behalf of the Jawoyn people to formulate a plan of management for the Katherine Gorge National Park, now known as Nitmiluk. The second part of the brief was to explore the practicability for the Jawoyns to enter into the tourist industry, and that led to the establishment of Manyallaluk Aboriginal Cultural Tours, an enterprise that is still operating to this day.

We were also invited to formulate a marketing plan for the Yulara Corporation, the owners of the soon-to-be-opened development at Uluru. It was by far the biggest project that we ever became involved with. The result of that brief saw us market a new range of holiday products worldwide under the NT Territory Holidays banner, featuring five-star accommodation and tourist services.

The success of that initiative led us to work with Ansett Airlines to package venturesome holiday experiences Australia-wide for the airline, again with five-star accommodation and services. Our consultancy business had become a very successful enterprise, and we accepted the Australian Tourism Award for marketing in 1986 for our Yulara Resort project, and in 1988 the consultancy received the award for tourism services.

•

Then the proverbial hit the fan. I opened the mail one morning and there staring at me was a letter from 'Costa, Plenty & More', one of those high-profile law practices situated in one of those expensive addresses, the type you know immediately are way out of your league. Well, I turned white, I can tell you, and immediately went into stress management mode. They were representing AAT Kings, who were alleging I was in breach of my contract and were demanding that all NT Territory Holiday brochures in travel agents throughout the land be withdrawn. Were they never going to stop?

I went to see Tony Garrison, our lawyer, and he said, 'Out of my league, Bill. We need advice.' So the inevitable happened and it was 'silks' at twenty paces. We told them to go screw themselves on the 'withdraw the brochure' issue. It was not mine to withdraw anyway; it was the Yulara board's and I was just managing the project. On the 'being in breach of my agreement' issue, the day eventually came when we went to war.

I was sitting in front of a desk with Tony at my elbow and Gerard, my Queen's Counsel, on the other side reading through my folder. Eventually he looked at me and asked, 'Now what is your version of all this?' or words to that effect.

'I did not sign an agreement not to work in the travel industry. I signed an agreement not to compete with them in the four-wheel-drive or coach tour industry, which I haven't. I believe that Page and McGeary were also satisfied that was the essence of the agreement when it was signed. Now they're attempting to read other issues into it.' I rested my case.

Gerard mulled over that for a minute, then picked up the phone and made the call to Page and McGeary's silk, and began to exchange pleasantries about family wellbeing.

'So what have we got here with this issue with my client?' he eventually asked. It was time to bring out the bugle and blow the call to arms, so to speak.

The debate began and Gerard kept turning to me, saying things like, 'Well, you did sign an agreement not to do this, and you did sign an agreement not to do that, and they are the owners of the AAT Kings name.' Bloody hell, I was thinking, whose side is this fellow on?

I suddenly felt indignant and told him, 'I really don't give a stuff about all of that bullshit. I signed an agreement not to go into the coach or four-wheel-drive tour operations—I haven't. I am involved in packaging fly/drive holidays that attract an entirely different market to theirs. My name is Bill King and I can be myself wherever and whenever I want. Tell them to go screw themselves.'

After passing that lot on and waiting for a reply, Gerard came back with, 'Well, there could be an instance where a client who might have taken an AAT Kings coach tour holiday buys an NT Territory Holidays fly/drive package.'

To my mind none of that had anything to do with the agreement I signed with Page and McGeary. 'Tell them, "Bullshit!"' I said.

He looked at me for a full minute again and shouted, 'YOU HAVE TO GIVE THEM SOMETHING!' Bloody hell, he was really pissed off. It took me by surprise, I can tell you, but I was even more indignant.

'I'll give 'em bloody nothing,' I told him. 'They have their AAT Kings brand; they have their Australian Adventure Tours brand. I never entered into any agreement not to work in the travel industry. Tell them to get on with their business and let me get on with mine.' Tony was nodding at my elbow.

Gerard gave me another long hard look and went back with that lot. I was thinking I was about to be shown the door, as he hung on and on and was gazing out of the window with a monster frown on his face. He said, 'Yes,' then the silence went on again, although his head was nodding up and down, and finally he flicked a switch on his phone and told me, 'They want you to sign an agreement not to use the words "Australian Adventure Tours" in any of your publications or advertising.'

I looked at him for a bit then asked, 'And?'

'That's it,' he said.

I was dumbfounded, I can tell you. 'That's it? That's all they want? We went through all that bullshit for that result? Of course I'll sign that agreement—not as an attachment to the old one, though,' I added. 'I want a new agreement with one paragraph stating precisely that, and not to take effect for another year, when the validity of our printed material expires.'

Gerard studied me for a minute or so again, then flicked the switch on his phone and began speaking with their silk. They had a bit of banter and a laugh or two as they agreed with what was said. As he hung up with a huge grin he told me, 'They said they quite like "Old Bill".' That was me they were referring to and I didn't give a shit whether they liked me or not, although it was probably better they did.

So it was done—much ado about nothing, and the whole exercise was just an expensive waste of time.

•

Not long after that, two Melbourne businessmen became involved in the travel industry and established a retail outlet, The Travel Professionals, in South Yarra. Obviously they were serious about furthering their investments as they then purchased the Wandana Travel retail chain from John Mitchell and Dennis Seward. It was soon after that Steve and I met the directors of that organisation and they made an offer to purchase our company.

And that was it. We had been in business for more than five years, built a very successful enterprise, and they made us an offer too hard to refuse. I must say that the two businesses were a perfect fit; they would control a chain of retail outlets with wholesale buying power, which in effect meant double the commission on sales.

•

I reckoned it was time for a well overdue sabbatical—I was ready to let the mind slip into neutral, to eliminate think-time and let somebody else tell me what to do. Thinking is bloody hard work, I find—that is probably why so few people indulge in it. But there would be no sitting around the house worrying about not having anything to worry about, and before long there were more new beginnings on the far horizon.

I'd been talking with John King and Bill Baker, who were heading up the Australian Tourist Commission office in Los Angeles. They were aware that we had sold our business interests and came up with this plan for me to visit the US and participate in a PR campaign. The idea was to visit key markets with yours truly doing radio talkback shows, television interviews, and interviews with journalists from leading magazines and newspapers as a follow-up to the very successful Paul Hogan 'Throw another shrimp on the barbie' campaign.

Well, why not? Although I did say that Val would have to come with me. I was tired of travelling around the world on my own.

Our job was to extol the wonders of Australia—the Great Barrier Reef, the outback, and the attractions and experiences the visitor can enjoy on a holiday Down Under. Hogan made a proposition to the American public to come to Australia; our job was to inform the prospective holiday-makers what they could do and see when they came.

Having spent so much time in the US, I was well aware that the market was big. However, it was not until this promotion got underway that I realised just how big. Never could I have imagined that one morning in New York I would have a one-hour television interview with Arthur Frommer on his travel show, with 13 million viewers on the other end of the little black lens. The radio was not short on listeners either; I did a talkback show one Sunday morning in Denver and asked the host how many people we were talking to. 'The show's syndicated. Probably about twenty million,' he said off-handedly. It made me feel quite insignificant.

Working in America on that promotion led to Val and me meeting with all manner of people, and was instrumental in us joining an American travel company with Australian interests to stage a series of travel agency educational seminars throughout the US.

We based ourselves in Los Angeles and I travelled on a Monday to wherever, then flew or drove to the next destination to conduct the functions while Val worked at arranging venues and invitations. The plan was to stage five or six workshops a week for two weeks, and during the third week swot up on attendees for the next round. We visited 114 cities in 26 states during the time we were involved in those projects, an amazing journey really, visiting places I had only read about, and some I never even knew existed. And if any soothsayer had ever told me, given my track record, that I would spend so much of my life being an educator, and be introduced as a 'walking library' on all things Australian, I would have said, 'Pull the other leg'.

We had some memorable drives, too, not the least being Route 66 from Los Angeles to Chicago, where we were delighted to experience a white Christmas, most certainly the only one we will ever have. Val and I enjoyed living in America. It really is a beautiful country: majestic mountains, painted deserts, and the displays of autumn colours in the eastern states are quite breathtaking. But, all good things come to an end and it was time to come home.

CHAPTER 28

KIMBERLEY CRUISING

I HAD NO SOONER put my foot back on Australian soil when I was approached by the representative of a company that was pioneering cruises along the Kimberley coast and was invited to join the ship as guest lecturer. I jumped at the chance. I had always wanted to travel the coastline, and the *Kimberley Explorer* offered that opportunity.

The voyage was to take us to from Broome to Cape Leveque and from there through the Buccaneer Archipelago to the Prince Regent River and King Cascade, before returning to Broome via the Lacepede Islands. The ship was equipped with two Zodiac inflatables for daily excursions to points of interest, while the majority of the voyage was undertaken at night. There was no GPS in those days, either, and the only charts available were those done by Phillip Parker King in 1820. I went to the bridge one night and the skipper was studying a chart with several lines and numbers on it. One line in particular, drawn in pencil across a blank space with arrows pointing in one direction, took my eye. It was a maritime 'mud map'. 'Who did that?' I asked.

'The skipper before me,' he replied, still looking at his homemade map and the radar screen. 'Uncharted waters,' he explained.

Beyond the windscreen of the bridge was a jet black wall that we were making headway into at a fair rate of knots. The blackness, however, was totally irrelevant to the skipper, who had his radar screen to steer by. For me, having no vision of what was out there was really scary. I kept thinking that there are 3000-odd islands off the Kimberley coast and they are still charting new ones. The only thing stopping us running into one was that little green screen on the console. I left the bridge and never went back again.

Our first stop was Cape Leveque, at the tip of the Dampier Peninsula, about 200 kilometres north of Broome. Here we went ashore, where the Indigenous women prepared a barramundi meal for the ship's complement in the traditional way. Wrapped in wet leaves and buried with hot rocks, the fish was steamed to perfection. The highlight, though, was damper cooked in the coals and smothered in honey gathered from the hives of native bush bees—a taste sensation. The Bardi people at Cape Leveque have come a long way since then, too, having realised the financial benefits to be gained by participating in the tourist industry. Today they have established a multi-award-winning wilderness camp called Kooljaman that provides overnight accommodation and extended stays with activities like barramundi fishing, snorkelling or just relaxing in a remote and delightful setting.

The second day of our voyage took us through the Buccaneer Archipelago, a region offering some of the most magnificent and colourful coastal scenery you could ever imagine. It is part of a prehistoric shoreline that was inundated millions of years ago, leaving peaks protruding from the sea to form nearly 1000 rocky islands and escarpments, many with small inlets and bays that shelter unspoiled and secluded beaches. It is the location of the horizontal waterfalls, where the huge tidal surge of some 12 metres gushes through the narrow gaps between the islands towards the coast on the high tide, and the reverse towards the Indian Ocean on the ebb.

Australia is the oldest landmass on Earth and the Kimberley is the oldest part of the continent. It is a region that was being weathered by time before the rest of the world emerged from the bowels of the earth. Its strange beauty and ancient slumbering spirit, however, belie the fact that it is a place where the traveller needs to proceed with extreme caution. It is a place where we saw spectacular sights like humpback and killer whales frolicking in the warm waters of the Indian Ocean, but we also saw innumerable venomous sea snakes, huge saltwater crocodiles and a sea alive with sharks.

It is also a treacherous coastline, subject to violent storms that have over the years claimed many ships with great loss of life. The *Encyclopedia of Australian Shipwrecks* lists hundreds of ships that have been lost along the Kimberley coast, along with some amazing stories of survival.

On a less dangerous note, the region is also rich in sea cucumbers, or trepang, and remnants of Macassan fishermen's camps are found all along the northwest coast. Tamarind trees, palms and other flora species from the tropical islands to the north indicate where you might find the skeletal remains of smokehouses and fire hearths. The sea cucumbers are about 25 centimetres in length and look like an overgrown garden slug. They are not just a simple 'catch and carry to market' either. The processing includes boiling, slitting, boiling again then gutting before drying and smoking to produce the final product, known as bêche-de-mer, a delicacy still in great demand in Asian markets and restaurants.

The Macassans, from the island of Sulawesi, as it is known today, fished the north of Australia for more than a thousand years, probably longer, and their distinctive vessels known as *praus* are depicted in Indigenous rock art and bark paintings in many locations across the top of the country. Naturally, over so many years, close ties developed between Indigenous groups and the Macassan fishermen, relationships that influenced both language and genetics. Macassan pidgin became a common language all along our northern coastline, not only with the Macassans but between different Indigenous tribes.

It is pretty evident why Australia was never colonised until the eighteenth century. In 1623 the Dutch explorer Jan Carstensz summed up the prevailing attitude pretty well when he described several armed clashes with the Aborigines and judged the place 'the most barren and arid region that could be found anywhere on earth; the inhabitants, too, are the most wretched and poorest creatures I have seen in my age or time.' On the strength of his report the Dutch government deemed the country to be unsuitable for habitation.

Traders from Asia, India and the Middle East had for many centuries been doing business in the islands just north of Australia, but they, too, had shown no interest whatsoever in the 'southern land'. Why would they? As far as they were concerned there was nothing to trade or plunder down here.

•

The next stop on the Kimberley cruise and an important point of interest was Careening Bay, which brings me to Lieutenant Phillip Parker King, who carved 'H.M.C. Mermaid 1820' on a giant forked boab tree growing near the beach. I had some interest in this bloke from way back, because whenever I came across the name 'King' among our early pioneers I used to delve into the genealogy stuff, to see if people involved in the development of the colony were in any way connected to my family. Phillip Parker King wasn't, but his story still captivated me.

His father Philip Gidley King arrived in 'New Holland' on the First Fleet as a second lieutenant on HMS *Sirius*, with the responsibility of establishing a penal settlement on Norfolk Island, where he was later to become governor, and where his son Phillip Parker was born in 1791.

The family returned to England where young Phillip joined the navy to become a qualified surveyor and scientific navigator, and was probably the first Australian-born citizen to become successful in the big world. It is odd that few Australians of today have ever heard of Phillip Parker King, but there are those who would argue he was Australia's greatest explorer and navigator. I wouldn't disagree with that. He finished what Matthew Flinders and Captain Cook left untouched, yet his name is hardly recognised.

In October 1817 the 26-year-old Phillip Parker King was given command of the cutter HM *Mermaid*, a tiny ship that only measured 56 feet, or 17 metres, from stem to stern, yet for the following three years he sailed her along the coastline of Australia, exploring and mapping the many bays and islands, including the first reliable inner channel on the Great Barrier Reef and Torres Strait. It was not until October 1820, however, that King reached the North West, where he sailed through a channel to the idyllic surrounds of Careening Bay, to carry out repairs to his vessel. The problems with the *Mermaid* turned out to be far more serious than first thought, so any further exploration was out of the question, which left no option other than to do a patch-up job and return to Sydney Cove.

By this time King's reputation as a naval hydrographer was unsurpassed, and he was appointed commander of HMS *Adventure*, which would accompany HMS *Beagle* to explore and survey the coast of Peru, Chile and Patagonia, with the renowned scientist Charles Darwin. He was to spend the next five years surveying the complex coastline of the Straits of Magellan.

While Phillip Parker King may not be as widely recognised as many other early explorers, he certainly was acknowledged by his peers as the greatest of Australian marine surveyors. The King River in Cambridge Gulf; King Sound, where Derby is located; King Bay at Dampier; Mount King near Kuri Bay; another Mount King, north of Halls Creek; the King River near Albany; and King Cascade on the Prince Regent River were all named in his honour.

However, Kings Peak, the highest point on the Cape Range at Exmouth Gulf, wasn't named after the navigator. It was named after Joseph King, my grandfather, and his half-brother William, who opened up the North West Cape when they settled there to establish Exmouth Gulf Station at the turn of the twentieth century.

•

I believe the voyage along the Prince Regent River reveals some of the most spectacular scenery in Australia. To enter the river in the late afternoon with the cliffs and escarpments reflecting the glow of an orange-red sun upon water of the deepest of blue is quite breathtaking, a spectacle only added to by the hundreds of booby birds wheeling and calling above our cruise ship. It was amazing.

Then we arrived at a place to be observed in an entirely different way. To look above as we entered this small anchorage at King Cascade and see the crystal clear water tumbling 50 metres down over the red rock tiers, where small clusters of ferns and other plant life had taken root, was truly beautiful. To turn one's back, however, and look down at the dark brooding water, black in the shadows of the surrounding escarpment, was really spooky, as it is a known haven for man-eating crocodiles.

One in particular was probably still in residence, the one involved in the dreadful tragedy that occurred on 29 March 1987, when 24-year-old US model Ginger Meadows, who was sailing as crew on a yacht heading back to the US from the Americas Cup, took an ill-advised swim to the base of the falls at low tide. It was when Meadows reached the waterfall that the crew on the yacht spotted the 3-metre crocodile stalking her across the sand that is exposed at the bottom of the falls at low tide. Now the big salties may only have small brains, but they are extraordinarily cunning, and this monster had positioned itself to obstruct any means of escape. Meadows heard the warning shouts from the boat and turned to see the animal just a few metres away. She was absolutely petrified and totally defenceless when the animal lunged and attacked her with terrifying ferocity. Those on the boat could do no more than watch in horror as the monster devoured her. The crew was eventually able to collect what remained of Meadows, and returned to civilisation to report the tragedy.

The final destination on our cruise was the Lacepede Islands. Named by the French navigator Nicolas Baudin in 1801, the three small flat and windswept atolls are the nesting grounds of thousands of booby birds and terns, who select their remote location to protect their rookeries from egg-stealing predators. We walked across the islands amid thousands of white fluffy booby chicks and also saw huge green turtles mating in the pristine waters at the edge.

I must admit I felt a tinge of sadness as we boarded the ship for the final leg back to Broome. Exploring the Kimberley coastline had re-awakened in me all the things I'd been selling to other people for the last thirty or so years—the love of the Australian bush and nature and the unique experiences it brings.

CHAPTER 29

GONE WEST

AFTER OUR TRAVELS IN America and following our cruise along the Kimberley coast we decided the time was right to open Glynt as an exclusive retreat. It was modelled along the lines of a small European hotel. We had a dining room to seat sixteen guests and four deluxe suites, each with king-size bed and its own bathroom and sitting room. The premises were fully licensed, with a lounge bar, where we had open fires in winter, and a huge garden room with views across Port Phillip Bay where we served breakfast, afternoon tea and the like. By now Glynt, a historic landmark that we had meticulously renovated, surrounded by two and a half acres of manicured garden, really was a spectacular property.

It did become a full-on business, particularly with our international clientele. We offered three-night packages with two days of sightseeing, taking guests to places of interest around the Mornington Peninsula: French Island, where koalas and other wildlife can be seen at close quarters, as well as Greens Bush, where they could walk among mobs of kangaroos in their natural habitat and observe northern hemisphere migratory birds in Western Port wetlands. Adding a wine tasting and lunch at a Mornington Peninsula vineyard to those enjoyable experiences ensures that you never have an unhappy customer. It is a region that has much to offer the visitor.

•

I awoke one Saturday morning, we had a full house, the dining room was fully booked and I had a French Island tour to operate. I would like to have stayed where I was, but I was the breakfast cook. I only thought about it for a minute or two then said to Val, 'I don't want to do this any more.' I had enjoyed our five years in hospitality but that feeling of needing to be doing something was gone, just like that.

The decision was made in that moment. We sold Glynt, with no intention of ever involving ourselves in business and the associated responsibilities again. We were well and truly ready and eager for a life of travel, leisure and entertainment.

'So you've retired?' people began asking.

'Not likely, just knocked off work to do other things,' was my reply. I find 'retired' a bloody awful word. My dictionary defines retirement, among other things, as 'obscurity, seclusion, withdrawal and loneliness'. I had so many things I wanted to do, I wondered where I was going to get the time to do them.

We had another house to build, and we did eventually settle on a property within walking distance of Main Street, Mornington. With its restaurants, café strip and shopping it's a lovely place to live, and that gave me time to reflect on projects that I had put aside for years, waiting for this moment. This included planning some extensive travel in Western Australia. While I had travelled a lot in the Kimberley I had never been south of Broome, and that part of the country was very important in our family lore.

Summer on the Mornington Peninsula and winter through the west was the plan. We had no timetable or itinerary, just a direction, with no obligations to be anywhere or with anybody. All we had to do was just 'be', moving along and staying where the mood took us, sometimes for a day or two, sometimes for a week or two.

For some time I had been aware that with the passing of my parents, Eileen and Billy King, went the last people I knew that had any real contact with my pioneering ancestors. Their stories about growing up with their parents and in particular their grandparents, immigrants who came to this country in sailing ships to start a new life, were stories that they passed on to me, and unless I recorded that information it would be lost for all time.

And so my fourth life began, the time had come to go walkabout once more, even though we were both reaching that time in life when you join the bad back, wonky-knee brigade, when your mind makes promises your body can't keep and everything hurts, and if it doesn't hurt it doesn't work. Obviously, camping was out of the question for us and we had spent plenty of time in a tent and swag anyway. It was no novelty any more, so we purchased a Supreme off-road caravan and a Nissan Patrol to tow it with.

It was always going to be a nostalgic journey. Nowadays as soon as I get on an open road my mind slips into neutral and the memories begin to flood back. Exactly like my old man—it must be hereditary.

•

We had intended to head north through Broken Hill, the Flinders Ranges and the Oodnadatta Track, for no other reason than it was one of the routes we took when we were heading to Ayers Rock on our coach tours more than 40 years prior. But that was not to be. There had been a bit of rain about and the dirt tracks north through South Australia had no appeal whatsoever. It was where I graduated to being a 'bogologist' back in the early 70s.

So it was up the South Road, now a highway that is very different indeed from when we drove to Ayers Rock in the 60s. Back then it was just a track that made its way from station to station, with the odd gate dividing paddocks and properties. People today could have no concept of how that track changed in the varying climatic conditions—mile after mile of bone-shaking corrugations when it was dry; in a big wet some places disappeared into lakes, in others you slogged your way through seemingly bottomless glue, then there were sections of bog hole after bog hole in the creek and river crossings where the big rigs that provisioned Alice Springs from Adelaide left their mark, and did they ever! Those were the days when the Ghan could be out for weeks, so Alice Springs' 20 000 or so people had to be fed by road.

Ayers Rock, of course, was our Mecca—it was where it all began. Way back in the 1960s we started taking groups along those dirt tracks from Melbourne to Ayers Rock in pretty ancient buses by today's standards. Sometimes we got there, sometimes we didn't; nobody cared. We had given it a go, our best shot. After the drought broke in the late 1960s it was not uncommon for passengers to alight and apply physical manpower to shove the monster through a muddy section. Then they had to alight again, and again, and yet again, to make 100 kilometres in a day. Sometimes we got back on time, sometimes we didn't.

Uluru, as the Indigenous people call it, is one of the most recognisable of Australia's natural features. Nine and a half kilometres around the base and 348 metres in height, it is the largest single rock in the world. The rock structure is coarse sandstone known as arkose, laid down around 600 million years ago beneath the great inland sea bed. Originally horizontal, the strata layers are now almost vertical, tilted by the earth's movement and shrinkage over millions of years.

Uluru is deeply significant to the Anangu people that inhabit the area. It harbours the stories of the mythological heroes who came to the region in the beginning of time. Their ancestors were believed to live in the image of man, but had the instincts of the animals or plants with which they lived as one. Knowledge and traditions were handed down through the generations by the way of songs and myths from the Dreamtime, to be remembered as the keys to survival in the harsh and unforgiving environment in which they live.

The Indigenous Australian is the supreme conservationist and over thousands of years they developed knowledge of the habits of the animals and the medicinal and food values of plant life. Water was the centre of the most important rituals and was the essence of life, especially for the nomadic desert dwellers. They had come to terms with the harsh conditions of inland Australia. Waterholes at Uluru were guarded by the fearful serpent *Wanambi*, the spirit that judges all mortals. In dry conditions the waterholes may be protected from the sun by branches and leaves, and hunting near waterholes was forbidden as a conservation measure.

To visit Uluru now gives me a weird feeling. The magnitude and variety of tourist services at Yulara is huge compared to the days when we camped under the northern side of the rock itself and showered in saltwater, with the odd brown snake slithering into the ablution block to warm his belly on the concrete floor. I once had a king brown poke his head under my door while I was showering: there I was, naked, defenceless and absolutely terrified, even more so when he slithered in for a circuit of my shower stall. And when I say the water at the rock was salty, I mean really salty. You would have to be dying of thirst to drink it. After a shower your hair was so hard after it dried you had to be careful or it would break. That's what I reckon happened to mine, it just broke off.

I also recall being stranded at the Rock for more than a week as the heavens really opened up—a spectacular sight, mind you, as the waterfalls literally poured over the edge where the dark stains are visible at ground level in dry times.

'When can we leave, Bill?' was the question I was constantly asked.

'After the first vehicle arrives from the outside world,' was my usual reply. It was better to be stuck there with some amenities than in some bog hole down the track.

There were plenty of dingoes around then, too. They would hang about looking for scraps, and although we never fed or encouraged them, some did. I was walking back from the shower one day and—whack—a rotten pair of socks that I had been wearing for a week disappeared out of my hand as a razor-sharp tooth shredded a finger. 'Bloody hell!' He frightened the daylights out of me. The dingo took off into the scrub with my socks but I saw him often after that. He was a nasty piece of work and wouldn't wait for things to be thrown in his direction. He would stalk and steal. When the Azaria Chamberlain tragedy happened I thought straight away that if a dingo did get the kid, it sure as hell was that one.

I always believed in the Yulara development. To my mind it was needed to launch Central Australia into the 21st century. The most recent addition to the complex, Longitude 131, is a magnificent wilderness retreat and I was quite flattered when the owners asked if they could name one of the lodges the 'Bill King Tent'.

Another place that was very special to me was Kings Canyon Resort, the project I had acted as the facilitator for, back in the mid 80s when Steve Gregg and I set up Destination Australia Marketing. I felt we made a contribution in developing it as a destination.

•

In the early days, after leaving Alice Springs to visit the gorges and chasms in the Western MacDonnell Ranges, we had to travel back through Alice to make our way to Ayers Rock via Kings Canyon, and that used to vex me no end. I hated going over the same ground twice. On one safari, 1970 it was, I was lamenting this fact to a couple of old blokes from the Haasts Bluff Aboriginal settlement, with whom I had struck up a conversation while camped at Glen Helen, and they told me about this abandoned mining track that they occasionally used when they wanted to knock over a kangaroo for some tucker. At the end of the track, they said, there was a 'jump up' or escarpment from which you can see mountains on the horizon to the south. Now there is only one mountain range to the south and that is the George Gills, where Kings Canyon is located.

I thought about it all night and reckoned if we gave it a go and failed it would only cost a day, and I could make that up later. So we set off really early the following morning, already heading in the wrong direction, when I told my folk the story of the 'shot line' put in by a bulldozer for geologists from the Mereenie gas field mob seeking sites for test drilling. Maybe it was an opportunity to find another route to Kings Canyon.

'What do you reckon?' I asked the punters. They sat there nodding and shaking their heads in turn as they looked to see what everybody else was doing, so they could say, 'It wasn't my fault,' if anything went astray. So we were on our way, which we were anyway.

We made our way along the Finke River bed, and then through Tyler Pass where we got some fantastic views of Gosse Bluff, that enormous and awesome crater forced up from the surrounding desert by the impact of an almighty object from outer space in the aeons of prehistory. But the going was really slow and I knew pretty early in the piece we weren't going to make Kings Canyon that day. We got to the 'jump up'; it's shown on maps these days as Camels Hump, which is oddly appropriate, because as we struggled to the top there grazing on the plains on the far side was the biggest mob of camels I had ever seen and what looked to me like the biggest bull camel in the world. He was enormous. He nearly fell over when he saw us and took off with his mob of cows and calves towards the Western Australian border with the speed of a thousand arrows.

The George Gill Ranges were a spectacular sight in the late afternoon sun, with Carmichael Crag glowing deep red about 60 or 70 kilometres away on the southern horizon. We set off in that general direction and as we were now travelling across country there were innumerable detours and washaways, every few metres in some places. The going was now really, really slow. About five o'clock we came across this lovely claypan—no bindi-eyes, no water about to encourage mozzies, plenty of firewood and copses of scrub for ablutions. It was lovely. 'Time to make camp,' I said.

I was also well aware that some of the punters would be out of their comfort zone and feeling a little agitated. Things were not going according to plan. What if the truck broke down or we had some kind of an accident? Ignoring the fact that we had a radio, they would still be thinking, 'Who would ever find us?' One had to be a firm and positive leader in these circumstances and get in first to stave off any muttering. That means get the camp set up ASAP. Tell them exactly where we are, even if you're not quite sure, give them the departure time and expected arrival time the following day, even if you really don't know. Sit 'em all down, open the Chateau Cardboard and get the tucker underway.

We got to Kings Canyon the next day and did the climb across to the Garden of Eden, then went around to our campsite at Reedy's rock hole, a crystal clear, spring fed pool, some 10 metres across, situated at the base of the escarpment.

A funny thing happened the following morning. Jim Cotterill, who ran Wallara Ranch with package tours to Kings Canyon, arrived in his old Bedford bus. It was a unique jigger, with Boeing 727 aeroplane tyres fitted on special wheels he had made, huge bald donuts to get him through the sand drifts. He was a handy bloke, Jim. Still about, too. Anybody travelling up the highway to Alice Springs will find him at Stuarts Well roadhouse.

Anyway, he arrived that morning with his punters peering out the window and a look of absolute shock on his face. 'How the bloody hell did you get here?' he asked. He thought he was going troppo. Wallara Ranch was right on the road to the canyon, and a bunyip couldn't sneak past without Jim knowing.

'I came across country from Glen Helen,' I told him.

'Bloody hell, the joint's getting as busy as Alice Springs,' he said. He and I with our respective groups had probably been the only people in there for the past couple of weeks.

Kings Canyon has something unique about it. Those abundant waterholes surrounded by primitive art and prehistoric relic plants were without equal. There could be no more rugged mountain range than the George Gills, with formations like the Lost City on their rim, yet here were these idyllic places, just like little pockets of paradise.

It was opened up for tourism by Jack Cotterill, Jim's father, in the early 1960s and today is a national park with the traditional name of Watarrka. In the early days it was thought by many to be named after me, because of the 'King' association and the fact that we began to promote the place pretty aggressively in the early 1970s. In later years, during the peak period, we had vehicles through there three or four days a week. Kings Creek, which flows from the canyon, was named by Earnest Giles in 1872.

Our next trip to the canyon was a few weeks later, with two vehicles in convoy, and even though we were travelling in the opposite direction, from Kings Canyon to Alice, I planned to take the 'new' track. But on leaving Carmichael Crag do you think I could find it? No way. There had been a bit of rain since our previous tour and our wheel tracks had disappeared. Heading south was fine, I had Carmichael Crag to get a bearing off; heading northeast was hopeless, with no tracks to follow.

When I lost sight of Carmichael Crag I had nothing to see other than thick scrub and didn't have a clue where to go. So, discretion being the better part of valour, I hung a U-ie and followed my tracks back whence I came. Bloody embarrassing, I can tell you, building up the punters for this new scenic journey to Alice Springs, taking them through unseen country that 'we' had opened up, modern-day explorers and all that, then having to backtrack with my tail between my legs.

In the late 1990s I received a phone call from somebody at the Northern Territory Tourism Commission saying the chief minister was going to open the track officially as a tourist drive, and as I was the person who pioneered the route I was invited to attend. Today it is shown on maps as the Mereenie Loop.

•

After the canyon Val and I headed through the Western MacDonnell Ranges to Alice Springs, the town that became the hub of our operations. In the early days our tours around the Red Centre spent a few days visiting the chasms and gorges that, apart from their scenic beauty, are the traditional lands of the Aranda people. They had the best-watered country in the whole of Central Australia, as the fissures within the ranges all contain deep permanent waterholes. The waterholes were very important in the daily lives of the people and were steeped in local mythology. They are said to be occupied by large water snakes. Some were uncompromising creatures that ate people who swam or lingered too long at the water's edge. The water snakes that inhabited Ormiston Gorge and Glen Helen, though, were said to be friendly and harmless. Glen Helen Gorge itself was one of the most important sites in the whole region, known as *Japala* in Aranda legend; it was where the first shapeless human beings emerged to spread out across the land. Spooky stuff.

The other important attraction in the Alice was the historic telegraph station, the very reason for the town being there at all. The telegraph line was the dream child of Charles Todd, and the project should be remembered as one of the great feats of Australian engineering. Todd's plan, accepted by the government of the time, was to construct a telegraph line from Port Augusta to Darwin across country that had only been traversed by one man, John McDouall Stuart, just eight years previously. At the same time an undersea cable was to be laid from Singapore to Batavia (now Jakarta), across Java, then undersea again to Darwin.

E.M. Bagot got the contract to construct the 500 miles of telegraph line north from Port Augusta. The firm Derwent and Dalwood got the contract for constructing 639 miles of telegraph line south from Darwin. This left a section of 626 miles in the middle for which there were no bids. 'Too bloody hard,' they all said. Not too hard for Mr Todd, though. He made the decision to build it himself. Not only that, Derwent and Dalwood went broke halfway through their project, so he finished their bit, too. Todd had eighteen months to build 3200 kilometres of telegraph line and eleven repeater stations—a mammoth task—but he made it happen.

The two ends of the wire were joined near Frew Ponds in August 1872, and the first cable to be sent was a congratulatory message to Todd, who was camped near the foot of Central Mount Stuart. The whole project was completed one month later.

Communication with England became instantaneous. Up until then if you wrote a letter to somebody in England, the earliest you could expect a reply would be seven or eight months. It could be said that the 'electric telegraph', as Todd used to call it, was a cornerstone of Australia's development as a nation.

Today the telegraph station in Alice Springs is maintained as a memorial to the blokes who completed the project using bullock wagons and horses for transport and picks and shovels to move earth.

•

After a brief stay in the Alice we took off, heading north to catch up with a few old cronies in Darwin, before travelling west along the Victoria Highway to Kununurra. Kununurra was a major provisioning location for our expeditions, so the cook on tour had to have the shopping list right.

Val and I set off to retrace that expedition and visit one of our old crew, Taffy Abbotts, who has established Mount Hart Station in the Kimberley as a tourist retreat, and it was certainly an easier journey than when we first tried to negotiate it back in the 70s.

We decided to stop in Broome for a week because the weather was good, then headed south into new territory, to begin our true mission—retracing the journeys and visiting the places my old man talked about when I was a small boy.

CHAPTER 30

IN SEARCH OF MY FAMILY

It had always been a dream of mine to visit the places that were significant to my family's history—the North West Cape which my ancestors pioneered, the Bangemall goldfields which my grandfather worked, the Bangemall Inn where my parents lived and where my story began. And now, finally, here I was.

My mother and father moved to Bangemall just after they married. They had met the year before when my father visited the Royal Melbourne Show seeking stud rams for Yardie Creek station, which he was managing at the time. My grandfather Joe invited the newly wed couple to come to Bangemall and run the pub with the view of taking it over in the future. I have no idea what my mother thought, but it was goodbye post office in Ormond where she was postmistress and onto the ship bound for Perth. Then in a 1926 Dodge tourer they set off on the 950-kilometre journey to Carnarvon, followed by 400-plus kilometres to Bangemall. I should add that my father's worldly possessions in those days, apart from his car, consisted of a suitcase of clothes, a travelling rug and a 44-calibre Winchester 73 lever action rifle.

After doing that journey in 1999, whatever respect I had for my father increased tenfold. To take a 1926 model car from Perth to Carnarvon was a feat of major proportions; to take it out to Bangemall was astounding. A two-wheel-drive car with skinny little tyres that had to be let down to traverse the sandy patches, and there are plenty of them, then pumped up with a hand pump when you got to the hard bits, and, when the tubes in the tyres were beyond repair, stuffed with herbage and grass to complete the journey. It was a feat of persistence and ingenuity.

My father had told me about that trip, laughing about the things they were confronted with, including floodways and washouts, but it was only after following in his wheel tracks that I gained any appreciation of what is was like back in the 1920s. He took a car built for city streets to an area that was still getting the supplies in by camel train.

The pub was originally named the Euranni Hotel and was built in the late 1890s. It was to remain the Euranni Hotel until January 1927, when Charlie Cornish bought it. The story goes that some bloke walked into the pub with a bag of nuggets, slammed them on the bar and shouted, 'That bangs 'em all'. Charlie just loved that, so he changed the pub's name to the Bangemall Inn and later sold the property and licence to my grandfather.

Joe also had two prospectors he grubstaked, Bob Reisbeck and Charlie Reid, who lived in a donga at the back of the pub in between expeditions. When Joe worked in Coolgardie at the turn of the century, he met Harold Lasseter, who talked about this fabulous reef of gold he had discovered deep in the Gibson Desert. Today the story of Lasseter's Reef is legendary. Some believe his story, many more don't. My grandfather believed him and for years financed Bob and Charlie to search the country where he thought the reef lay. There were several other official expeditions manned, including two by Lasseter himself, the second of which was to claim his life. Ion Idriess, the renowned author, did visit Bangemall and spent many hours talking with Joe when researching his book, *Lasseter's Last Ride*.

When Joe first went prospecting in the Gascoyne region in the 1890s, he and a couple of blokes went deep into the Gibson Desert beyond the Carnarvon and Brassey ranges and he could clearly remember coming across some country that was distinctive, and exactly how Lasseter described it. Lasseter was delirious, on foot and near death when found by an Afghan camel driver with his little bag of gold samples way out near the Canning Stock Route in 1897. Joe always said Lasseter didn't have a clue where he found the stuff, but it was more likely to be 500 kilometres west of where he was searching, and where he passed away in 1931.

Charlie and Bob had minimal success on their prospecting expeditions. On one occasion Charlie failed to manage his water supply, staying on a site where they found colour for too long, pushing his luck on the water to sustain his return to Bangemall. He never made it back alive. My father was one of the men who went out to look for him and brought the body back to the inn where they buried him. When we visited Bangemall in 1999 the current owner told us of the anonymous grave nearby. I told them it was Charlie Reid's.

My mother never said much about her time at the Bangemall Inn, but it is not hard to imagine the feelings of a young lady from a suburb of Melbourne being thrust into the harshness of the Australian outback. What's more, it was a man's world, and a pretty rough one at that. In later years when my mother was asked about her time in Bangemall, she said it was not the end of the earth but if you stood on the verandah you could see it.

After Bangemall we headed north again to Exmouth Gulf, another important location in my quest to follow in the footsteps of my family. There were no roads or tracks through the giant sand dunes when my grandfather and his half-brother William took up the lease in 1908 and the only access was by the coastal trader SS *Geraldton* and a small dinghy to ferry supplies in and wool bales out. My father began working at Exmouth Gulf Station as a seventeen-year-old in 1918. At that time they were shearing 20 000 sheep. The bales had to be hauled to the beach landing by the horse team and then ferried, three at a time, in the rowboat to the *Geraldton* anchored offshore.

The permanent white population of the North West Cape at that time numbered eleven—the three Kings, William, Joseph and Billy; the two Campbell brothers at Yardie Creek, on the Indian Ocean side of the Cape Range; and Harold Wilson, the lighthouse keeper at Vlamingh Head, his wife, their two children, and two helpers, who came and went.

There were two Indigenous groups living on the cape. The Yardie mob numbered about 30 and their traditional hunting land was to the west of the Cape Range. The Kooburra mob of similar number camped at a waterhole in the limestone, where the town of Exmouth is situated today, and they fished and hunted on the east side of the Cape Range.

My old man worked at the station until 1924, when he had the opportunity to join a new trucking company in Carnarvon, founded by Charles Kingsford Smith and Keith Anderson, the yet-to-be famous aviators. Always infatuated with motor transport, Billy began taking rigs on the long roads north, battling the heat, rivers and harsh terrain.

My father was with Kingsford Smith for a year, and then went to work for the Campbell brothers at Yardie Creek Station. The brothers had decided to live in Perth and needed an experienced person to manage the property. Among the memorabilia my old man left was a letter of appointment as manager, also an order for supplies (written on the back of an envelope) to be shipped in on the SS *Geraldton*. Apart from bags of flour, tea, sugar, onions, potatoes and the like, the order included twenty cases of beer, ten cases of whisky, and ten cases of Penfolds Red Label port. It was obviously very thirsty work on an outback sheep station.

Today the old Yardie lease is the national park on the Indian Ocean side of the North West Cape, and the homestead and shearers quarters are established as a tourist park. It is quite amazing that they have survived, really, when the other three original properties on the cape have been decimated by cyclones.

My father also left photographs taken in the early 1920s of Aboriginal tribesmen and women living the traditional life, wading through Yardie Creek, catching fish with three-pronged fishing spears and netting them with woven vines. When Val and I did the boat tour through the gorge at Yardie Creek on our visit, the tour guide said the Indigenous people left the area in the latter part of the nineteenth century, due to some sickness. I had photographs of them there 25 years after that.

It was with some trepidation that we drove down a track marked on a local map as King Road to call at Exmouth Gulf Station. It had been devastated by Cyclone Vance only two months before. The homestead and half the woolshed were gone, and the whole place would have to be rebuilt. John and Linda Lefroy, however, could not have been more welcoming—John's grandfather had purchased the lease from the King estate in 1932.

•

We had been on the road for three and a half months by then, following in the footsteps of my parents. It had been a fantastic journey and there was still so much more we wanted to see and do, but that was for another day. It was to be the first of five journeys, during which we covered 65 000 kilometres in search of my ancestors. We had no idea, then, that researching my family's history would take us to nearly every corner of the Swan River Colony, from Greenbushes to Geraldton, Mount Magnet to Marble Bar, Coolgardie to Cossack and so much more in between.

A copy of the family history that I wrote and a copy of my father's photo album are now in the council library in Exmouth, so history has been preserved.

My family's history could best be described as unusual. Both of my great-grandfathers on the paternal side were sent to the Swan River Colony by the powers that be, but for very different reasons. Juan Bancells was a Catalan born in Massanet de la Selva who became a monk of the Benedictine Order at the famous monastery of Montserrat, in Spain. He was sent to the colony by the Pope with a group of monks under the leadership of Dom Rosenda Salvado in 1853. Their assignment was to build and establish a monastery and mission at a place called Batgi Batgi, north of Perth, today known as New Norcia, and recognised as an important part of our national heritage.

The second great-grandfather, William Graham Ashton from Newcastle on Tyne, was sent to the Swan River Colony at about the same time. However, he was a 'guest' of Queen Victoria for six years, having been convicted of breaking and entering a coach house. His assignment was to work on the construction of his accommodation at Fremantle prison.

There would be few people on the planet, I would imagine, who have descended from a Spanish Benedictine monk and an English convict on their father's side and an English ship's deserter and a judge of the High Court of Ireland on their mother's side. It is a fascinating story for another time.

•

There would always be another day, another adventure. I had learned over the years that no two journeys would ever be the same. Behind every sand dune, by every waterhole and on every mountain lay the mysteries of the Australian outback. It will always be this way—a harsh, unpredictable land watched over by the spirits of the Dreamtime, and its secrets will only be unfolded to those who travel beyond the fringe.

POSTSCRIPT

We've done a lot over the years, Val and me, but I must say it is no easy task writing about it, always conscious that you are on your own ego trip. If you've got this far, though, I assume you've found some passages of interest in my involvement with Australia's fledgling tourism industry.

This whole exercise began when I gave number-three son, Bradley, a copy of our family history. 'Family history?' he said. 'I thought you were writing about *our* family. You were never here when I was a kid and we had no idea what you were doing or where.'

So it was into my boxes of stuff—diaries, scrapbooks, old correspondence and the like—to see what there was to be found, and when I began to unearth this material, I became increasingly surprised at the depth of the human mind, particularly my own. I had always thought my powers of retention left a lot to be desired, but after reading articles and documents and revisiting old haunts it was like passing through a progression of doors, each one leading to a long-forgotten memory.

There is another question that I am often asked—what were the most memorable of all those happenings—and those that come readily to mind are the ones that gave me a sense of achievement and a feeling of pride.

First and foremost was the creation of Bill King's Northern Safaris. It was a dream that gradually became a way of life, a life that took me to so many places and introduced me to so many people in this great country of ours. The success of that enterprise is still very evident today. AAT Kings, as the business is now known, still operates tours at Uluru National Park that we began in the 1960s, and the Bill King 'tent' at Longitude 131 is a permanent fixture that gives me a feeling of belonging.

Being no more than a graduate of the university of life, I was never going to be presented with a cap and gown, but over the years I have been honoured by people and organisations that have recognised contributions they considered worthy of acknowledgement. I reckon that may be my cap and gown, as there is no greater honour than to be acclaimed by one's peers.

So the second of those memorable moments came in 1984, when I accepted the Australian Tourism Award for Excellence in the category of transport. I felt deeply honoured to be nominated and even more so when selected by the judging panel as the recipient. It is now housed with a display of memorabilia on the Bill King Wall at the National Road Transport Museum in Alice Springs, and I was again honoured by that organisation when I was inducted into the museum's Road Transport Operators' Hall of Fame in 2006.

The third recollection of an accomplishment began when Steve Gregg and I established Destination Australia Marketing. In the following five years we were involved in many successful ventures and it was gratifying indeed to accept the Australian Tourism Award for tourism marketing in 1986, and again in 1988 for tourism services.

My fourth important moment came in 1996, when I was nominated by Tourism Victoria for the Australian Tourism Award for excellence in the category of outstanding contribution by an individual, and was judged the winner and presented with a trophy by Tourism Minister John Moore at a function at the Burswood Casino in Perth.

POSTSCRIPT

I found that presentation to be a defining moment in time and did not attend a travel function for ten years afterwards. When I looked around the audience at the presentations, I saw young and vibrant people, the new leaders in an industry that was flourishing, and I was a yesterday person. I didn't mind that, I felt very comfortable just slipping away into the past. The future was in good hands.

The fifth and final important moment came at the anniversary of the Inbound Tour Operators of Australia organisation, known today as the Australian Tourism Export Council, when I was inducted as the first honorary life member of that organisation and presented with a memento with the following inscription:

Vision
A leader's job is to look into the future and to
see the organization, not as it is . . . but as it can become.
Celebrating 30 years of ATEC
In recognition of your leadership
Bill King, Chairman
1983–1984

FURTHER READING

Beddoes, Thomas (1850). *Death's Jest Book*, Pickering: London.
Blainey, Geoffrey (1975). *Triumph of the Nomads*, Macmillan Co.: Melbourne.
Brock, Daniel George (1975). *To the Desert with Sturt*, The Royal Geographical Society of Australia: South Australian branch.
Clark, C.M.H. (1978). *A History of Australia IV: The earth abideth forever—1851–1858*, Melbourne University Press: Melbourne.
Durack, Mary (1959). *Kings in Grass Castles*, Constable & Co.: London.
Hansard Report (9 February 1977). *The Significance and Potential of Tourism*, Australian Commonwealth Government: Canberra.
Hicks, Doug 'Unimog—Out Back with Precious Cargo', *Australian Trucking Action*, May 1983.
Joachim, Kenneth, 'The Joy of Being in the Outback', *The Herald and Weekly Times*, 12 February 1977.
Idriess, Ion (1931). *Lasseter's Last Ride*, Angus & Robertson: Sydney.
——(1936). *The Cattle King*, Angus & Robertson: Sydney.
MacDonald, Alix, 'Swinging Safari', *New Idea*, 28 November 1970.
McDonald, Rhonda (1985). *Gold in the Gascoyne*, Hesperian Press: Victoria Park. WA.
——(1991). *Winning the Gascoyne*, Hesperian Press: Victoria Park. WA.
MG Media Communications (1996). *ITOA: 25 years serving inbound tourism—1971–1996*, Inbound Tourism Organisation of Australia: Sydney.
Miles, Lois, 'The Curse of Burke's Bones', *The Australian Women's Weekly*, 6 April 1977.
Mitchell, Thomas (1839). *Three Expeditions into the Interior of Eastern Australia*. Published by T.W. Boone: London.
Moorehead, Alan (1965). *Cooper's Creek*, The Reprint Society: London.
Mudie, Ian (1968). *The Heroic Journey of John McDouall Stuart*, Angus & Robertson: Sydney
Roberts, Tony (1983). *Frontier Justice: A History of the Gulf Country to 1900*, Queensland University Press: Brisbane.
Roff, Derek (1983). *Ayers Rock and the Olgas*, Lansdowne Press: Sydney.
Slater, Peter (1970). *A Field Guide To Australian Birds—Non Passerines*, Rigby Limited: Adelaide.
——*A Field Guide To Australian Birds: Volume Two—Passerines*, Rigby Limited: Adelaide.

ACRONYMS

AAT (Australian Accommodation and Tours; Australian Adventure Tours)
ADC (Aboriginal Development Corporation)
AFTA (Australian Federation of Travel Agents)
ATC (Australian Tourist Commission)
ATEC (Australian Tourism Export Council), formally ITOA
ATE (Australian Tourism Exchange)
ATS (Australian Travel Service)
CKD (Completely Knocked Down)
DAM (Destination Australia Marketing)
FIT (Free Independent Traveller)
ITB (International Tourism Bourse)
ITOA (Inbound Tour Operators of Australia)
NTTC (Northern Territory Tourist Commission)
TAA (Trans Australia Airlines)
VFR (Visit Friends and Relatives)

INDEX

AAT 142, 223
   sale of Bill King's Northern Safaris to 223–8
   see also AAT Kings
AAT Kings 191, 261
   legal action 267–70
Abbotts, Taffy 290
Abeles, Sir Peter 259
Aboriginal art 17–18
   Arnhem Land 17
   Bynguano Range 18
   Chariots of Fire carvings 160–2
   desert art 17–18
   Kimberley 17
   rock art 18, 160–2
   see also Mootwingee rock peckings
Aboriginal land permits 159–60
Aboriginal people, poor treatment of, 85
Adelaide River 165
air packages 69, 177, 187
   see also Ansett Airlines
Alice Springs 39, 108, 111, 180, 288–90
   base in 129, 191
Allen, Bluey 153
Amata Aboriginal settlement 159, 160
Anangu people 283
Anderson, Keith 294
Anna Creek Station 93, 108–9, 196
Ansett Airlines 69, 133, 177, 187, 191
   pilots' strike 193–4
Ansett Pioneer 211–12
Ansett, Reg 145
Aranda people 289–90

Arnhem Land 12, 165, 167
Ashton, William Graham 296
Astley, David 237
Atlanta 146
Australian Adventure Tours 259
Australian Federation of Travel Agents (AFTA) 242–3
Australian Pacific Tours 259
Australian Tourism Export Council (ATEC) 243
   life membership 299
Australian Tourist Commission (ATC) 142–7, 148–9, 178, 179, 189, 211, 222, 240, 244, 245, 256, 261
   Asian road show 248
   Destination Australia Marketplace 216–17
   German road show 201, 203–8
   German wholesalers trip 215–17
   Singapore office 247–8
   UK office 209
   US road show 142–7
   US PR campaign 271–2
Australian Trek magazine 189
Australian Women's Weekly 154–5
awards: Australian Tourism Award for Excellence for outstanding contribution 298
   Australian Tourism Award for marketing 267, 298
   National Tourism Award for Excellence 259, 298
   Travel Trade Brochure of the Year Award 135–6, 142

INDEX

Ayers Rock, viii, ix, 15, 39, 130, 180, 352–3, 283
  see also Uluru
Ayers Rock Air Safaris 130

Bagot, E.M. 289
Baker, Bill 271
Balcanoona 60
Ballantine, Derek 105–6
Bancells, Juan 1, 295–6
Bangemall goldfields 1, 291
Bangemall Inn 1, 2, 10, 291
Bardi people 274
Barkly Highway 32
Barkly Tableland 65, 87
Baudin, Nicolas 279
Bennelong 244
Bentley, Ron 115, 121
Berlin 205–6
Bill King's Australian Adventure Tours 226, 237, 260
  international marketing 243
Bill King's Northern Safaris viii, 28, 298
  first-ever tour 29–40
  see also tours
Bill King's Red Centre Tours 180–1
Birdsville 133
Birdsville Track 106, 108, 133
Blanchwater Station 64
Blunsom, Tony 226
Bo-Bo [dog] 71–2, 76–9
Boggy Hole 130
Boomerang Travel 210–11
Borroloola 84, 165
Bouchaud, Leon 'Beau' 135, 137, 139, 187
Boulder 115
Bowen Downs Station 63, 64, 65
Bowler, Professor Jim 32
Brachina 60
Brahe, William 33, 34
Briscoe, Penny 260
British Airways Arts and Adventure Club 210
brochures 81, 83, 187, 226
  award-winning 135–6, 142
  see also marketing

Brock, Daniel 56–8; diary 58
Broken Hill 15–16, 49, 267, 282
Brooks, Steve 253
Broome 164, 273, 279, 290
Brown, John 238, 256, 257, 258
Brunette Downs Station 90
Bryant, Tottie 42
Buccaneer Archipelago 273, 274
Buchanan, Nat 65–6
Buck, Bob 157
Buckley, Reverend Sydney 4
buffalo culling 165
Bungapidu, Michael 244
Burke and Wills 12, 24, 38
  base camp 64
  Camp 76, 24
  Cooper Creek 24
  tour 15–27
  see also Dig Tree
Burke, Robert O'Hara 12
  death 35
  grave 152
  see also Burke and Wills
Burketown 25
Bushwackers, The 253
Bwung Gul dance group 243–4, 246
Byrnes, Di 180

Caldwell, Bill 100
Calkoen, Alfred 100
Cameron Corner 52
Cameron, John 53
Camooweal 25
Campbell brothers 294
camping, 31, 36, 171–2
  bathing 36
  Chateau Cardboard ix, 21, 37, 67–8, 287
  meals 21–2, 67–8
  toilets 35, 171, 172
Canning Stock Route 293
Cape Leveque 273, 274
Capricorn Travel 266
Captain Cook Cruises 241
Careening Bay 276
Carnarvon 3, 291–2
Caroline Pool 162

Castle, Keith 180
Central Australian Tourist Association (CATA) 180
Central Land Council 159, 160
Centralian Tours 82–3
Centurion Transport Engineering 251
Chamberlain, Azaria 285
Channel Country 67, 133
Chariots of Fire, rock carvings 160–2
Chung, Ah 33
Clarke, Dymphna 38
Clarke, Manning 37–8
Cloncurry 25
Cobbler Desert 53–6
  drilling rig 54–5, 59, 62–3
Cobra Station 3; *see also* Bangemall goldfields
Coburg Heidelberg Omnibus Company 4, 8
  midweek charter business 11
  outback tours 12
  ski weekends 11
  tours to Ayers Rock 11–12
Cocky's Camp 130
Cohen, Barry 179, 238, 256
Collins, Henry 63
Conroy, Dennis 133
Conway, Ian 39
Coober Pedy 37, 41–6, 113, 196
  missing tourists 44–6
  see also Nayler, Faye
Cooinda 166
Coolgardie 1, 115, 156
Cooper Creek 12, 55, 56, 112, 150, 151–2, 220
  Burke and Wills site 24
Copley 59–63
Corbett, Ken 211
Corner Country 20, 52, 149–50
Cornish, Charlie 292, 293
Cornish, Ronald 256
Cotterill, Jack 287
Cotterill, Jim 180, 287
Coward Springs 93
Crocodile Harry 42–4
crocodiles 42, 44, 163, 166, 181, 182–6, 219

Cromb, Alan 7
cultural tourism 257
Curdimurka 112
Curtin Springs Station 39–40
Cycad Gorge 130
Cyclone Tracy 127–8

Dajarra 25
Dampier Peninsula 274
Darwin 127, 164, 165, 290
  base in 260
Darwin, Charles 277
Davies, Barney 23, 101–2
Davies Camp 159–60
Davies, Jenny 252
Davies, Jos 23, 102
Dawson, Caroline 105
Dawson, Colonel Mac 30
Dawson, Diane 105
Dean, Gordon 256
deaths of tourists 218–19
Denning, Alan 11
Depot Glen 49, 51
Derby 164
Derham, Lady 261–2A
Derham, Sir Peter 245, 261
  Red Hill Estate 262
Desai, Morarji 213
Destination Australia Marketing 266, 285, 298
Dhulparippa, Murphy 244
Dig Tree 34, 64, 133, 152, 206; *see also* Burke and Wills
dingo fence 150
dingoes 284–5
Docker River Aboriginal settlement 131, 156
Doyle, Bob 135, 231
Dreke, Manfred 203, 206
Drysdale, Sir Russell 23
Dunn, Carmel 91
Dunstan, Keith 27
Dunstan, Kim 247–8
Durack, Mary 66
Durack, Patrick 66
Durrell, Edna 137–9

INDEX

East Alligator River 165–6; *see also* crocodiles
education, role on tour ix, 170
Ellis, Rennie 14, 52–3, 105, 135, 187
Emu Bottom 252
Esperance 115
Evenden, Harley 123
Everingham, Paul 237, 252
Exmouth Gulf 293–5
Exmouth Gulf Station 1, 2, 293, 295
Eyre, Edward John 49, 132

Farrands, Bruce 162
Finke 110
fishing camp 181–6
FitzGerald, Brigadier Lawrence 35, 37
Flackl, Val 236, 260
Fleming, John 203, 204, 210
Flinders Ranges 108, 282
Fort Grey 52
Fraser, Malcolm 178, 201, 238
Frewena 32
Frewena Roadhouse 87–90
　grader incident 88–90
Frommer, Arthur 271
Fryer, Ray 183

Garland, Alan 20, 21, 22
Garland, Jenny 20, 21
Gauci, Joe 73
Geikie Gorge 163
Gerritsen, John 19, 97–8
Ghan, track 109–11
Gibb River Road 163–4, 167
Gibb River Station 163
Gibson Desert 156
Giles, Ernest 12, 19, 38, 132, 138
Giles Meteorological Station 156
Gilheaney, James 215
Glaser, Paul 240–1, 246
Gleeson, Bobby 70–1, 72, 76
Glen Helen 180, 285, 287, 289
Glen Helen Gorge 289
Glennon, Billy 5
Glenormiston Station 24
Glynt 262–4
　as exclusive retreat 280–1

sale 281
Godfrey, Bob 144
Gol Gol Station 52; *see also* Lake Mungo
Goldman, Ruth 125
Gosse, E.W. 138
Gosse Bluff 130, 286
Gray, Robin 256
Grayden, Johnny, 6, 7
Great Sandy Desert 214
Green, Gil 180
Gregg, Steve 236, 260, 266, 285, 298
Grey, Mick 169, 195
Greyhound 15, 146
　in USA 146
Gulf Country 84–5
Gunbarrel Highway 156

Haasts Bluff Aboriginal settlement 285
Hair tour 70–5, 81
Hall, Charles 162
Hampel, Trevor 105–6
Hardy, Sir James 259
Harrison, Peter 169
Hart, Pro 16
Hartigan, Peter 169
Hawke, Bob 238, 256, 257
Hawker, Frank 76
Haworth, Trevor 241
Herald (Melbourne) 189–90
Hermannsburg 106
　Lutheran mission 130
Hewitt, Ron 244
Hicks, Doug 253
Hill, Nick 69
Hill Hill Station 64, 65
Hodgkinson, Frank 23
Hogan, Paul 271
Holiday (ABC TV) 188
Holiday (UK) 222
Homewood, Helen 105
Hook, Jeff 27
Howitt, Alfred 35, 36
Hutchinson, Frank 249
Hutchinson, Jim 42
Hutchinson, Willie 42

Idriess, Ion 66, 156, 292
Inbound Tour Operators of Australia (ITOA) 239–42, 299
　book 242
　chairman 241–2, 245, 258
　US promotion with Qantas 245
　US trade mission 240–1
inbound tourism market 221, 239–42
incentives 147
Indian Pacific train 15
inland telegraph line 289–90
Innamincka 153–4
insurance, public risk 117–18, 120
Inter Air Voss 191
International Tourism Bourse (ITB) 221–2, 229, 243–5
itineraries 69

Jawoyn people 267
Joachim, Kenneth 189–90
Johns, Barry 120
Johnson, Bruce 219

Kakadu National Park 165, 166
Kalgoorlie 115, 131, 214
Katherine 165
Katherine Gorge 165
　National Park 267
Kelly, Joy 180
Kelly, Ren 180
Kennedy, Bob 191
Kensington Travel 211
Khan, Esan 33
Kidman, Sidney 66–7
Kimberley 12, 160, 164, 273–9
　shipwrecks 275–6
Kimberley Explorer 273–9
King, Alan 9–10, 90–1
King, Bill: birth, 2
　car renovation 8
　engagement 7
　first block of land 7
　first car 6
　first job 4–5
　heart attack vii, 229–32
　honeymoon 8
　marriage 7
　motorcycles 5
　rehabilitation 233–6
　relationship issues 120–1, 128–9
King, Billy (Snr) [father] 1, 3–4, 291–2, 294
　death 282
King, Bradley viii, 297
King Cascade 273
King, Eileen [mother] 2, 291–2; death 282
King, John (ATC) 271
King, John (explorer) 34, 206–7; death 35; rescue 35
King, Joseph [grandfather] 2, 277, 291–3, 294
King, Lieutenant Phillip Parker 273, 276–7
King, Martin viii, 119, 264
　birth 8
King, Melissa viii
King, Philip Gidley 276
King, Ron 9–10, 28, 136, 229, 231
King, Russell viii, 119, 126, 169, 194, 264
　birth 8
King, Susan viii
King, Valerie 8, 10, 29, 71–2, 73, 75, 76–8, 81–2, 104, 136, 181, 182, 191–2, 196, 217, 218, 223, 226, 231, 233, 234, 262–3, 266, 271–2, 281, 288–9, 295, 297
　fishing tale 183–4
　relationship issues 120–1, 128–9
　see also West, Valerie
King, William 2, 277, 294
Kingchega Station 34, 52
Kingoonya 42
　breakdown at 196–7
Kings Canyon 130, 180, 194, 285–6
Kings Canyon Resort 285
Kings Creek Station 39
Kings Peak 277
Kingsford Smith, Charles: Gascoyne Trading Company 108, 294
Kngwarreye, Emily 18
Knox, John 11, 12, 87, 89, 142, 145, 169, 196–200, 223, 231
Kooburra people 294

INDEX

Kulgera 86–7
Kununurra 290
Kyatt, Don 174

Lacepede Islands 273, 278–9
Laidlaw, Wally 4, 8
Lake Cadibarrawirracanna 113, 133
Lake Eyre: flooding of 107
Lake Mungo 32–3, 52
  Mungo Man 32–3
  Mungo Woman 32
Landells, George 33
Lasseter, Harold Bell 132, 156–8, 292–3
Lasseter's Cave 156–7
Lasseter's Reef 292
Laverton 131
Lefroy, John 295
Lefroy, Linda 295
Leichhardt, Ludwig 23–5
  Safari 133
Leis, Manfred 169
Lempad 101
Lightning Ridge 41
Limb, Bobby 259
Long, Jack 145
Longitude 131 resort 39, 285, 298; *see also* Yulara Resort
Longstaff, Sir John 34
Lynch, Phillip 201

MacDonald, Alix 105
McGeary, Geoff 259, 260, 264, 268
McGlynn, Meredith 222
Mahomet, Dost 33–4
Maidens Hotel 15, 33
Manyallaluk Aboriginal Cultural Tours 267
marketing 67–9, 103–4
  posters 84
  role of Val King 81–2
  see also brochures
Marks, Stan 189, 207–8, 215
Marrakai Plains 165
Marree 112
Martin, Alan 21, 78, 99, 100, 101, 102
Mary River 165

Maryvale Station 110
Maxwell, Don 105
Meadows, Ginger 278
media, 188–9
  Italian journalists 149–54, 189
  Skylab 215
  Uluru 253
Mednis, Karlis 100, 101–2
Mee, Russell 122, 123
Meekatharra 3
Menindee 15, 33, 52
Mereenie Loop 287
Mereenie Track 17–18
Mildura 49, 108, 137
Miles, Lois 154–5
Mills, Corrine 106
Milnes, Brian 211–12
Milparinka 20, 21
Miners Right newspaper 2
Misty the horse 16–17
Mitchell, John 270
Mitchell, Major Thomas 56–8
Mongeeta 253
Moomba gas field 55
Moore, John 298
Moore, Ray 59
Mootwingee 17; rock peckings [paintings] 18, 97
More, Geoffrey 69
Mount Hart Station 290
Mt Isa 90–1
Mununggurr, Robert 246, 247
Mutjuntjarra people 42
Muttaburra 63

Nashville 146
national parks, tourists and 97–8, 255–9
National Road Transport Museum:
  Bill King Wall 298
  Road Transport Operators' Hall of Fame 298
National Tourism Awards for Excellence 258–9, 298
Nayler, Faye 41–2, 44, 46, 113
  Opal Cave 41–2, 113
  partner Sue 41

New Idea article 105
New Norcia 296
Newton, Dallas 265
Ngukurr Aboriginal settlement 188
Nicholls, Ralph 243–4, 246, 247
Nicholls, Sir Douglas 243
Nitebook, Mr 56–8
Nitmiluk, *see* Katherine Gorge National Park
Noakes, Brian 73, 74
North West Cape 291
Northern Safaris, *see* Bill King's Northern Safaris
Northern Territory Parks and Wildlife Service 165
Northern Territory Tourist Bureau 135
Northern Territory Tourist Commission 237
Nullarbor Plain 32, 49, 115, 131
Nunn, Dick 106

Old Halls Creek 162
Olgas, The 214
Olympia [employee] 78–80
Oodnadatta Track 37, 62–3, 85, 108–9, 112, 130, 195, 282
opals, *see* Coober Pedy
Opitz, Judy 166
Opitz, Tom 166
Orientos Station 151
Ormiston Gorge 98, 289

Page, Mayer 259, 260, 268
painting schools 20–3, 99–106
  Bali 101
  Cooper Creek 102
  Merimbula 100, 116
  Milparinka 21, 102
  Mount Buffalo 100
  Omeo 100
  Peri Lake 100–1
  Tibooburra 101–2
  see also Martin, Alan
Palm Valley 106, 130, 137, 139, 249
Palmos, Frank 189
Parachilna Gorge 60
passenger types 171–3

Perks, Sergeant Owen 106
Petyerre, Gloria 18
Phillip, Governor Arthur 244
Poole, Eric 237
Poole, James 51–2
Port Roper 181
Possum, Clifford 18
Powers, John 91–2
  Shindig 91–2
Prince Regent River 273, 277–8
Pugh, Clifton 23
Pwerle, Minnie 18

Qantas: agreement 236–7
  Jetabout Holidays 237
  US tourism promotion with ITOA 245, 246–7
Quebec 147

Rasp, Charles 16
Razer, Helen viii
Red Rover Tours 220
Redford, Harry 63–5
Redford, Thomas 63
Redford Trail 65
Reid, Charlie 292
Reisbeck, Bob 292, 293
Renton, Bruce 149, 152, 154, 189
Richards, Bill 137, 139
rock art, *see* Aboriginal art
Rockhampton Downs Station 87, 88
Roper Bar 167, 182
Roper River 188
Rose, Graham 14, 19–20, 21–2, 25–6, 27, 49, 70–1, 72, 77, 85, 169
Ross River 180
Ross, John 105
Rowe, John 245, 256
Roy and Vera 174–6
Rynia, Joan 115
Rynia, Peter 169, 195
Rynia, Robyn 202, 218

S.R. Evans Motorcycles 4–5
Saltbush Bill 94–6
Salvado, Dom Rosenda 295
Santos Station 151

INDEX

Schultz, Alby 26–7
Select Committee on Tourism 201
Severin, Pete 39–40
Seward, Dennis 270
Shaddick, Brian 84, 85–6, 126, 169, 194
Siklos, Peter 211, 215
Silverton 16
　film sets 16
　pub 16
Simmons, Len 225, 227, 236, 237, 239, 248, 260
Simpson Desert 56
Skipworth, Lindsay 108
Skylab 212–15
Slattery, John 162
Smith, Greg 252
Smyth, Brian 118–19, 120
snakes 55–6, 152, 182–3, 186, 289
South Alligator River 166
special-interest tours 103–4
Stacey, Wesley 52–3
staff 168–76
　training manual 169–70
Staff, Dennis 261
Starliner 11
Steele, Mike 220
Stevens, Riley 21–2, 59, 60
Stewart, Frank 178
Strzelecki Track 53–6, 64, 65
Stuart, John McDouall 42, 49, 138, 289
Sturt, Charles 12, 38, 56–8
　journal 58
　search for great inland sea 49
　tour 47–58
Surveyor General's Corner 157
Swan Hill 15
Swan River Colony 1

Tanami Desert 160, 162
Tanami Track 162, 167, 195
Tasmanian Parks and Wildlife Service 256
Tasmanian tourism 255–6
Tasmanian Tourist Commission 256
Tempe Downs Station 157
Theldarpa Station 22

Thorpe, Lesbia 100
Three Ways 87
Tibooburra 20, 23, 49, 150, 174
Toby the Camel 22–3
Todd, Charles 289–90
Todero, Arthur 148–9, 152, 154, 189, 203, 204, 207
toilets, *see* camping
Top End 160; *see also* Darwin, Kakadu
touring life, *see* camping
Tourism Advisory Council 258
tours: Alice Springs and Ayers Rock 30, 69, 114
　Burke and Wills 13, 15–27, 29, 206
　Charles Sturt, 47–58
　fishing camp 181–6
　Gunbarrel Safari 130, 132
　Leichhardt Safari 133, 134
　Highlights of the Centre and Top End Safari 136
　new Alice Springs-based 129–30
　Northern Frontier Safari 161–7
　Papua New Guinea Highland Sing Sing 202
　Red Centre Safaris 180–1, 216
　Seek the Rare Parrot 202–3, 215
　special-interest 103–4
　Summer in the Mountains 192
　Tasmanian west coast 192
　West of Alice Safari 130, 131
trade shows: Germany 201, 203–8, 221–2
　United States 141–7
Trans-Australian Airways (TAA) 236, 253, 259
Transport Workers Union 118–19
travel industry, funding for 177–9
Travel Professionals, The 270
travel shows, *see* trade shows
Travel Trade Brochure of the Year Award 135–6, 142; *see also* brochures
Tuando, Mr 56–8
Tuit, Len 111–12
Tunbridge, Richard 203, 204, 210
Tunnel Creek 163

Twilight Cove 131
Tyler Pass 286

Ubirr Rock 166
UDP Falls 166
Uluru 39, 252–3, 283–4; see also Ayers Rock
Uluru–Kata Tjuta National Park 252
Urandangi 25
Urapunga Station 183, 188

vehicles: Bedford M series four-wheel-drive 141–2, 148, 187, 249
 Big Ben 148, 187, 194, 250
 breakdowns 194–200
 Desert Cruiser 122–3, 172, 188, 250
 first year, 47–8
 Gertrude 85, 86, 92–3, 114, 136, 188, 196
 Katherine 148
 Little Ben 136, 148, 187, 250
 maintenance 82, 115
 Olga 122, 148, 187
 passenger comfort 48–9
 reliability 194–200
 Unimog 250–4
Ven, Karyn 252
VFR market 209–10
Victorian Department of Conservation, Forests and Lands 256–7
von Brockhausen, Hans 252
von Däniken, Erich 162
Voss, Helmut 191

Wagstaff, Bob 169, 192, 195–6
Waka Station 52–3
Walkabout magazine 27–8, 29, 104–5
Walker, Bill 209
Wallara Ranch 194, 287
Walls of China 32; see also Lake Mungo
Walsh, Georgina 215
Wandana Travel 270
Warburton Aboriginal settlement 131
Warri Gate 150

Watarrka National Park, 267; see also Kings Canyon
Waterfall Creek 166
Watson, Jeffrey 188
Watts, Terry 103–4
Weatherly, Ian 'Sticko' 169, 184–5, 188, 190, 202, 217–18
Weihmanns, Götz 189, 203
Welch, Mr 35
Wellbrock, Heinz 203, 204, 205
West, Valerie 5–6, 7; see also King, Valerie
West Wyalong 87
White Cliffs, opal tour 78–80, 81
Whitlam, Gough 178, 238
William Creek, 133
 pub 93–6
Williams, Buddy 188
Williams, Gus 106
Williams, Ric 253
Wills, William John, 12
 death 35
 see also Burke and Wills
Wilpena Pound 59
Wilson, Harold 294
Wimble, Ted 9
Windjana Gorge 163
Winter, Debbie 137, 139
Wolfe Creek Meteorite Crater 162
Wolfe, Dusty 84, 108–11, 169
Woods, Stanley 4, 5
Woods, Tom 4, 5
Woomera 197
World Tourism Day 259
Wright, Billy 240
Wyndham 164

Yanyuwa people 84
Yardie Creek Station 1, 291, 294
Yardie people 294
Yellow Water Billabong 166
Yemmerrawanyea, grave 244
Yulara Resort, 284–5
 marketing plan 267
Yule, John 100
Yuntruwanta people 35
Yunupingu, David 246, 247